A-Z

of
alternative
therapy

A-Z

of

alternative

therapy

BLITZ EDITIONS

Published by Blitz Editions
an imprint of Bookmart Ltd
Registered Number 2372865
Trading as Bookmart Ltd
Desford Road
Enderby
Leicester LE9 5AD

ISBN: 1 85605 224 9

Material previously published in 1992 as part of the encyclopedia set *Know Yourself* (Fabbri Publishing Ltd).

Editorial and design: Brown Packaging Ltd,
255-257 Liverpool Road, London N1 1LX

Printed in the Czech Republic
51742

CONTENTS

For ease of reference, **The A-Z of Alternative Therapy** has been divided into three colour-coded sections: *Your Health, Understanding Yourself* and *Looking Good. Your Health* entries are green, *Understanding Yourself* is red and *Looking Good* is purple. The entries in *Your Health* provide practical guidance on how to use alternative therapies to improve your overall health; *Looking Good* entries feature the best alternative choices for beauty care; and *Understanding Yourself* entries show you how to understand your emotional self, using a whole range of alternative therapies.

Acupuncture is a medical treatment that has been practised in China for more than 5000 years, but has only really gained acceptance as an 'alternative medicine' in the West in the last 20 years.

Traditional acupuncture is based on the theory that an energy force, the Chi, flows through our body along 12 special channels called meridians. As long as the force can flow freely we remain healthy, but if the meridians get blocked we become ill.

Acupuncturists use fine needles which are inserted in specific points to unblock the meridians and restore the flow of Chi. According to the theory of acupuncture, there are a number of points on the body which are entrances or exits for Chi. As long ago as the 14th Century, Chinese doctors identified 657 acupuncture points, while today over 1000 points are recognised by acupuncturists.

What happens when you visit an acupuncturist?

Before they can treat you, acupuncturists have to make a diagnosis. They will do this by carefully

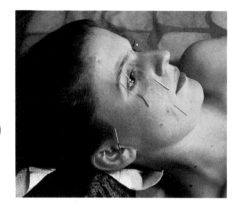

An acupuncturist treating a patient for a persistent headache.

observing the colour and the texture of your skin, whether or not your eyes shine, how you stand, gesture, breathe and even the tone of your voice. They will also ask you questions and give you a full physical examination. Finally, they will take your pulse, not like a conventional doctor, but using 12 pulse points. There is one for each meridian, and six on each wrist. Each pulse point is identified with a particular internal organ and tells the acupuncturist which meridian needs to be unblocked.

Once the diagnosis has been made, the treatment will begin. Sterile needles are inserted at the acupuncture points indicated on a chart, which are often far removed from where the

symptoms are felt. The needles are very fine, only 1/17,000 of an inch thick. In the past they may have been made of bone, silver or gold, but they are now made of stainless steel.

The needles are inserted vertically, at an angle, or almost horizontally, just under the skin or up to an inch deep. They may be left undisturbed or stimulated by the acupuncturist, who may twirl or pump them by hand or pass a small electric current through them. The needles can be left in the acupuncture point for up to 30 minutes and up to 20 needles may be inserted.

Uses of acupuncture

No one is really sure how acupuncture works but there is little doubt that it can work well. It is particularly effective for the treatment of pain, especially arthritis, neuralgia, back pain, headaches, PMT and period pain.

In 1979, the World Health Organisation published a list of illnesses acupuncture could help. It includes respiratory disorders like acute sinusitis, bronchitis and colds, eye disorders such as conjunctivitis, digestive disorders like constipation, diarrhoea and the pain caused by a duodenal ulcer, headaches, migraines and muscular disorders like sciatica, 'tennis elbow' or a 'frozen shoulder'. The most publicised use of acupuncture in this

ACUPRESSURE

Acupressure is concerned with specific points of the body, and is chiefly used to stimulate Chi energy and so relieve pain such as headaches, period pain, back pain and neck tension.

These points relate to different parts and functions of the body which lie along the energy channels and are chosen according to the specific pain being treated. You can teach yourself acupressure from various books, but it's always advisable to have at least one consultation with a trained expert.

Once you have chosen your point, you should apply approximately 20lbs of pressure for 30 seconds (try pressing your hands down on a pair of bathroom scales to see how much this is). Here are some examples of acupressure you can do at home.

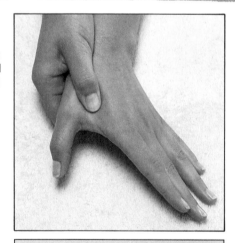

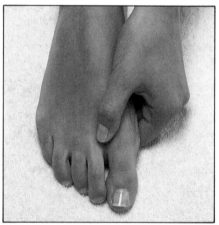

TAKE CARE WITH ACUPRESSURE

● Do not do it if you are pregnant
● If your headache is different from the usual frontal headache, or causes vomiting, see your doctor
● Do not use in conjunction with drugs or alcohol

Above left: For headaches, press the thumb and forefinger together to form a fleshy mound. The pressure point is at the top of the mound between the two bones.

Above: For headaches that are caused by nervous tension or anger, try pressing the point that is located on the top of the foot, between the big and second toes.

YOUR HEALTH

country is to treat addictions like smoking and overeating. Although it does work for some, a lot depends on the patient's motivation.

Ear acupuncture is often used to treat smokers and overeaters. A needle is inserted in one of 120 acupuncture points on the ear, and sometimes a staple is used which the patient wears

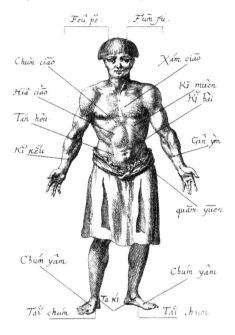

A medieval Chinese body map, showing some of the most important sites in the body.

continuously so you can stimulate it yourself when you feel a craving.

Acupuncture is also effective as an anaesthetic. In China, exhibitions were given to Western doctors and journalists, of patients undergoing major surgery while completely conscious, their pain being controlled by acupuncture needles. So far, its use as an anaesthetic has not caught on in the West, though it is sometimes used to control pain in childbirth.

Natural painkillers

Attempts to prove the existence of Chi have been unsuccessful, but modern theorists have come up with explanations of their own. It's possible that acupuncture works by either stimulating the body to produce more of its natural painkillers (endorphins) or by blocking the passage of pain impulses.

In the hands of a qualified practitioner, acupuncture is safe and it can be effective. It is not though, suitable for severe infections, cancer or in a medical emergency. If there is any doubt over a diagnosis you should visit your doctor. Acupuncture is particularly useful for long-term chronic ailments which have not been helped by conventional treatment, and for the drug-free control of pain.

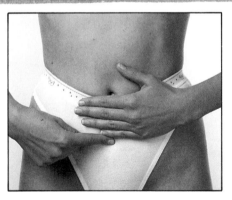

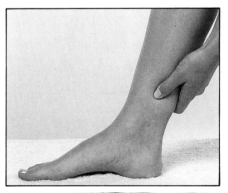

Left: This point, Guanyuan, is four fingers' width below the navel, and in line with it. This relieves PMT and period pain.

Below left: To help ease PMT or period pain, find the ankle bone on the inside of your leg. This point, Sanyinjiao, is four fingers' width up from the bone, and just off the border of the tibia (the long shin bone in your leg).

HOW TO CHOOSE AN ACUPUNCTURIST

In order for acupuncture to be safe, conditions must be hygienic to avoid the transmission of infections like AIDS and hepatitis.

The therapist must have a good knowledge of anatomy. It is important to choose a fully qualified and experienced acupuncturist Training for acupuncturists varies greatly, from short courses, favoured by doctors, to intensive three-year courses.

⚫ The best way to choose is by personal recommendation. Ask friends, family or colleagues who have had acupuncture.
⚫ Ask your doctor for advice. He shouldn't be offended, and will probably know local therapists.
⚫ A good acupuncturist will practise in clean, properly equipped premises. If you're not happy with what you see, leave.
⚫ If it makes you feel more comfortable, you can visit a medically qualified doctor who is also an acupuncturist. He may, however, only have taken a short course in acupuncture.
⚫ Be careful when choosing an acupuncturist. Telephone or write to the regulatory bodies in your area and ask for lists of their members and their qualifications. Also ask to be sent information describing the various qualifications.
⚫ Before you make an appointment, telephone the practice. A reputable therapist will be quite prepared to tell you about his practice and how he may be able to help you.

YOUR HEALTH

Did you know?

* It is said that the origins of acupuncture date back thousands of years, to when the Chinese noticed that soldiers who had received arrow wounds gained relief from ailments that had been troubling them for years.
* Before the Iron Age, sharp sticks and thorns were used to perform acupuncture. Sometimes stones were used to scratch the skin at the acupuncture point - this method is still practised by some African tribes.
* If you are nervous of needles you may prefer to try shiatsu, an ancient Japanese practice that is based upon a similar theory to acupuncture but which uses pressure-point massage with the fingertips.

Aerobics are exercises such as swimming, jogging and cycling where you get out of breath and your heart and lungs get a good workout.

While you're exercising, oxygen is carried in the blood supply to the working muscles where it releases energy from

the body's stores of glycogen, sugar and fat. If fat isn't broken down in this way, it will be deposited on the muscles, which then become flabby and weak.

You can do aerobic exercises at specially arranged classes, at home, in the swimming pool, while cycling to work... and nearly everyone can benefit from them.

The exercise session

You should build up your exercise sessions gradually and gently. If you're not very fit, start off with five to 10-minute sessions, and slowly build up your exercise time. Consider starting with low impact aerobics, which involves keeping one foot on the ground.

As with any sport, you should do some warm-up exercises first. Loosen up your body and warm up your muscles and joints with a few bending and stretching exercises before you begin, concentrating on the muscles you will be using. If you're going to cycle, for example, you will need to pay special attention to your legs. Similarly, after the exercise session, you will need to wind down: if you suddenly stop, you may feel dizzy or faint, so repeat the sequence you used for

warming up and then spend a few moments relaxing flat on your back.

The benefits

If you exercise for between 20 and 40 minutes three times a week, you will become much fitter. Aerobics is also good for the heart: the heart muscle becomes stronger, and the heart can then pump more blood with less effort.

An aerobics class begins the warming up exercises before a session.

JANE FONDA

At school, Jane Fonda was an awkward, clumsy and fat girl who dieted and binged excessively.

Throughout her successful modelling and acting career, the Hollywood emphasis on looks filled Jane with anxiety and, although she was an extremely beautiful woman, she continued to supplement her crazy diet with cigarettes, coffee, amphetamines and diuretic pills.

It was only when she became pregnant at the age of 30 that Jane began to take care of her body. She realised that physical fitness and a good diet would solve her problems.

Ten years later, in 1977, Jane Fonda taught her first exercise class, creating 'The Workout'; she opened her first studio the following year.

'The Workout' is a series of exercises which are both fun and

strenuous. They are designed to burn off calories, tone up the body, and strengthen the heart and lungs. They are based on the repetition of movements, stretches and aerobics, and are all accompanied by music.

✔ DO

✔ Aim to exercise regularly for maximum benefit: half an hour three times a week is ideal.

✔ Perform warm-up and wind-down exercises at each session.

✔ Wear suitable clothes, such as a leotard or tracksuit, which will allow freedom of movement while providing support.

✔ Wear snug padded training shoes to prevent jarring and jolting.

✔ See a doctor if you hurt yourself.

✗ DON'T

✗ Overdo it. Exercise until you can feel your heart and lungs working well, but never push yourself too far: over-exertion hurts and isn't good for you.

✗ Exercise if you're pregnant without seeking medical advice.

✗ Exercise on a full stomach as the blood will be diverted to the muscles, depriving the stomach of oxygen, and this may give you cramp and nausea.

✗ Embark on aerobic exercise if you have a family history of heart disease without taking medical advice.

The way we use our bodies expresses how we feel about ourselves and the world around us. But years of slouching, tension and laziness, have encouraged us to fall into bad habits, which, according to the Alexander principle, may do us harm.

While acting with an Australian dramatic company, Frederick Matthias Alexander (1869–1955) was continually losing his voice and suffering from hoarseness. He studied his movements in front of a mirror, and discovered that the way he pulled his head back when speaking was constricting his larynx

Bad posture causes tension, aches and pains. The Alexander Technique can help you to correct these bad habits, and improve you both physically and mentally.

and therefore leading to hoarseness. Thus began the creation of the Alexander Technique.

What is it?
The Alexander Technique encompasses a whole philosophy of coordination and

very easy to slip back into bad habits, though! Try not to give in to them. For example, when you carry a bag don't hunch up your shoulders as this tenses the neck and half the back.

Who can it help?
It is particularly useful for musicians, dentists, hairdressers, sports enthusiasts and dancers who are constantly suffering from bad posture, tension and stress, brought on by repetitive and exaggerated movements. Violinists, for example, hunch their shoulders up and twist their arms when

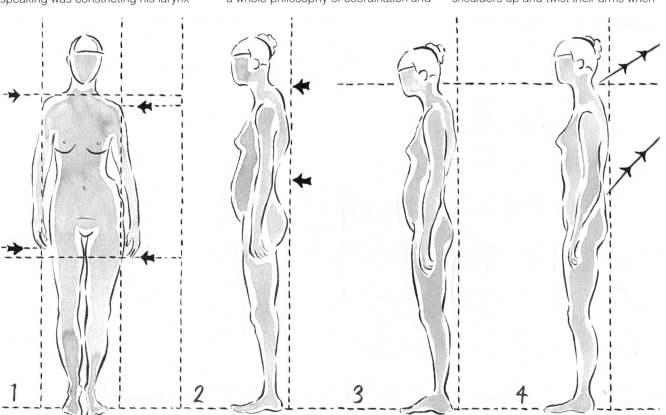

1 2 3 4

There are certain key areas that the Alexander Technique works on, to improve all-round physique. Diagram 1 (above) illustrates a common postural problem: one leg is bent, causing one hip to be pushed higher than the other and creating lop-sided shoulders. This is often connected to the problems in diagram 2, where the neck is held too far forward, causing a humped back and putting pressure on the windpipe. In diagram 3, the neck is again held incorrectly, making the lower back arch, the pelvis tip and the abdomen stick out.

Diagram 4 represents an improved posture. The dotted lines show the 'lengthening' and straightening of the neck and lower spine, which will have benefits for the body as a whole.

movement that concentrates on getting rid of stress and bad posture. It is based on a series of gentle exercises and movements that teach you how to sit, move and stand the way you are anatomically designed to. It is adjusted to your individual needs, and isn't based on rigid rules of 'correct' posture. A qualified teacher will explore areas of tension in your body and give you a feeling of poise, increased awareness and physical well-being. She may suggest things you could do to improve your posture, like straightening a curved spine or relaxing hunched shoulders.

The basic movements include 'letting the neck be free', 'letting the head go forward and up' in relation to the torso and neck, which in turn 'lengthens and widens' the body. It's

playing the violin, but once the Alexander Technique has taught them to 'let go' of these bad habits they can perform more easily and comfortably.

> "{The Alexander technique} gives us all the things we have been looking for in a system of physical education... and along with this a heightening of consciousness on all levels."
>
> *Aldous Huxley*

YOUR HEALTH

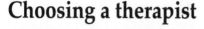

Alternative medicine is becoming increasingly popular as patients look outside orthodox medicine to help with problems or simply to make them feel better.

There are now many thousands of therapists practising some form of complementary therapy. Some therapies don't use any drugs at all, while others use only herbal and natural remedies. Despite the growing success of alternative medicine though, there is still little scientific evidence of its value. Many of the therapies are based on the concept of treating the 'whole person'' and it is this approach; combined with the extra time and attention a therapist can give you, which helps a patient to feel better.

The term 'Alternative Medecine' covers a large number of varied therapies. Some of the most common treatments are outlined below, but for more detail see under individual alphabetic entries.

Acupuncture
Needles are inserted into some of the body's acupuncture points and manipulated in order to release blocked flows of energy. It is most commonly used to relieve pain, such as arthritis, migraine and period pain; and to cure addictions, such as smoking.

Chiropractic
A recent scientific study has indicated that chiropractic is more likely to help

From left: fig, strawberry, mint and camomile.

patients with low back pain than orthodox medicine. Chiropractors believe that maladjustments and misalignments of the spine cause joint strain. After taking a full personal history and using an x-ray, they manipulate the relevant part of the spine by hand. It can also be used to help neck, shoulder and arm problems, migraine, asthma, arthritis and even stress.

Herbalism
Practitioners believe that only plant materials should be used to treat

disease in order to help the body's restorative powers.

Homeopathy
This has been used to treat a wide range of diseases. It is based on the principle that like is cured by like. For example, an allergy sufferer may be injected with a minute amount of an allergen.

Osteopathy
Used mainly to treat back pain, sciatica, and muscular and spinal problems, by both manipulating and massaging the affected joints.

Choosing a therapist

As yet there are insufficient guidelines which cover all alternative therapies, so in order to protect yourself, you must make your own investigations and follow a few simple rules.

● Make sure that the practitioner you choose is qualified and experienced. It is advisable to check the therapist's qualifications with the relevant regulatory body because in some fields, people can call themselves alternative practitioners after minimal training. Some practitioners are also qualified doctors.

● Have you obtained a medical diagnosis first? You should do this before seeing an alternative therapist to rule out the possibility of any serious disease or problem which require orthodox treatment.

● Are the premises clean and hygienic? This is essential if you are seeing an acupuncturist because of the risk posed by dirty needles.

● Do not take herbal and homeopathic remedies without supervision — most may be harmless, but some can cause poisoning and liver damage if taken in large quantities

> **" Traditional wisdom... sees illness as a disorder of the whole person, involving not only the patient's body, but also his mind, his self-image, his dependence on the physical and social environment, as well as his relation to the cosmos... "**
>
> *Fritjof Capra*

> **" There is more wisdom in your body than in your deepest philosophy. "**
>
> *Friedrich Nietzsche*

YOUR HEALTH

Swimming is one of the best exercises you can do. It will improve your balance and coordination, and will help to tone up your whole body.
(Telegraph Colour Library / Action Images)

In the SWIM

Exercising in water is a great way to meet friends and unwind, but it's also a good way to tone up your muscles in a safe and therapeutic environment.

Aquafit is a form of exercise which everyone can enjoy. A number of pools have set aside time for swimming/exercise classes (usually called aquarobics) so you can get fit without being splashed by children or battered by divers.

Try to go to your local pool twice a week and exercise for half an hour, and after three weeks you should start seeing some great results. It's a good way to get your body into shape, and in many ways is not as difficult as exercising on land. It's particularly good for people who are unfit, the overweight and the old.

Make your first session a gentle one and slowly build up your speed and strength at following sessions; you could repeat the same exercise a few more times, do it a little faster, or even adapt the exercise to make it more challenging.

Exercising in water has many advantages, which are partly due to the fact that water counteracts the effect of

Water Exercises

Here are some basic water exercises to tone up your muscles. Try them out for 30 minutes twice a week and you'll be amazed how much better you feel and look.

Exercise 1: Arms, tummy and bottom

1 Hold onto bar or ledge at side of pool. Make sure your feet can't touch the bottom. Curl up your body into a ball, tucking both knees into your chest.

2 Return to starting position, still holding on, and slowly curve spine backwards by stretching legs out behind you. Make sure you keep your head tucked in.

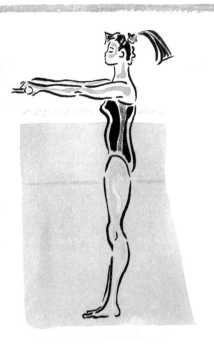

Exercise 2: Arms

1 Stand facing side of pool in chest-deep water and hold onto the bar or ledge.

2 Let go of bar with left hand and swing it behind you in an anticlockwise direction. Carry on turning until your left hand reaches the bar and stretch it out until it's as far away from your right hand as possible.

3 Let go with your right hand and turn in the same direction until you can touch the side again. You'll now be facing the edge of the pool. Carry on like this until the water gets too deep and then change directions.

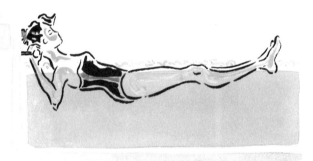

Exercise 3: Shoulders

1 Float on your back, and hold onto the bar.

2 Slowly pull your knees up to your chin, being careful to keep them together. Then stretch out your legs and body as far as possible without letting go of the rail.

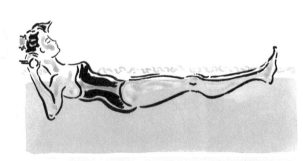
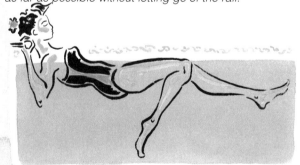

Exercise 4: Legs

1 Float on your back, and hold onto the bar with both hands. You must make sure your knees are touching each other throughout the whole exercise, and that they also remain just below the surface of the water.

2 Bend your left knee so your foot is underneath you, as if you're trying to kick your bottom. Straighten your left leg and at the same time bend your right knee. Keep your knees together – only the leg below the joint should be moving. You'll feel the muscle in the front of your thigh pulling.

DO

✔ Relax — if you're a nervous non-swimmer, afraid of getting water in your eyes, or even concerned about your new hair style, you'll not be relaxed and won't be getting the most from these exercises.

✔ Go to a pool which plays music over its public address system — it's much easier and more relaxing to exercise to music than to a silence.

✔ Rest for half an hour when you've finished — give yourself time to get your breath back.

DON'T

✗ Exercise if it hurts — it's not an endurance test so don't overdo it.

✗ Use a pool which has cold water — you won't get any of the therapeutic benefits.

✗ Exercise if you have any medical problems — get your doctor's advice first.

gravity. It's good for people with aching or painful joints as the joints are buoyed up and floated slightly apart, so that movements which are normally painful don't hurt at all.

Fitness and balance

As well as helping easy and painless movement, water also makes exercising a lot more effective. This is because water is 1000 times denser than air so the simplest movement, like walking, is more difficult as the 'drag' in the water makes the muscles work much harder than normally.

Water exercises will also improve your balance and coordination. In water, all movements are slower than on land, so it's much easier to keep your balance as you have time to steady yourself. Try to use the water as if it isn't there; do the exercises slowly and gracefully, not awkwardly, and make sure you're balanced perfectly.

People are becoming more and more health and fitness orientated and this has been reflected in the increase in the number of public swimming pools over the last twenty years.

Swimming is one of the best

- **Most aquafit exercises take place in shallow water, so non-swimmers can join in too - but do warn the instructor if you can't swim.**
- **Take care not to over-do the exercises - the body is so well supported in the water that you may not notice when muscles are becoming tired.**
- **Swimming and gentle aquafit is a particularly good form of exercise**

exercises you can do. It will help to tone up your whole body, particularly the arms, shoulders and legs. If you swim at a steady rate, you will burn up between five and fifteen calories a minute.

For maximum benefit, try to swim three times a week for half an hour. Start slowly, and gradually build up your speed.

Fragrant Remedies

Aromatherapy is an increasingly popular form of alternative medicine. As well as smelling wonderful, aromatherapy oils are good for the mind and body, and are used to treat many different complaints.

Aromatherapy literally means 'treatment with smells' and is the practice of using essential oils extracted from plants to improve and enhance health and appearance. The uses of aromatherapy vary widely, ranging from soothing dry or sensitive skin, to treating depression and stress.

Aromatherapy was first practised by the Chinese 3000 years ago, but the term 'aromatherapy' was actually coined by the French chemist René Maurice Gattefosse who discovered the healing power of essential oils quite by accident. He burnt his hand badly whilst doing an experiment and he treated it with the closest thing — lavender oil. Much to his surprise the burn was instantly soothed and healed very quickly.

Essential oils

The oils used in aromatherapy are called essential oils. They are highly concentrated scented droplets of liquid that are greatly valued for their therapeutic powers (see Choosing essential oils).

The oils are extracted in minute quantities from flowers, stems, roots or bark of various plants. The process of extraction is expensive and time consuming. For example, it takes 90kg of rose petals to produce just 600ml of essential oil. Other plants are more productive — the same amount of eucalyptus leaves will produce over 8.5 litres of oil.

Essential oils also vary in their potency depending on the time of day, month or season they are gathered. For example, jasmine is particularly fragrant at midnight.

Most essential oils are sold in 2fl oz bottles which hold about 15-30 drops of essential oil. Be careful when you buy an essential oil though, as many manufacturers sell impure oils that are cheaper, but not nearly as effective as the real thing. Watch out for a range of oils that are all the same price. Pure essential oils should vary in price as some oils, for example jasmine, neroli and rose, are more difficult to obtain and should therefore be more expensive.

Once you have bought an essential oil, store it in a cool, dark place. If you leave the bottle in the sunlight, the oil will quickly lose its fragrance and will no longer be effective. Essential oils are also very volatile so don't forget to put the tops back on once you have used them or they will evaporate and you'll be left with an empty bottle.

What are they used for?

Essential oils are used to treat a variety of complaints and can be used in many different ways (see box on treatments).

Many of the oils, for example eucalyptus, lemon and pine, have antiseptic and antibacterial properties that are useful for treating colds and coughs, and for cleansing infected wounds.

Essential oils are also used to soothe the nerves and are commonly used to treat stress-related problems, such as tension and insomnia. Some oils, for example thyme and rosemary, will help to reduce inflammation, ease aching bones and joints, and relieve the pain of arthritis and rheumatism.

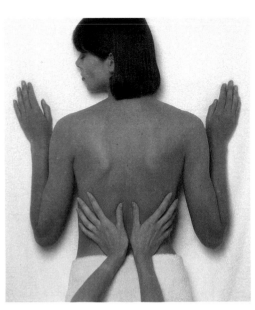

A massage using essential oils can be extremely therapeutic.

Massage

A common use of essential oils is in massage. Combined with massage, the essential oils will help you to relax and will relieve stress and tension. They will also improve your blood circulation and get rid of dead skin cells, leaving your skin looking smooth and healthy.

Essential oils are extremely concentrated and should always be diluted in a carrier oil such as sunflower or grape seed before being applied to the skin as they may irritate it. Add 4-6 drops of an essential oil of your choice to 10ml of a cheaper carrier oil. The amount of oil you need will vary — some people need more dilute solutions, while others need stronger ones. Don't make up more aromatherapy oil than you need though, as once you have mixed it with a carrier oil it will only last for two to three weeks.

If you don't have time to prepare your own oil, you can buy ready mixed oils. The Body Shop, for example, has a range of aromatherapy oils for about £3 each which are already diluted and ready for use.

The oil should be massaged into the body using smooth, firm strokes that warm the skin and thus help the oil to penetrate the skin. Depending on the essential oil you are using, it will take between 10 and 100 minutes for it to be properly absorbed. Once you've had the treatment, give your body time to absorb the oils and benefit from them — don't head straight for the shower.

AROMATHERAPY TREATMENTS

The following techniques are all easy to use at home, but stick to the recommended number of drops of essential oil per treatment. The oils are extremely concentrated and if you use too much you may reverse their beneficial effects.

Room freshener

If your bedroom smells of yesterday's socks or today's breakfast, use essential oils to freshen it up and get rid of stale lingering odours.

Add a few drops of your favourite essential oil to a dish of warm water and carefully place it on top of a radiator. The heat from the radiator will evaporate the oil and the aroma will quickly fill the room. Thyme, pine, lavender and eucalyptus are antiseptics and are very good air fresheners.

Alternatively, you can buy incense burners from most herbal shops. Add a few drops of oil to a small amount of warm water in the cavity at the top of the incense burner. Then place a lighted candle underneath the oil. The heat from the candle will vaporise the oil.

Vaporisers are small rings of fire-proof material that you can buy from most herbalists. Find a lamp and turn it on, then sit the ring on top of the light bulb and lightly squeeze a few drops of oil onto the ring. The heat from the bulb makes the oil vaporise and will fill your home with a beautiful fragrance.

Aromatic baths

If you're suffering from stress, fatigue, aches and pains or insomnia, you will find it's extremely soothing to relax in an aromatic bath.

Fill your bath with warm water, choose an oil, and add 5-10 drops to the bath. Mix the oil in and relax in the bath for about 10 minutes. The essential oil will be absorbed into your skin and it will also vaporise so you will be inhaling it in the steam. A good tip is to keep the door and windows closed so you get the total benefit from this treatment.

Inhalants

If you suffer from colds, coughs, headaches, stress or sinus trouble, one of the following inhalants may be the answer to your problems. Don't try inhalants though, if you suffer from asthma.

Take a bowl containing one pint of very hot water and squeeze 5-10 drops of the oil into it. Cover your head with a towel and keep your head about nine inches above the water; inhale the steam for 5-10 minutes. Don't do this more than three times a day. Menthol is good for treating respiratory problems and eucalyptus is excellent for easing sinus problems.

A practical alternative to the bowl of water, is to put 5-8 drops of the oil on a hanky or tissue and breathe in the aroma with four slow but deep breaths.

Pot pourri

If your bowl of pot pourri is tired and stale, sprinkle a couple of drops of an essential oil over it. This will quickly revitalise it and it will soon be fresh and fragrant again.

AROMATHERAPY

CHOOSING ESSENTIAL OILS

The oils listed here are commonly available and can treat a variety of ailments. Use our guide to help you select an oil that will successfully treat your complaints.

Camomile: soothes dry, sensitive and allergic skins. Also has a calming effect. Should be avoided during pregnancy. Mixes well with lavender, ylang ylang, peppermint and geranium.

Eucalyptus: an excellent decongestant so is good for coughs and colds. Helps relieve muscular aches and pains, and is refreshing. Mixes well with lemon and lavender.

Geranium: a refreshing oil that will help you to relax. Also an astringent, and will ease menstrual problems and cleanse the skin. Blends well with all oils.

Juniper: good for tension and for relieving rheumatic symptoms. Also helps fluid retention and is an astringent so is good for oily skin. Should be avoided during pregnancy. Mixes well with rosemary.

Rosemary: refreshing and good for oily skin, especially when used in a face mask. Also helps relieve fluid retention and cellulite. Said to improve memory. It is very good for the digestion. Should be avoided during pregnancy. Mixes well with juniper.

Lavender: soothes problem skin and helps relieve tension, headaches and insomnia. Mixes well with geranium, peppermint and eucalyptus.

Neroli: a good anti-depressant and relaxant. Will also soothe dry, irritated skin.

Peppermint: has a refreshing, cooling effect on hot skin. Also acts as a decongestant. Should be avoided during pregnancy. Mixes well with camomile and sandalwood.

Pine: a refreshing antiseptic and excellent air freshener. Helps ease sinus problems and 'flu.

Sandalwood: soothes dry skin and can help relieve sore throats and coughs. It is an important part of mixtures that are used for soothing massage after bathing. Renowned for its unproven aphrodisiac qualities. Mixes well with lemon. Is one of the most expensive oils.

Rose: a relaxing, anti-depressant that helps to ease stress and headaches.

Ylang Ylang: very richly perfumed. Relaxing, can relieve depression and insomnia.

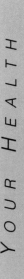

YOUR HEALTH

Safety First

• Never take essential oils internally unless under the instructions of a qualified aromatherapist.
• Keep essential oils away from the eyes.
• Always dilute essential oils before using them on the skin, unless specifically instructed
• Store essential oils out of the reach of children and in a cool dark place.
• If you suffer from asthma or any other allergic condition such as dermatitis or hay fever, seek the advice of an aromatherapy practitioner before using essential oils.

Bach flower remedies are pure plant essences that are preserved in brandy. They are used to treat emotional and mental problems, which some practitioners believe are the root of all illnesses.

Dr Edward Bach (1880-1936) was a Harley Street physician who graduated from Birmingham University and University College Hospital, London. He believed that mental and emotional problems were the underlying cause of illness and that practitioners should concentrate on relieving them rather than the symptoms. He was convinced that fear, depression or worry, for example, would lower the body's resistance to disease.

In 1930, he abandoned his practice and moved to the countryside where he developed his theory which is based on English flowers found in the fields and trees of the countryside.

The remedies

Dr Bach found the remedies by searching the countryside and succeeded in identifying 38 flowers that appeared to have healing qualities. He made the remedies by cutting off the heads of particular flowers (see *plant essences*, right) and floating them on a bowl of water in sunlight for a few hours. The essence of the flower was transferred to the water. He then threw the flowers away but kept and bottled the water. Dr Bach also made remedies from flowers growing on trees. He did this by boiling the blossoms in a pan of water for half an hour, and bottling the water.

Bach flower remedies now tend to be preserved in brandy though, which helps to preserve them and makes them last much longer. They are relatively inexpensive and can be bought from most herbalists. All you have to do is choose the remedy you

think would be best for you and put two drops on your tongue or dilute the drops in a glass of mineral water and drink it. You can take the remedy up to four times a day and for as long as you need. A few weeks should be long enough to sort out most problems, but sometimes it could take a couple of months or so.

Practitioners argue that if your emotional or mental state is temporary, the remedy should work immediately. If, however, it is a more serious problem, it may take longer for the remedy to work.

> " There is no true healing unless there is a change in outlook, peace of mind, and inner happiness. "
>
> Dr Edward Bach

PLANT ESSENCES

Bach divided the 38 plant remedies into seven groups, according to the problems they treat. Follow our guide and experiment to see which remedy would work for you.

◉ *For fear:* mimulus, cherry plum, aspen, rock rose, red chestnut.
◉ *For uncertainty:* scleranthus, gentian, gorse, hornbeam, wild oat, cerato.
◉ *For insufficient interest in present circumstances:* clematis, honeysuckle, wild rose, olive, white chestnut, mustard, chestnut bud.
◉ *For loneliness:* water violet, impatiens, heather.
◉ *For oversensitivity to influences and ideas:* agrimony, centaury, walnut, holly.
◉ *For over-care of the welfare of others:* chicory, vine, beech, rock water, vervain.
◉ *For despondency or despair:* pine, elm, sweet chestnut, larch, star-of-Bethlehem, willow, oak, crab apple.

RESCUE REMEDY

Bach 'rescue remedy' is a combination of five plant remedies — cherry plum, clematis, rock rose, impatiens and star-of-Bethlehem.

If you put a few drops of the rescue remedy on your tongue or take some in water, it will help to soothe, calm and reassure you. It will also help you overcome any feelings of trauma, anguish, bereavement or panic you may have.

YOUR HEALTH

Callan Pinckney's Callanetics

Callanetics is a programme of exercises unlike most others. Instead of the rigorous exercises we are accustomed to, Callanetics consists of toning up your body using gentle movements that make the muscles work deeply.

Callan Pinckney was born with spinal curvature, one hip higher than the other and feet that were turned inwards so badly she had to wear leg braces for seven years. In 1961, Callan left her home in Georgia and travelled the world for 10 years, taking various menial jobs in order to supplement her savings.

During that time, she carried a very heavy backpack which put a great deal of strain on her back, knees and shoulders. She also suffered from malnutrition and dysentery. After years of mistreating her body and suffering from back ache, she became aware of the need to look after her body and, after returning to the United States in 1972, she began experimenting with various exercise techniques in an attempt to ease her pain and improve her posture.

Callan discovered that if she altered her position by less than an inch her back stopped hurting. She developed these precise movements and was amazed to see how much stronger and firmer her body was becoming. As a result of this discovery, Callan began tutoring students in the privacy of their own homes and she slowly built up her hour-long programme of exercises.

The exercise programme

Callan stresses that before you start the exercise programme, you should always do a warm-up. These preliminary exercises will gently stretch your muscles and help to prevent you from injuring yourself. They will also prepare your muscles for the demanding programme and thus make the exercises more effective. Callan sees her exercises as a successful way of sculpting the body — around her studio she has a number of sculptures which she changes every couple of weeks to give her students something new and inspiring to look at.

The total Callanetics programme can be completed in less than an hour, depending on your strength and stamina, and you should try to do the exercises twice a week. One of the main attractions of this programme of exercises is that it doesn't take long before you start seeing some results — it takes hours and not weeks. The exercises are also popular because they can be done by people of all ages and, although they are much more popular with women, many men do them as well.

The exercises are varied and concentrate on particular areas of the body, for example the tummy, bottom, thighs, legs and neck. But they can look deceptively easy! The important thing to remember though, is that you should not exercise until it hurts. If you're not supple or flexible enough to do some of the exercises and they hurt, don't force

CALLANETICS

After the birth of her first child, the Duchess of York was somewhat overweight (above left). Callanetics put her back in shape again (above right).

stamina, speed, body control and awareness, and will help you to relax both mentally and physically.

You should not judge your success by your weight — Callanetics may actually make you put weight on! So don't jump on the scales after each exercise session as it may discourage you — use a tape measure instead and you will be surprised how quickly you can lose the extra inches. If you stick with it, you may drop two or even three dress sizes as the excess flab is replaced with muscle (which actually weighs more than flab).

yourself to do them. You should build up your strength and flexibility slowly — if you force your body to do something it doesn't want to do, you may end up doing yourself a serious injury.

You can do the exercises anywhere, providing you are comfortable and have enough space to stretch and lie down without bumping into anything. It is best though, to do your exercises in full view of a long mirror so you can see what's happening to your body while you're exercising and make sure you're doing them correctly. (The chances are that if you find the exercises easy, you're probably not doing them correctly.)

The benefits

The exercises consist of precise, concentrated and gentle movements — no more than half an inch in any direction. The exercises work deeply and as you become stronger you'll be able to increase the number of times you do them.

As well as tightening and toning up your body, the exercises will help to improve your coordination, balance,

Useful Information

Books
Callanetics, Century Hutchinson Ltd, £7.99
Callanetics Countdown, Arrow Books Ltd, £7.99
Callanetics for Your Back, Ebury Press, £7.99

Videos
Beginning Callanetics, £9.99
Callanetics, £9.99
Super Callanetics, £9.99

The above publications are all written by Callan Pinckney.

INNER THIGH SQUEEZE

One of the most common complaints women have about their bodies is their thighs. The following exercise is part of Callan Pinckney's hour-long programme which she says will help tone up your inner thighs.

Sit on the floor in front of a chair with your legs stretched out in front of you. Rest your hands on the floor by the side of your hips to give you support and place the arch of your feet on the outside of the chair legs.

Relax your shoulders and head, allowing them to fall slightly forward to avoid putting pressure on your lower back. Tightly squeeze your feet and legs together, as if you're trying to crush the chair legs, and count to 100 slowly. You should be able to feel your inner thighs working.

YOUR HEALTH

A VERSATILE HERB

Camomile is a plant that grows wild in England. It is widely used for its cosmetic and medicinal properties and is an ingredient in many products, such as cleansers, shampoos, tea, toothpaste and mouthwashes.

There are two varieties of camomile: German camomile (or true camomile) and Roman camomile. Some experts argue that the German variety is the more medicinal but most people don't distinguish between the two varieties.

The name camomile comes from the Greek word 'chamaimelon'. Chamai means 'on the ground' and melon means 'apple'. It was called this because of the relaxing fragrance of the leaves. The Ancient Egyptians used camomile for its wonderful healing qualities and Greek physicians prescribed it for fevers and for female problems, such as premenstrual tension. And it is believed to have been used in England as early as 1265.

Camomile grows naturally in England on wasteland and along country lanes. It grows to a height of about 60cm and is quite easy to recognise. The plant has a tall stem and little white flowers that have yellow centres which contain the soothing properties. The bright green leaves are apple-scented, and give off a fragrance that is very relaxing.

What are its uses?

Camomile is mainly grown for its oil which is used in a wide variety of cosmetic products, including cleansers, soaps, astringents and body splashes. Camomile suits all skin types, particularly sensitive, dry and delicate skins. It is pleasantly soothing and moisturising and will help to ease various skin complaints such as eczema, acne, inflammations, sunburn and allergies. Camomile is also commonly used in shampoos and conditioners for blonde hair as it helps to enhance the natural highlights and lighten the hair.

CAMOMILE AND CHILDREN

Camomile is particularly good for children because it is very low in toxicity and is therefore very safe.

If your baby is suffering with an irritating nappy rash, make a cool compress of camomile and gently apply it to the area that is sore and painful. Camomile will also help to ease insomnia so if your child finds it difficult to get to sleep at nights make her a cup of warm camomile tea about half an hour before it's time for her to go to bed. It will help her to relax and will stop her from having any disturbing nightmares.

Camomile contains azulene which has anti-bacterial and healing properties and it is a popular ingredient in toothpastes and mouthwashes. It is used to treat many conditions, including skin inflammations, rheumatism and nervous tension. The small, yellow flowers can also be used to make refreshingly fragrant camomile tea which has been drunk for centuries. It is a popular drink as it helps to relieve headaches, indigestion, period pains and stress — it will even help to relax the face muscles.

A herbal bath

Camomile essential oil is used to treat depression, insomnia, and digestive and menstrual problems — it is a refreshing and relaxing oil that eases aching joints and will help you to unwind. A relaxing camomile bath may be just what you need if you're feeling tired and need to relax. Add about 10 drops of camomile essential oil to your bath — it will help to moisturise your skin, and ease aching muscles.

If you can't get hold of camomile essential oil, a very good alternative is to take three or four camomile teabags or a handful of dried camomile flowers and wrap them up in a piece of fine gauze so you have a bag of herbs. Immerse the bag in your bath water and relax as it releases the therapeutic properties into the water. You can also make a body scrub in the same way by adding a little bran to the bag of herbs and gently rubbing it over your body to exfoliate your skin and get rid of all the grime and dead skin cells.

Alternatively, you could make an infusion by pouring two cups of boiling water over half a cup of dried camomile flowers. Leave it to infuse for about 10 minutes, then drain off the flowers and add the water to your bath. Don't put the herbs straight into the bath, though, as you'll end up with bits of flowers clogging up the drain, and sticking to both you and to the bath.

The therapeutic and anti-bacterial properties of camomile make it a very popular ingredient in a wide range of products.

RECIPES FOR BEAUTY

HERBAL TEA

1 tsp (5ml) dried camomile flowers
1 cup boiling water

Add the dried camomile flowers to a warmed teapot. Pour boiling water over the dried herbs and leave it for at least 10 minutes to infuse.

FOOT BATH

1 oz (25g) camomile
1/2 oz (10g) thyme
1/2 oz (10g) rosemary
1 oz (25g) peppermint
1 oz (25g) marjoram

Mix the dried herbs. Take two dessert spoons of the herbs and add to one litre of water. Boil for five minutes, then cool and pour into a bowl. Bathe your feet in it — you'll find it's very soothing for tired and aching feet.

FACE STEAM

3 tbsp (40g) dried camomile flowers
3 pints (1.5 litres) boiling water

Remove all your make-up and tie your hair back so it doesn't get in your way. Put the dried camomile flowers in a bowl and pour 1.5 litres of boiling water over the top, stirring with a wooden spoon as you do so. Drape a towel over your head and the bowl, and keep your face about 30cm above the water. Relax and inhale the steam for approximately ten minutes, then rinse your face with cool water. Steaming your face with camomile will help to soothe and cleanse your skin.

CAMOMILE CLEANSER

2 tbsp (25g) dried camomile flowers
1/4 pint (125ml) creamy milk

Heat the milk and camomile for half an hour but don't bring it up to the boil. Leave it to infuse for about two hours. Strain and throw away the flowers. Squeeze a little onto a ball of cotton wool and apply to your face. The cleanser will last for about a week if you keep it in the fridge.

Helpful Hints

• Camomile tea is particularly recommended after a course of antibiotics.
• For itchy skin and sunburn conditions, try dabbing the affected area with cotton wool which has been soaked in ice-cold camomile tea.

ORIENTAL OUTLOOK

If you have difficulty believing that your astrological sun-sign has some influence on your destiny, then you will have to suspend your disbelief entirely in order to come to terms with Chinese astrology!

Instead of dividing the population up into rough twelfths, according to their date of birth, as Western astrology does, the Oriental system ascribes us a set of characteristics according to the year in which we were born. Each year is named after one of twelve animals, and when that twelve-year cycle ends, another begins.

Animal years

The story goes that Buddha felt the Chinese needed a complete overhaul. So he called a meeting of all the animals on New Year's Eve — but only twelve of them turned up: the rat, the ox (or buffalo), the tiger, the cat (sometimes known as the rabbit), the dragon, the snake, the horse, the goat, the monkey, the rooster, the dog, and the pig.

Buddha honoured the twelve animals listed above by giving each of them a year of their own, from which the human beings born then took certain characteristics. For example, those born in the year of the Rat assume the qualities of intellect, sociability — and manipulation — characteristics usually ascribed to that much-maligned rodent.

But with Chinese astrology there are no planetary movements to take into consideration or arcane books to consult: it's a great deal simpler than its Western counterpart. And it's easier for us to see whether it works or not! On the whole, Chinese astrology is gaining popularity in the West because it seems to come up with the goods. Even if it's not the most subtle of systems it can still have a lesson or two for us — and it's also a lot of fun.

East meets west

Western sun-sign astrology fits in amazingly well with the Chinese version. Your sun-sign will give you a subtler, more detailed insight into your Chinese animal. Add all the details of your sun-sign characteristics (see Astrology) to those of your Chinese Animal Year and you will almost certainly understand yourself and your destiny much better.

CELEBRITY HOROSCOPES

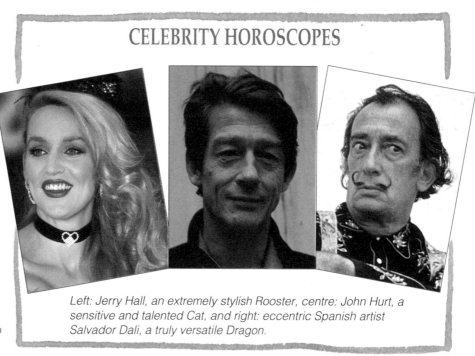

Left: Jerry Hall, an extremely stylish Rooster, centre: John Hurt, a sensitive and talented Cat, and right: eccentric Spanish artist Salvador Dali, a truly versatile Dragon.

THE RAT

YEARS OF THE RAT

January 31 1900 to February 19 1901
February 18 1912 to February 6 1913
February 5 1924 to January 25 1925
January 24 1936 to February 11 1937
February 10 1948 to January 29 1949
January 28 1960 to February 15 1961
February 15 1972 to February 2 1973
February 2 1984 to February 19 1985
February 19 1996 to February 6 1997

Rats are well-mannered, charming, romantic, natural actors who can make others laugh or cry with equal ease – and they also have a tendency to be nit-picking, manipulative, self-tortured and self-pitying.

PARTNERS

They're at their best with the daring Dragon, whose wisdom will calm them down and point them in the right direction. The plodding Ox also brings them down a peg or two – in the nicest way! Monkeys are very attractive to Rats, although they may not be faithful. Beware of romance with a Horse or a Cat. Horses are too self-centred and may bewilder the Rat with conflicting demands. Cats are too introverted for the outgoing Rat.

FAMOUS RATS

Marlon Brando, Prince Charles, Lauren Bacall and Shakespeare.

THE OX

YEARS OF THE OX

February 19 1901 to February 8 1902
February 6 1913 to January 26 1914
January 25 1925 to February 13 1926
February 11 1937 to January 31 1938
January 29 1949 to February 17 1950
February 15 1961 to February 5 1962
February 3 1973 to January 22 1974
February 20 1985 to February 8 1986
February 7 1997 to January 27 1998

Oxen are powerful, determined, weighty (in more senses than one!), charismatic, natural leaders, style-setters, brave, loyal, long-suffering, disciplinarians – and bossy, stubborn, bad losers, stick-in-the-muds, jealous and rather oafish.

PARTNERS

The best partner for the Ox is a typical Rooster – flashier than the plodder, and therefore a perfect complement. Charming Rats and slithery Snakes also make compatible partners for the Ox, although the Snake may find difficulty in not slithering into someone else's arms! It will be peace, perfect peace, to the point of tedium if one Ox marries another, but utter disaster if the Ox teams up with the capricious Goat or the over-vivacious Tiger.

FAMOUS OXEN

Napoleon Bonaparte, Adolf Hitler, Richard Gere and Princess Diana.

THE TIGER

YEARS OF THE TIGER

February 8 1902 to January 29 1903
January 26 1914 to February 14 1915
February 13 1926 to February 2 1927
January 31 1938 to February 19 1939
February 17 1950 to February 6 1951
February 5 1962 to January 25 1963
January 23 1974 to February 10 1975
February 9 1986 to January 28 1987
January 28 1998 to February 15 1999

Tigers are spontaneous, generous, sexy, brave, honourable, wise, noble, magnetic, profound, charismatic hypersensitive, unyielding, slapdash, rebellious, vain, live dangerously – and to hell with the consequences!

PARTNERS

Tigers do not suffer fools gladly, but they often admire and respect the Horse more than any other Year. The Dragon and the Dog are also possible partners as long as mutual loyalty is maintained, but the wily Monkey may be too fidgety and dangerous even for the Tiger! Pigs are possible partners but usually have to sacrifice a cherished part of their lives. The Cat is too similar to the Tiger for any union between them to work for very long.

FAMOUS TIGERS

Marilyn Monroe, Tom Cruise, Princess Anne and the Queen.

THE CAT

YEARS OF THE CAT
January 29 1903 to February 16 1904
February 14 1915 to February 3 1916
February 2 1927 to January 23 1928
February 19 1939 to February 8 1940
February 6 1951 to January 27 1952
January 25 1963 to February 13 1964
February 11 1975 to January 30 1976
January 29 1987 to February 16 1988
February 16 1999 to February 4 2000

Cats are refined, shrewd, scrupulous, calm, hospitable, clever, tactful, companionable – but they can also be moody, wimpish, hypersensitive, egocentric, jacks of all trades and somewhat withdrawn.

PARTNERS
Dreamy, artistic Goats are most attractive to Cats, and – unlikely as it may sound – Dogs also make loyal partners. Pigs love the refined Cat and add their own brand of elegance to a union with one, but Snakes and Horses are too pedestrian, while Dragons and Roosters tend to make the sparks fly! It's possible for two Cats together to live in harmony – but Cats are difficult to live with and many will have more than one marriage.

FAMOUS CATS
Frank Sinatra, Eva Peron, Albert Einstein and John Hurt.

THE DRAGON

YEARS OF THE DRAGON
February 16 1904 to February 4 1905
February 13 1916 to January 23 1917
January 23 1928 to February 10 1929
February 8 1940 to January 27 1941
January 27 1952 to February 14 1953
February 13 1964 to February 2 1965
January 31 1976 to February 17 1977
February 17 1988 to February 5 1989

Dragons are vivacious, lucky (for their family and partners too), optimistic, intuitive, psychic, enthusiastic, generous and ethereal. However, they can sometimes be rather demanding, disruptive, loud, egocentric, self-tortured, over-impressionable and forcefully judgmental.

PARTNERS
The quick-witted and guileful Monkey complements the Dragon, although some Monkeys may run rings around them. The Rat and the Rooster can also provide plenty of security for the self-doubting Dragon. The Tiger can be a good match, although some concessions will have to be made by both partners quite early on in their relationship. But the Dragon should take care not to get involved with Oxen or Dogs. who don't have time for the Dragon's self-doubt.

FAMOUS DRAGONS
Salvador Dali, Joan of Arc, George Bernard Shaw and John Lennon.

THE SNAKE

YEARS OF THE SNAKE
February 4 1905 to January 25 1906
January 23 1917 to February 11 1918
February 10 1929 to January 30 1930
January 27 1941 to February 15 1942
February 14 1953 to February 3 1954
February 21 1965 to January 21 1966
February 18 1977 to February 6 1978
February 6 1989 to January 26 1990

Snakes are elegant, intuitive, attractive, sympathetic, quiet, wise, serene and philosophical – but they also have the tendency to be self-critical, lazy, mean, possessive, vindictive, underhand, disloyal and rather showy.

PARTNERS
Slow, loyal Oxen make perfect partners for the flirtatious Snake, while Roosters provide a lively home, with a somewhat stormy atmosphere! Fascinating and magnetic Dragons are favourites of the Snake, who can break the habits of a lifetime and remain loyal to them. Tigers are far too difficult to handle. Dogs and Pigs give the Snake much-needed freedom, but remember that neither will enjoy being taken for a ride.

FAMOUS SNAKES
Pablo Picasso, Aretha Franklin, Jackie Onassis – and John F Kennedy.

THE HORSE

YEARS OF THE HORSE
January 25 1906 to February 13 1907*
February 11 1918 to February 1 1919
January 30 1930 to February 17 1931
February 15 1942 to February 5 1943
February 3 1954 to January 24 1955
January 21 1966 to February 9 1967*
February 7 1978 to January 27 1979
January 27 1990 to February 14 1991
*Years of the Fire Horse – every 60 years.

Horses are charming, well-spoken, sensual, hard-working, tough, quick-thinking, companionable – and egocentric, insensitive, bullying and weak. Those born in the Year of the Fire Horse (see above) are said to be rare and strangely lucky, although they are not so lucky for their families.

Fire Horses are talented, psychic, witty and destined for greatness. But also headstrong, controversial, egocentric, hypersensitive and lonely.

PARTNERS
Tigers, Goats and Dogs make the best partners for the self-doubting Horse. All three signs keep the Horse amused and provide a secure home, but the Tiger will win the most respect and be by far the most compatible sexually. Roosters are superficially attractive, but mutual nit-picking can kill romance. Pigs and Oxen are too earthy and Monkeys are too deceitful.

FAMOUS HORSES
Barbra Streisand and Paul McCartney.

THE GOAT

YEARS OF THE GOAT
February 13 1907 to February 2 1908
February 1 1919 to February 20 1920
February 17 1931 to February 6 1932
February 5 1943 to January 25 1944
January 24 1955 to February 12 1956
February 9 1967 to January 29 1968
January 28 1979 to February 15 1980
February 15 1991 to February 3 1992

Goats are homelovers, mild-mannered, artistic, delicate, peaceloving, persevering, endearing – but also changeable, undisciplined, fussy, gloomy, unpunctual, and are easily led.

PARTNERS
Cats are by far the best partners for the dreamy Goat. Good organisers and refined, Cats provide the sort of home that suits a Goat's inner needs, while Pigs are good with money, protective and loyal. Monkeys will get to the heart of the matter for a Goat, and Horses will be only too pleased to help out with a beloved Goat's burdens. Avoid Dogs or Oxen – they'll take you apart in no time.

FAMOUS GOATS
Florence Nightingale, Mick Jagger, Robert De Niro and Mel Gibson.

THE MONKEY

YEARS OF THE MONKEY
February 2 1908 to January 22 1909
February 20 1920 to February 8 1921
February 6 1932 to January 26 1933
January 25 1944 to February 13 1945
February 12 1956 to January 31 1957
January 29 1968 to February 16 1969
February 16 1980 to February 4 1981
February 4 1992 to January 22 1993

Monkeys are witty, quick-thinking, incisive, clever, inventive, passionate, energetic, enthusiastic, vivacious, assertive, adaptable – and also deceitful, manipulative, two-faced, unfaithful, opportunistic, verbose and superficial.

PARTNERS
The ever-versatile Dragon will ensure the easily bored Monkey never (or rarely!) strays, and the Rat adores the Monkey for his energy and wit. Tigers arouse the Monkey's passion, but the Tiger tends to slope off from time to time, leaving the Monkey panting with unsatisfied passion! Pigs make secure mates, but Oxen live for their children, which won't please the sexy Monkey. Dogs and Horses don't suit the dilettante Monkey.

FAMOUS MONKEYS
The Marquis de Sade, Yul Brynner, Diana Ross and Elizabeth Taylor.

THE ROOSTER

YEARS OF THE ROOSTER

January 22 1909 to February 10 1910
February 8 1921 to January 28 1922
January 26 1933 to February 14 1934
February 13 1945 to February 2 1946
January 31 1957 to February 16 1958
February 17 1969 to February 5 1970
February 5 1981 to January 24 1982
February 23 1993 to February 9 1994

Roosters are full of vitality, frank, open, stylish, enthusiastic, adventurous, inventive, interesting, generous and confident – but they also have a tendency to be braggarts, vain, loud, caustic, pompous and they are changeable.

PARTNERS

The brave Dragon is very lucky for the Rooster, who may even be happy to take a back seat and revel in his partner's success! The Ox will provide some much-needed security, while the Snake and the Rooster often make a beautiful couple who enjoy meaningful discussions. Rats can get on with the showy Rooster, but not Cats – sharp tongues on both sides don't make life easy. Other Roosters should also keep their distance.

FAMOUS ROOSTERS

Errol Flynn, Katherine Hepburn, Joan Collins and Jerry Hall.

THE DOG

YEARS OF THE DOG

February 10 1910 to January 30 1911
January 28 1922 to February 16 1923
February 14 1934 to February 4 1935
February 2 1946 to January 22 1947
February 16 1958 to February 8 1959
February 6 1970 to January 26 1971
January 25 1982 to February 12 1983
February 10 1994 to January 30 1995

Dogs are brave, loyal, trustworthy, discreet, faithful, dutiful, generous-spirited, selfless, modest and conventional – but on the other hand, they can be introspective, anxious, temperamental, cynical, pessimistic, obstinate, self-righteous and extremely judgmental.

PARTNERS

Dogs find Tigers beautifully self-assured. Worriers by nature, Dogs admire anyone who rises above daily cares. The Cat is understanding, the Pig encourages the unwary Dog to live a little, and the Horse provides encouragement to get on with the bolder schemes in life. But two Dogs together may make for a pessimistic household where little gets done. Rats, Dragons, Goats and Roosters all provide too many conflicts, while Snakes are too showy for the Dog.

FAMOUS DOGS

Shirley MacLaine, Elvis Presley, Winston Churchill and Sophia Loren.

THE PIG

YEARS OF THE PIG

January 30 1911 to February 18 1912
February 16 1923 to February 5 1924
February 4 1935 to January 24 1936
January 22 1947 to February 10 1948
February 8 1959 to January 28 1960
January 27 1971 to February 14 1972
February 13 1983 to February 1 1984
January 31 1995 to February 18 1996

Pigs are truthful, loyal, sensitive, sympathetic, scrupulous, sensual, obliging, peaceloving, refined and have a sense of fair play – but they can also tend to be naive, overindulgent, lazy, pushovers, gullible and insecure.

PARTNERS

The best mate for the Pig is the Cat, who may be shocked by his huge sexual appetite, but will always be flattered by it! Dragons may make protective partners, but should be aware how easy it is to deceive the gullible Pig. For this reason, the guileful Monkey makes the worst partner. Roosters and Snakes may take advantage of his good nature, while the Tiger isn't straightforward enough for the pure-minded Pig.

FAMOUS PIGS

Ernest Hemingway, Woody Allen, Barbara Cartland and Elton John.

WHAT'S IN A CHINESE YEAR?
The Chinese believe that the different animal years affect us in various ways, according to the characteristics of each animal.

YEARS OF THE RAT
These years are lucky, especially for summer babies, years that are generally good for storing up provisions against rainy days, and for planting and setting things in motion. Good years to look deeply into finances and investments – whatever you do, expect the unexpected and don't count your chickens!

YEARS OF THE OX
These are lucky years for those Oxen who were born in the winter months, these years benefit the sudden rise of dictators and harsh regimes, but are also good for crops and harvests and environmental issues – although conservationists may have a fight on their hands with big corporations or governments.

YEARS OF THE TIGER
This is a time of upheaval, catastrophe and disaster, not just locally but on a global scale, this sudden change is reflected in many individual lives. It's a time to be calm and turn to inner resources, to make the most of security and to try to be positive no matter what happens.

YEARS OF THE CAT
Justice prevails in the year of the Cat; perhaps the end of conflict is marked in these years, and there are strong movements towards learning, self-improvement and profound thought. It's a time for the philosopher and the playwright, not the soldier or the politician.

YEARS OF THE DRAGON
These are times for celebration, for indulging in legend and myth, for harking back to one's roots, for the resurgence of archetypal images such as King Arthur and Merlin. Don't expect any rewards of these times to be anything other than fleeting, but there will be many memories to cherish.

YEARS OF THE SNAKE
Past indiscretions and betrayals have a way of coming to a head, both globally and closer to home, in Snake years. Upheavals of all sorts can be expected – finances need watching, although they will tend to be tight and dangerously close to breaking point. But on a more optimistic note, at least romance is starred for success.

YEARS OF THE HORSE
These are active years, years in which to throw away the useless and worn-out and to build a new future energetically and with optimism. It's hard work but the rewards in future years will be considerable. You may come out of a Horse year a different person from the one who entered it.

YEARS OF THE GOAT
Disaster approaches, financially and politically – then, at the last minute, we're all saved by someone or something who, although pushed to the limits, carries all before them. We must all learn to think on our feet and improvise, to think laterally and to throw out outmoded concepts and traditions. The Arts always benefit from Years of the Goat.

YEARS OF THE MONKEY
The unexpected always takes precedence in these years. It's a time of reckless abandon, taking risks, putting your money where your mouth is, and forgetting staid old plans. In these years we should accept new ideas, take up challenges on a grand scale. Individuals will be able to succeed in the year of the Monkey where companies and governments are likely to fail.

YEARS OF THE ROOSTER
War is on the horizon, but the answer really does lie in the soil – and it would be better for all of us to get back to our roots, learning to be practical, inventive and creative. Those who have the knack for thinking in unusual ways should manage to make it to the top of the ladder.

YEARS OF THE DOG
Times of thinking of others and for compassion, these years are best for communal living or community work, for charities to blossom and for any wrongs to be righted. They are not, however, such good times for the rat race or for selfish individualism, for the conservative or traditional.

YEARS OF THE PIG
The end of the 12-year cycle sees us looking back and weighing up the pros and the cons of humanity's leap forward (or step back!). Realistic and often sobering phases, nevertheless the overwhelming feeling is positive, taking the good and learning from the bad.

The Chinese Years

RAT	1900	1912	1924	1936	1948	1960	1972	1984	1996
OX	1901	1913	1925	1937	1949	1961	1973	1985	1997
TIGER	1902	1914	1926	1938	1950	1962	1974	1986	1998
CAT	1903	1915	1927	1939	1951	1963	1975	1987	1999
DRAGON	1904	1916	1928	1940	1952	1964	1976	1988	2000
SNAKE	1905	1917	1929	1941	1953	1965	1977	1989	
HORSE	1906	1918	1930	1942	1954	1966	1978	1990	
GOAT	1907	1919	1931	1943	1955	1967	1979	1991	
MONKEY	1908	1920	1932	1944	1956	1968	1980	1992	
ROOSTER	1909	1921	1933	1945	1957	1969	1981	1993	
DOG	1910	1922	1934	1946	1958	1970	1982	1994	
PIG	1911	1923	1935	1947	1959	1971	1983	1995	

Manipulative Treatment

Chiropractic is an alternative therapy that has been around for 100 years. It isn't available on the NHS but many people believe it's more effective than conventional physiotherapy if you suffer with chronic low back pain.

Chiropractic is a system of spinal manipulation that is used to relieve low back pain and a number of other disorders that are associated with the spinal column and with the nervous system. The technique is an alternative form of treatment to conventional medicine. It is normally used by chiropractors and involves the manipulation and massage of one or two specific vertebrae of the spine. This differs from the technique that is used by osteopaths, who tend to manipulate and massage a wider area of the back, including soft tissue. Chiropractors also use x-rays to locate the troublesome vertebrae.

How chiropractic started

The practice of spinal manipulation goes back many centuries. Hippocrates wrote about it 2000 years ago and ancient Egyptian manuscripts refer to the practice. The word chiropractic is derived from the Greek for 'hand' — cheiro — and 'to use' — practikos. Literally, 'chiropractic' means 'done by hand' or manipulation. However, it is only in the last 100 years that chiropractic has actually been developed and refined into a major system of healing. Today, chiropractic is the third largest health profession in the world after conventional medicine and dentistry.

The person responsible for the development of chiropractic was a Canadian-born merchant called Daniel David Palmer (1845-1913), who was based in Iowa in the United States. He is said to have performed the first chiropractic adjustment in 1895. In 1898 he established the Palmer College of Chiropractic in Davenport, Iowa, and a few years later in 1910 his book 'The Science, Art and Philosophy of Chiropractic', was published.

Today, America has one chiropractor for every 13,000 people and chiropractic is regarded as a mainstream part of health care. The popularity of chiropractic varies though from country to country. In Switzerland, for example, there is one chiropractor for every 74,000 people, while in the UK there is only one for every 260,000 people. In the US and Australia there are more chiropractors than osteopaths, while in the UK osteopaths outnumber chiropractors.

What chiropractic can do for you

If you have low back pain, such as lumbago, a slipped disc or sciatica, a chiropractor may be able to alleviate it or even banish the problem altogether. About half the patients who consult a chiropractor are suffering from low back pain.

Chiropractors also treat a wide range of other chronic problems. These ailments include common aches and pains such as neck, shoulder and arm pain, headaches, migraine, dizzy spells, pins and needles, hip and knee problems, arthritis and muscular aches and pains. Sports injuries that are not relieved by conventional techniques such as physiotherapy often respond well to a programme of chiropractic treatment, and, indeed, some sports personalities travel with their own chiropractor.

Pregnant women commonly suffer from low back pain, caused by poor posture and by the weight of the baby

CHOOSING A CHIROPRACTOR

It is important you choose your chiropractor very carefully – don't just pick someone out of the 'phone book. Ask around and see if a friend can recommend someone.

A personal recommendation is always the best way to choose a chiropractor. For example, you may know of someone who has already seen a chiropractor and is very happy with the results. Alternatively, if your doctor is not against alternative therapies, she may be able to suggest someone who is in your area. You could also ask an acupuncturist, a homeopath or other alternative practitioner who you already know, as they will probably know of other alternative therapists in their area.

A letter of referral from your doctor will give your chiropractor useful information about your complaint. Your doctor may appear unenthusiastic about the use of chiropractic to try to help alleviate your back pain, so follow the procedure outlined below before booking yourself an appointment with your chosen chiropractor.

which increases the stress and pressure on the spine. It should be noted, however, that if you are pregnant or hope to be so, you should not be x-rayed unless it is absolutely essential as the foetus may be harmed.

Before you look for a chiropractor

Before you go to a chiropractor, it is wise to consult your doctor and discuss the possible reasons for your back pain. She may refer you to a hospital specialist and you may also be advised to have a course of physiotherapy. This procedure should eliminate the sorts of problems that a chiropractor would not be qualified to treat.

After this course of events your doctor should also be satisfied that no harm can be done if you choose to consult a chiropractor. Doctors are trained in conventional medicine, and many are still more than a little sceptical about the merits of alternative therapies such as chiropractic. Very few chiropractors are actually qualified medical doctors. Some doctors, however, recognise that alternative practitioners often secure notable successes, particularly in chronic cases in which there is no particular reason for pain that has existed for a long time.

If you find your own doctor is resistant to chiropractic in general, you could suggest that she takes a look at a paper published in the 'British Medical Journal', 2 June 1990, Vol 300, No 6737, pp1431-1437. This journal is read widely by doctors and medical specialists and possesses impeccable credentials. The paper describes a study that set out to compare the

effectiveness of chiropractic with hospital out-patient treatment.

The study reported that 'Chiropractic was particularly effective in those with fairly intractable pain — that is, those with a history of severe pain.' It also showed that chiropractic was significantly more effective than traditional physiotherapy. Furthermore, the report suggested that chiropractic treatment could often be more cost-effective than other forms of treatment for back problems.

What's involved?

Once you have chosen a chiropractor (see box above), you will probably need to have a series of consultations. The first consultation will be taken up with the practitioner asking you various questions in order to establish your medical history and determine what your present problem is. She will carry out a physical examination and will probably takes x-rays of your back. The chiropractor therefore determines at this first consultation whether or not chiropractic treatment will help you in any way. She may decide that it won't and refer you back to your doctor.

Treatment usually begins on your second consultation. Your chiropractor will ask you to take off your outer clothes, but she will not ask you to remove your underwear. You may be asked to stand, sit or lie on the chiropractic couch. The practitioner will make specific adjustments to the vertebrae of your spine with her hands. You may feel 'things happening' to your back and tingling sensations, but the treatment is not normally painful.

Will it work?

The British Medical Journal published a study that claimed that people with chronic back pain were significantly more likely to respond to chiropractic treatment than sufferers with a recent, acute problem. However, chiropractic can show spectacular results. In one case, a woman noticed a pain down her left leg, and within days was immobilised. Successive doctors gave her various forms of medication, including muscle relaxant tablets, valium and anti-inflammatories. She was in bed for a month and in agony for most of that time. She then saw a chiropractor. After her second treatment, the woman was able to walk for the first time in five weeks. And within the year her back was completely pain-free.

Some patients experience an immediate improvement after they have had the chiropractic treatment. Others need the benefit of four or five sessions before things start to happen. Once you are better, you may not need to have any further treatment, although you may be advised to have a check up a month or two later. Patients who are suffering with chronic problems may need to have regular monthly treatments.

What does it cost?

Like other forms of health care, treatment is not cheap. The first consultation will usually take an hour and a half to two hours and there will be an additional charge for x-rays if these are necessary. Subsequent sessions will probably cost less but you may need to visit the chiropractor half a dozen times. However, for people who have suffered chronic pain for years, or are now experiencing sudden and agonising pain, this may not seem a great deal of money to pay.

" Look well to the spine. For many diseases have their origin in dislocations of the vertebral column."

COLOURING IN YOUR LIFE

Are you 'green with envy', 'seeing red' or 'feeling blue'? Colours can have a very real effect on our emotions and health. Einstein analysed the physical properties of light – but what about its psychological influences?

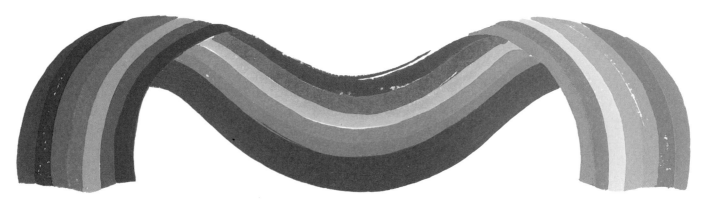

Although we have always used colours to describe our moods, colour therapy has formalised these connections. Colour therapists aim to increase our awareness of the power of colour in our everyday lives, and help to put it to work for us. Colour can be 'applied' simply by surrounding yourself with a particular colour, but professional colour therapists use a special lamp to beam the colour around you in rhythmic bursts, varying the intensity according to the amount of colour required.

What is colour?

Although we think of colour as something tangible — pigments or dyes, for example, it is in fact reflected light. Light, although it appears colourless, is actually a spectrum of colours. The colours can be seen as a rainbow of colour if white light is aimed through a prism. (Sunlight passing through raindrops to produce a rainbow is a natural display of the spectrum.)

Different pigments reflect different colours, so that, for example a red object reflects the red part of the spectrum, while a white object reflects the whole spectrum. Each basic colour can be altered by the addition of black pigment, to make a darker shade (which absorbs a lot of light), and white, to make a paler tint (which reflects a lot of light). Besides these changes there are many subtle gradations of colour through the spectrum; the red band of colour, for example, embraces literally

thousands of hues, from the palest white-pink to the deepest and most vibrant tones. Other colours are complex mixtures: peach is a variation of orange, for example.

The various colours that make up the spectrum are basically different vibrations. In general, the faster the vibration the 'warmer' the colour (such as red); the slower the vibration the 'cooler' the colour (such as blue). Red makes us active, passionate and, when taken to extreme, rebellious. Blue calms us, makes us reflective, and can render us emotionally chilly if we surround ourselves with it.

Absorbing colour

The effect of colour — whether in our clothes, decor or even in the food we eat — is powerful. Over the centuries, artists have developed many theories about the influence of colour, and colour theory is now used by interior designers, particularly in institutions like hospitals and hotels, to make patients and clients relaxed and happy.

Recent research has shown that yellow surroundings can calm even the most violent schizophrenic patients, and a pink bedroom can have a tranquillising effect on a hyperactive child. Green, the colour of nature, also calms, but at the same time it acts as a bridge between the most positive aspects of the blues and the reds, and provides a balance in our lives.

For most of us, the effects of colour are subconscious: walking into an office

with a grey colour scheme may make us feel shy and unenthusiastic, but perhaps we put it down to the working environment rather than the influence of the colour of the decor.

Picking up the vibrations

Everyone responds to colour — even, it has been shown, people blind from birth. Because colour is vibration, and not purely visual, the blind can learn to pick it up through their fingertips. After a little practice, they can differentiate the colours with 100 per cent accuracy. Many theorists believe that these vibrations have an influence on our brain patterns, and this is the reason that colour can have such a strong effect on our emotions. The theories have been taken a step further by some philosophers, psychologists and musicians who combine musical vibrations with colour vibrations to create complete environments. The jolly background music and relaxed colour schemes of supermarkets are just one example of how these ideas can be put into practice.

WARNING

Never use colour therapy as a substitute for medical treatment, and do not use this summary to diagnose illness.

BLACK

Not strictly a colour, but non-reflective pigment which gives depth and power to the colours. It is often associated with death and mourning. If worn by a woman, for example, it may show a desire to be seen as mysterious and powerful. It absorbs all other colours, and can be seen to take and give nothing in return. Rooms decorated with black may indicate eccentricity, but may also show an obsession with death and dying, with negativity and all that opposes warmth and love. Black can be dramatic, but few personalities are strong enough to combat its negative effects. An attraction to black may indicate a need for emotional support.

If a child paints a black picture, or paints over a normal picture with black, it is a sign that they are profoundly distressed and need help and cuddles.

GREY

A mixture of white and black, grey has a negative aura. It is the colour of self-denial, of self-martyrdom and of repression. Adding a little pink tone to it will immediately make its effect more bearable. Pink-tinged grey can be very flattering if worn by middle-aged women, but it would help to combine something stronger with it – red or yellow. Grey is also associated with stress and mental fatigue.

Like sheep, timid, inhibited and fearful people go for grey, and being surrounded by it can be depressing.

BROWN

The earth colour is associated with stability, but also with a tendency to be backward-looking and uninspired. Brown encourages practicality, but can keep our minds closed to higher matters. If you are attracted to brown, you probably have confidence and freedom from worry, but you might consider balancing its effects by introducing the opposite colour from the spectrum – minty green – to encourage you to put your mental powers to better use.

Brown is one of the colours of nature, associated with working with one's hands and the land: don't let its earthiness turn you blind to emotional matters, or make you too stodgy.

RED

Vital, creative and fizzing with energy, red is the opposite of brown. All the colours in the red band have a greater or lesser effect on energy levels and even on blood pressure. It inflames sexual passion and anger, and if used to excess can boil over into destruction. People who buy red cars are the perfect example of the influence of red: they use the car as a sex symbol, to arouse the excitement

A red rag to a bull? It is no accident that the red flag is the international symbol for revolution.

of possible partners, and they drive more aggressively. People who are attracted by red like to be out in front – where they can get the recognition of others. They react quickly to the people around them and may be rather overemotional. Wear red if you are low on energy or feel cold. You can even feel warmer simply by visualising this fiery colour. Don't wear it if you are agitated, have heart trouble or any sort of inflammation.

Pink combines the excitement and strength of the red element of the spectrum with the softness of white.

ORANGE

Like red, orange is energising, but is a great life-changer, with less potential for negative power. People who love life are attracted to orange, and people who are depressed, lonely or lacking in motivation can benefit from having the vibrations of orange around them. Its many therapeutic qualities include being good for gallstones, chest conditions, arthritis, sexual frustration and repressed creativity. Vegetarians particularly need orange in their lives to add zest. Anyone who feels hemmed in or directionless should introduce some of the vitality of orange into their lives.

A little orange goes a long way: one or two pieces of kitchen equipment or an orange scarf may be all you need to feel an immediate beneficial effect. Beware of 'overdosing' on orange – it can turn liveliness into restlessness.

It's not just the vitamins in an orange that are good for you: the very colour of the fruit you eat can have a beneficial effect on your health.

YELLOW

The colour associated with sunshine and sunny dispositions – but it is too strong for those suffering the extreme emotional distress of a nervous breakdown (green or blue are more helpful). Under normal conditions it can lift our spirits, cheer the sick and help activate our digestion. Lovers of yellow are good communicators – and sometimes talk too much. People drawn to strong yellow may be conceited or arrogant, whereas those who like the softest hues may be lacking in courage (the 'yellow' coward). Rich golds are deemed to be one of the most exalted colours and should not be worn by anyone except the most spiritual of people.

Golden yellow, the colour of the sun god Apollo, is an exalted colour and one of those associated with God and spirituality.

GREEN

This colour is the natural balancer between the power of red and that of blue. Green is the colour of self-esteem and may be disliked by those who have just come through a traumatic time because it will seek to balance and bring aspects of the trauma back to the surface in order to do so.

As well as balance, green brings harmony and hope, but too much of it can deprive us of the challenges and problems we need in order to evolve and thrive. It is soporific and can drain us of energy. The yellower tones of green indicate a more flexible personality with an adventurous trait, while the

Green is perfect for those who are agitated and need to relax – a walk through woods or a park will bring its power to you.

bluer tones of green suggest an optimistic and hopeful personality, with more spirituality than the other tones of green.

If you are drawn to green, be careful to add a little red or orange into your surroundings to bring a lively element into your life and compensate for your naturally tranquil temperament.

UNDERSTANDING YOURSELF

BLUE

Contemplation and thoughtfulness are linked with blue.

'True blue' is the colour of honesty and loyalty. It is also noble, as in the concept of 'blue blood'. The Virgin Mary is portrayed as wearing a blue veil or robe, for this is the colour of serenity, perfection and protection.

By meditating on or visualising blue it is possible to prevent nightmares and ward off the psychic attacks experienced by poltergeist victims. It is a cooling colour, and should be worn on very hot days. Blue has a sedative effect, so it can help if you are easily flustered or frightened. On the other hand, it can be too pacific, so those drawn to blue may be easily led or taken advantage of. Too much blue may lead to a 'holier than thou' attitude, so be prepared to tone it down with the happy-go-lucky influence of orange.

Physically it is good for patients suffering from shock, inflammation and nervous breakdowns but it is also a cold colour, so avoid it if you have bad circulation.

INDIGO

Those who are attracted to indigo are drawn to the higher things, perhaps even the occult. It should improve your intellectual abilities and bring special insight into the world around you.

Midnight blue is a profound and mysterious colour. It eliminates fear and timidity and helps give us a natural authority and inner calmness. Don't let it distract you from everyday, practical matters. You can temper its influence by introducing pink, to bring affection and sympathy to your personality. Conversely, people who have too much red in their lives could well be advised to add some indigo, to add a deeper dimension to their existence.

Indigo brings a sophisticated, executive appeal to rooms where it is used for furnishings. It is good for treating varicose veins, diseases of the nervous system, boils and ulcers, skin disorders and it cleanses the blood.

VIOLET

Violet points the way towards selfless service to humanity, and great spirituality.

At the end of our normally visible spectrum, violet is immensely powerful and may be too strong for many people. It is associated with creativity, with access to higher worlds and dimensions. Leonardo da Vinci used to meditate upon it and Beethoven had violet curtains at his window. If you cannot channel the creativity it brings it may make you feel very ill through its power: if the forces are not harnessed they may become very negative. The term 'shrinking violet' is apt both in terms of the shape of the violet flower and the influence of violet as a colour – those attracted to it are often shy. Physically, it is very useful for those suffering from excessive emotional agitation, but it is not advised to use it on clinically depressed people. Balance its influence with the all-time balancer, green.

Violet has a good effect on compulsive eaters, calming them down and helping to drain away the compulsion.

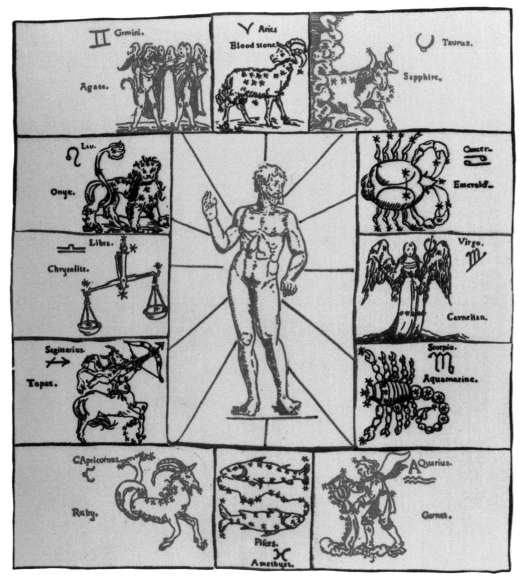

Power of Crystals

Since the beginning of civilisation men and women have decked themselves out with gems and brilliantly coloured crystals - not simply for decoration, but because these stones are believed to have magical and healing powers.

Today there is a growing belief that crystals hold the key to our physical, emotional and spiritual health. The word crystal comes from the Greek 'crystallos', which means 'clear ice' or 'frozen water', and in ancient times it was actually believed that crystals were made by the gods, who froze sacred water as it poured down from the heavens.

Russian scientist Nikola Tesla (1856-1943) wrote: "In a crystal we have the clear evidence of a formative life principle and though we cannot understand the life of a crystal it is nonetheless a living being."

These days the scientific value of crystals is well known. They are used in radios (the first wirelesses were known as 'crystal sets'), in watches and in computers. But there is much more to crystals than this.

The healing power of crystals

Enthusiasts for crystals have made great claims for them. In experiments conducted in the USA in 1980 by Dael Walker, Director of the Crystal Awareness Institute and a convert to the power of crystals, out of 234 muscle-pain sufferers who held a crystal in their hand, it was claimed that 227 reported an almost immediate reduction of pain. Dael Walker wrote: "... the crystal

WARNING

PLEASE NOTE: crystal therapy should never be used instead of orthodox medical treatment.

CRACKING THE CRYSTAL CODE

There are hundreds of different types of crystal, of all hues and combinations of colours. Some are precious, others semi-precious but both are equally effective. The size of the crystal is not important. It is not crucial to see a crystal therapist before you try out this therapy; quite often you will be more relaxed and receptive if you are on your own. Here are some of the properties that have been claimed for some of the most common crystals:

AMETHYST
This purple-and-white stone (above) is a wonderful healing tool. It puts us in touch with our intuition and stimulates self-healing. It's marvellous for insomnia if kept under the pillow, and helps straighten out the overemotional and frightened. This is a good beginner's crystal.

AQUAMARINE
Known also as the 'water stone', it can help prevent seasickness, gets rid of water retention and helps purify drinking water. It's especially good to place in your daily glass of water. Aquamarine also clears away negativity and helps clear thinking.

BLOODSTONE
As the name suggests, it helps people with blood disorders, such as menstrual problems or even nose bleeds! It helps cleanse the blood and also is believed to make us more courageous and able to face difficulties calmly.

CORAL
A wonderful aid to digestion, coral helps to overcome toothache and gum problems – although it is no substitute for proper dental hygiene! It also encourages self-esteem and positive thinking, balancing out feelings of worry about what other people think of us. It is good for children, as therapists believe it helps prevent any ill effects of falls and tumbles.

DIAMOND
This precious gem is a powerful crystal. It is believed to stimulate a sense of direction in life and help strengthen one's courage. Just wearing one in a ring will not, however, give you these qualities. Like any other crystal, you have to build up a personal relationship with it by talking to it, stroking it and cleaning it regularly.

EMERALD
The stone of true love, it can help generate insight into a relationship – which may or may not be welcome! It also bestows psychic ability, heals inflammation and promotes a feeling of inner peace and relaxation.

GARNET
This stone is good for balancing out sexual problems. Both overactive sexuality and repressed urges will benefit from the power of the garnet. It also encourages assertiveness and helps to regularise blood pressure.

KUNZITE
Discovered as recently as 1902, this stunning pink stone is superb for women who have gynaecological problems that are due to difficulties in accepting their femininity, and also for women who need to come to terms with all aspects of their sexuality. It is a reassuring, healing, calming stone.

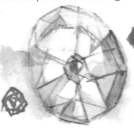

LAPIS LAZULI

Honoured as a royal stone by the ancients, this blue-and-gold stone has always been believed to open the inner vision, to create a link between this world and the invisible realm. High priests used to wear it ground up as eye make-up, and in jewellery during rituals. It is good for anyone undergoing a spiritual awakening or instruction in a particular religion.

OPAL

This highly sensitive stone has had a 'bad press'. There are still many people around who believe it is unlucky, but its reputation is the result of a story by the writer Sir Walter Scott – and has no truth in it at all! Opal does need to be treated with care, for it chips easily. It's a water stone and loves being soaked in cold water and benefits from being left in the moonlight from time to time. Opals reveal the state of your physical and emotional energy, being dull when it's low, and brilliant when it's high again.

PEARL

A stone of triumph over adversity, of making the most of an unpromising start, it is a gem of hope and inner strength. If a pearl loses its lustre, it is unlikely to regain it – it is believed to have lost its life force.

QUARTZ

Clear quartz (above) has stimulating male qualities and opaque or milky quartz is the receptive, female stone. If you're given to brooding upon the unfairness of life, hold on to the clear quartz. If you need rest and insight, choose the milky sort. Rose quartz is gentle – useful in times of high emotion, like the break-up of a relationship, or bereavement.

SAPPHIRE

A stone of control, it helps overcome temptation and guides one's thoughts on to higher things! Star sapphires are deemed especially significant, for they help guide people whose dreams and ambitions will one day benefit humanity.

TOURMALINE

This stone (above) refuses to absorb or retain any negativity. It is a stone of transition, both physical and emotional, and its beauty helps the processes of birth, menopause and death, as well as other rites of passage. It is good for people who feel the world is against them, and for those who have a great need to forgive – especially themselves.

TURQUOISE

Ancient symbol of the sky, this stone benefits lungs and throat, and because it contains a good deal of copper it is a superb conductor for the healing force. It's also said to be excellent for those who are terrified of speaking in public or of appearing physically or emotionally weak.

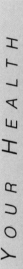

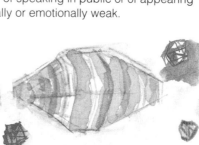

responds to thoughts and emotions and interacts with the mind. It increases thought energy and emotional power. Reduction of stress and pain and accelerated healing are ordinary paths of crystal energy balancing. We have whole systems of simple but effective methods to reduce healing time by at least half of the accepted standards."

So although orthodox scientific experiments have provided no clear evidence, the proponents of crystal therapy are very enthusiastic.

Choosing a crystal

So how do you go about acquiring and using these beautiful and — some claim — magical stones? Many crystal therapists believe that the most special stones in our lives come to us as gifts, or are just found by us. Somehow they come to us, without any effort on our part. Others are bought in the usual way, but even here you should be careful to take some time over your choice. Faced with hundreds of different crystals, it may be tempting to buy the most beautiful, but that may not be the right choice for you, or for the work you want your crystal to do. Experts say that you should hold the palm of your hand over the crystals. When it hovers over the right crystal for you, your hand may start to feel warm or tingly after a few seconds.

Caring for your crystal

Once you have acquired your crystal, it should be cleaned. Do this by immersing it completely in a bowl of pure sea water or warm water and sea salt, for 36-70 hours. Cleanse your crystals when you first get them and every few weeks after that. Keep crystals in the sunlight, although it has been claimed that some, such as opals, enjoy soaking up the moonlight too — so keep these on a window ledge during nights when the moon is bright. It may sound somewhat far-fetched, but adherents to crystal therapy say that this is a sound way of revitalising these mysterious and powerful stones.

Using your crystal

Enthusiasts of crystal therapy even go so far as to claim that to establish a therapeutic relationship with your crystal you should talk to it, breathe into it and keep it with you. If you need to be more assertive, then keep a small crystal in your right-hand pocket. This is because the left half of the brain, which governs the right side of the body, deals with

CRYSTAL FOLLOWERS

Tina Turner, Charles Dance and Shirley MacLaine are all great believers in the power of crystals to enhance one's life.

Raunchy American rock star, Tina Turner. *Sophisticated English actor, Charles Dance.* *American film star, Shirley MacLaine.*

clarity of thinking and male qualities. If you lack the warmer feelings or are out of touch with your intuition, keep one in your left-hand pocket. This reflects the fact that the right half of the brain, which governs the left side of the body, deals with more psychic, female qualities. Using crystals in this way can stimulate the qualities you are most in need of.

Some people swear that sleeping with a crystal, or keeping one within 3 ft (0.9m) of you during the night, can have a curiously beneficial effect. They even claim that the crystal moves around inside the bed, depending on the benefit you need most. Enthusiasts cite the case of one woman who was suffering from earache. Apparently, although she went to bed with the crystal under her feet, when she woke in the morning she found that the crystal had moved up the bed and was nestling close to her ear. Moreover, her earache was cured!

Another claim for crystals is that, if you drink a glass of water in which a (cleansed) crystal has been soaking for 24 hours, you will feel revitalised. To get the full benefit of this, enthusiasts claim, you should drink a glass of such water every day. Another secret — which is said to be good for jet lag — is to hold a crystal on your thymus, a gland found about 4-5in (10-13cm) below your throat, for about five minutes. This is supposed to energise your body and mind and help calm you down.

The belief is that crystals can be used to help in a host of everyday situations. If a wilting plant, for example, is surrounded by a ring of small

crystals, or if one or two are put in its soil, the plant will revive. It is also said that animals are helped by being given crystal-vitalised water to drink regularly — they apparently become noticeably perkier. It is even claimed that if you keep a crystal under the bonnet of your car or pass one a short distance from your computer screen, both these machines will respond to you much better!

Like many of the so-called New Age therapies, crystal therapy may seem somewhat far-fetched — even slightly insane. But even some of the most sceptical of critics have ended up becoming converts to this elegant and comforting therapy.

"Sit down before the fact like a child, and be prepared to give up every preconceived notion. Follow humbly wherever and to whatever abysses Nature leads, or you shall learn nothing."

T H Huxley

"Sermons in stones, and good in everything."

William Shakespeare

A REFRESHING SLICE

Are you suffering from tired eyes? Or are you a little burnt from your annual holiday in the sun? You need look no further than your local supermarket for the solution to your problems.

Cucumber (*Cucumis sativus*) is a vegetable that grows on a trailing plant. It is a major food crop in tropical, subtropical and temperate regions, and is on sale all year round in your local supermarkets and grocers. Cucumber was widely eaten by the Ancient Greeks and the Romans and was considered to be a delicacy in the East.

However, it was not until the 16th century that cucumbers were cultivated on a wide scale. Cucumber is largely composed of water and is therefore very low in calories and extremely popular with slimmers. Cucumber is an essential ingredient in many different types of salad, is often chopped into strips and dunked into an array of cheese or spicy dips, and can even be made into light mousses. A small salad will supply you with many vital vitamins, minerals and fibre and is a healthy choice of meal. When you're buying a cucumber, choose the smallish, smooth-skinned ones as the larger ones can be less tender and have tougher skins.

Cosmetic properties

Cucumber is very refreshing and cooling because of the large amount of water it contains. It is widely used in cosmetics because it has gentle, soothing properties which are ideal for sensitive or dry skin that tend to be irritated by harsher products.

Cucumber is an astringent and is therefore an effective and popular ingredient in a wide range of toners. A skin toner should be gently applied to the skin with a piece of cotton wool after cleansing and before moisturising your face. It will remove excess oil from the skin and will stimulate and tone up the complexion.

Because of its astringent properties, cucumber is also commonly used in face masks to help combat oily skin and leave your skin glowing and healthy. If you smooth a

RECIPES FOR LOOKING GOOD

Skin care products containing cucumber are easy to make and very effective. You can buy the necessary ingredients from your local supermarket and chemist.

CUCUMBER TONIC

¹/₂ cucumber
2 lemons
1 orange
1 apple
2 tbsp (30ml) pure alcohol
2 tbsp (30 ml) rose-water

Peel the cucumber and apple, and then mash them thoroughly with a fork. Wrap the pulp in a square of fine gauze and squeeze the juice out into a bowl. Then squeeze the juice out of the lemons and orange and mix it with the cucumber and apple. Finally, add the alcohol and rose-water and mix well. Pour the tonic into a clean, labelled bottle and use twice a day after cleansing.

CUCUMBER CLEANSER

¹/₄ cucumber
¹/₄ pint (140ml) milk

Peel and mash the cucumber. Then wrap the pulp in a piece of gauze and squeeze out the juice. Mix the pulp, peel and milk together and shake well for five minutes. Leave for three hours. Then strain and pour into a labelled bottle and refrigerate. The cleanser will last for about two to three days.

cucumber mask over your face and leave it on for 10 to 15 minutes, it will leave your skin feeling fresh and smooth, while cleansing it and helping to stimulate the circulation.

Cucumber is also used in a range of cleansers which are formulated for oily, normal or combination skin, and in some soaps and hand creams. You can try out the effects of cucumber before buying skin care products. Peel and mash a piece of cucumber and squeeze the resulting pulp until you end up with some cucumber juice. Strain the juice to remove all the bits of cucumber.

Gently smooth this juice over your face. You'll find it has a moisturising and soothing effect on the skin, and will help to brighten your complexion. Another useful tip, if you've been in the sun and want to cover up a few freckles, is to mix a little cucumber and lemon juice together and smooth the mixture over your freckles — it will help to bleach them and make them less noticeable.

Medicinal properties
Cucumber has valuable diuretic properties (helps to increase the flow of urine) so it is excellent to eat if you have

a swollen stomach as a result of water retention or chronic constipation. Because of these properties, and the fact that cucumber also helps to dissolve uric acid, it is commonly used to treat kidney and bladder problems.

Cucumber also has a high water content so it is very soothing when applied to skin inflammations and sores. Its healing properties make it a popular ingredient in after-sun lotions, as it is very cooling and will effectively soothe the pain and discomfort that is caused by excessive exposure to the sun's harmful ultraviolet rays.

SWOLLEN EYES

Do you suffer from strained or tired eyes as a result of artificial light, smoky atmospheres or too many late nights? A couple of slices of cucumber may be the answer.

If your eyes are tired or inflamed, cut off two slices of cucumber and lie down somewhere where you won't be disturbed. Close your eyes and place the two pieces of cucumber over your eyelids. Relax for 10 minutes. Cucumber is a natural eye brightener and is very refreshing. You will find it helps to soothe your eyes and reduce any inflammation or swelling. If, however, you have eyes that are extremely sensitive, it's advisable not to use cucumber.

" He had... a project for extracting sun-beams out of cucumbers, which were to be put into vials... and let out to warm the air in raw inclement summers. "

Jonathan Swift

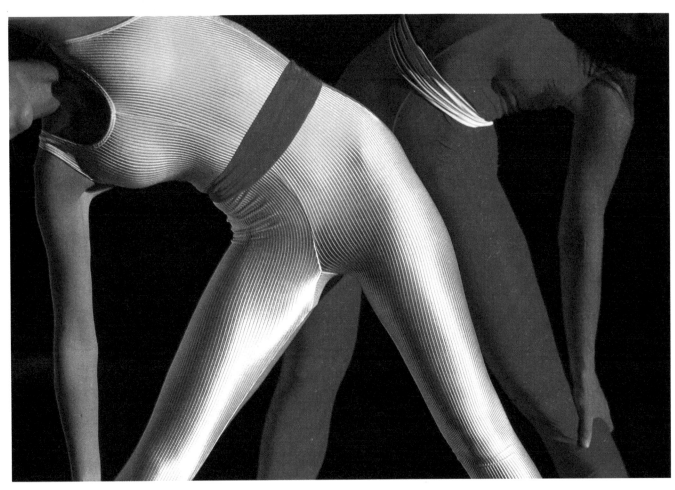

Dance For Joy

Dance is one of the most ancient forms of human self-expression. People have danced for joy, in celebration of births and marriages, and at festivals, for many centuries. With its essential elements of movement, gesture and rhythm — with or without music — dance has long been used to express feelings and emotions that cannot adequately be shown in any other way.

Most western education fails to put us in touch with our entire selves, neglecting the physical in favour of the mental. Alternative therapies and methods of healing, however, often incorporate elements of dance and movement within their theories. Yoga, for example, includes some dance techniques and it, too, encourages a physical grace and harmony, improving the body's sense of balance and the individual's sense of unity in the physical and mental dimensions.

Dance therapy, dance classes and exercise programmes such as

Dance therapy is the perfect way of developing a physical sense of grace and harmony, exercising in a group and getting rid of tension.

Dancercise all draw on the unique attraction of dance to develop a sense of self, to get rid of feelings of tension, stress and aggression and to promote positive feelings of poise, harmony and joy. As well as all this, the carefully controlled breathing and quite strenuous exercise involved in dance therapy will make you physically fit.

The elements of dance
Dance is the continuous movement of the body, according to prescribed sequences of steps, to a certain rhythm and within a given space.

Its essential elements are:
● Centring (the awareness of your physical centre, which enables you to move and to hold yourself), which is

also an intrinsic part of yoga.
● Gravity.
● Balance.
● Posture.
● Gesture.
● Rhythm.
● Movement in space (spatial orientation).
● Correct breathing (crucial to dance, bringing extra oxygen to your body and lending your movements fluency and harmony).

Dancing for mind and body
Because we associate dance with feelings of happiness and exuberance, dance and dance therapy have the ability to make us happy and outgoing.

Dance therapy inspires a unique form of creative self-expression, and at the same time, it encourages physical fitness. Dance can be described as rhythmic and sustained aerobic exercise: it improves the action of the heart, tones up the circulation and develops all the muscles of the body.

All this contributes to a sense of well-being as well as general physical fitness. Dance also improves your physical balance and your posture. It's noticeable that those people who are happy and fulfilled tend to adopt a positive and confident posture, while those who face difficulties in life will habitually assume a slouching, negative posture. The positive psychological effects of dance and dance therapy are profound and can hardly be overestimated.

Dance therapy helps to banish tension, alleviate anxiety and invigorate you. Specifically, it can be useful for those who suffer back problems, headaches, migraine, asthma, hayfever, eczema, dizzy spells (if they are caused by anxiety), constipation and all those general aches and pains that have no medical cause.

It is interesting that dance therapy is used in the treatment of autistic children and as a therapy for the mentally impaired. The benefits of dance as a physical means to creative expression which bypasses the intellectual self have long been recognised.

How did it start?

Primitive man intuitively appreciated the profound psychological benefits of dance, although he attributed its benefits to a belief that we could communicate through dance with the unseen spirit world. People danced to celebrate a birth, to heal the sick, to mourn a death, to pray for good hunting, for rain and for victory in battle.

The physical and psychological benefits of dance inspired healers to use dance as a part of their armoury, and witch doctors in tribal communities have traditionally favoured dance as a therapy — some still do.

The therapy of dance has long been recognised in the West, too. Rudolf Laban (1879-1959) for example, endorsed the therapeutic value of dance and taught it, in England, together with psychotherapy, as a means of improving mental health. In America, after the Second World War, Marion Chace introduced another form of dance therapy. Within a decade, dance therapy was firmly established on both sides of the Atlantic, with classes available in every large town.

Types of dance therapy

There is enormous variation from class to class, so, if you find one teacher doesn't suit you, do try another. Every

FLOORWORK

These exercises are performed on the floor in a sitting, lying or kneeling position. The intention is to work certain muscle groups in isolation, while bearing the minimum weight. At the first level, you will learn simple stretches and contractions, while at higher levels, floorwork involves such movements as heel in hand stretches, hip spirals and side falls.

One famous dance teacher explains: "You must remember that you are on the floor to work, not to rest. Use it not merely to sit on, but also to push down against. In any floor position you should hold your body in such a way that if you were suddenly lifted up you would come away in one piece like a statue, and not with your legs dangling."

Spine stretch
Tempo: medium.

1 Sit on the floor with your back straight, your knees bent, the soles of your feet together and your hand resting on your ankles. Take a deep breath.
2 Counting to eight twice, and breathing out steadily, gradually lean over until your head is as close to your feet as possible. Aim your forehead towards the arches of your feet.
3 Return to the sitting position, again counting to eight twice, this time breathing in steadily. Repeat.

Spine curve
Tempo: Slow waltz

1 Sit on the floor with your back straight, legs crossed and arms stretched in front of you at shoulder height, with your hands clasped.
2 To a count of three, tighten your buttock muscles and tilt your pelvis forwards, gradually feeling your spine lengthen and stretch as it curves outwards. At the same time, stretch your arms forwards, but try to keep your head at the same level throughout the exercise.
3 Return to the original position, sitting on your two pelvic bones, again to a count of three. Repeat three times.

CENTREWORK

The next area to concentrate on is improving the alignment of your body and concentrating on your centre. Coordination, alignment and balance are the keys, as you hold each of the positions in turn. The five basic positions of dance are the fundamentals of classical ballet and dance the world over. Once you have mastered the basic positions, centrework moves on to special exercises to enable you to shift your body weight, while retaining alignment and balance.

First position
With legs turned out or parallel, position the heels together and hold your arms down in a shallow curve.

Second position
With legs turned out or parallel, move the feet apart, so that your heels are in line with your shoulders, and your feet point outwards diagonally. Raise your arms to shoulder height, curving forward slightly.

Third position
Position one leg just in front of the other, so that your heels and ankles just cross each other. Hold your arms downwards, in a gentle curve.

« Fourth position
Move one leg forward, so that your feet are separated, and an imaginary line joining the centre of each foot is at right angles to the line joining your shoulders. Curve your arms forwards.

« Fifth position
Overlap the feet, so that the heel of one touches the toe of the other, with the legs and hips turned outwards and buttocks held in. Raise your arms up into an arch above your head, or hold them down as for Position 1.

Pliés and Relevés

In classical ballet, each of the five basic positions is practised further. Try breathing in as you bend down to a *plié* and breathing out as you return to the basic position. Then breathe in again as you stretch up to a *relevé*. Count evenly through each movement, in fours or threes.

Plié means folded, and involves bending the knees. There are different ways of 'folding': to start with, practise half *pliés*, with your heels on the floor.

Relevé means raised up, and involves going up on to the balls of your feet. If you are well-balanced in the basic positions, a *relevé* should be easy to do.

WILL DANCE THERAPY HELP ME?

If you answer 'yes' to most of these questions, you will probably enjoy and benefit from dance therapy.

- Do you tend to feel easily depressed?
- Do you walk badly – do your shoulders ache?
- Have you a tendency to bump into things and trip over?
- Do you dislike what you see in the mirror?
- Do you puff and pant after running for a bus?
- Do your find it difficult to get to sleep at night and wake up still feeling tired?
- Do your joints, especially the hip joints, feel stiff?
- Do you find it tiring to walk briskly and talk at the same time?

teacher has her own method. What is important is the sequencing of the movements and steps.

Some teachers take their inspiration from classical ballet, some from modern dance ballet, others from ballroom, jazz or tap, while still others may favour belly dancing. Some teachers incorporate elements of all these types of dance.

Getting to work

It is important that any class, at whatever level of proficiency it may be,

DO

- ✔ Warm up gradually with limbering up exercises.
- ✔ Massage your feet
- ✔ Tie back long hair
- ✔ Concentrate on the rhythm – an essential element of dance.
- ✔ Observe and memorise the type, fequency, intensity and duration of each exercise so that you can practise at home.
- ✔ Check with your doctor before starting if you have a heart or lung condition or other chronic illness.

DON'T

- ✗ Wear jewellery – particularly pendants and bracelets, which may interfere with your movements.
- ✗ Join a class if you are pregnant or very overweight.
- ✗ Go to a class if you have just eaten, are very tired, ill or cold.
- ✗ Go on with a class if you become excessively tired or breathless, if you get a pain or tight feeling in the chest, arm, back or joints, or if you feel dizzy or get a headache.

starts with limbering up exercises, just as you would for any exercise session. After that, dance classes progress through the three main technical areas of dance: floorwork, centring and moving in space (see the diagrams on the previous page for examples of floorwork and centring).

The design of a dance exercise programme should be based on an understanding of the logical progression of ideas for movement in a properly balanced sequence. Combined with interesting and creative ideas for the body action, this contributes to a stimulating atmosphere and, ultimately, the achievement of physical and psychological harmony.

The music you choose to work to must be something you enjoy listening to. Enjoyment is part of the therapy. Count as you listen to the sound — you will find most exercises work to a count of eight, but some work to triple time (*ONE* two three, *ONE*, two three). Check the speed of the count: start with a slow or medium tempo, and then choose faster music as you gain experience and confidence.

Useful Information

- Enquire at your local library for details of classes in your area. Your local leisure centre may also run classes. An acupuncturist or naturopath may be able to recommend a dance therapist.
- *The Dance Workshop* (Allen and Unwin, London 1986) by Robert Cohan, former Artistic Director of the London Contemporary Dance Theatre: a useful book which explains many of the principles of dance, and gives a wide range of exercises.

Life Rhythms

In the course of a single day, temperature, blood pressure and heart rate all vary. They are subject to diurnal (or daily) rhythms – just one of several types of regular cycles ruled by our biological clocks.

Almost everything in the natural world seems to work according to a rhythm — night and day, the tides and seasons, annual plant and migration cycles. The human body, too, is subject to specific rhythms; and certain major life events seem to occur at pre-set times.

Birth patterns

Take childbirth. Labour, so statistics reveal, most frequently begins at night — inconvenient for hospital staff, perhaps, but at a point when the mother is most likely to be resting and relaxed. There is more to birth patterns, too. A greater number of children are born in the spring, for instance. Here, some form of safety factor may be at work, since these babies are almost always slightly heavier and more robust. One New England study has even indicated that those born in March live four years longer, on average. Those born in May, on the other hand, have been shown to score more highly in IQ tests, according to a New York survey.

In spite of the birth pattern, sexual intercourse takes place most frequently between April and June. Most people die at around 4 am. Statistics such as these concern the longer cycles of life. But what of those daily patterns which we tend to take more or less for granted? Infants do not have an established 24-hour clock, as any new parent will readily tell you. It seems, therefore, that diurnal rhythms become established partly through an imposed environment, but probably more substantially through complex genetic coding and chemical activity.

No one can specify what organ controls the body clock, or what triggers its mechanism. But current opinion tends to point to certain cells in the hypothalamus, part of the brain.

Peaks and troughs

In the course of just one day, there are many physical changes that occur, some of them quite surprising. Scientists have shown, for example, that we are usually about 2cm taller on waking than we are later in the day. The explanation is not that mysterious.

It seems that during sleep, fluid swells the discs between the vertebrae, resulting in increased body length which becomes lost with movement.

THE CYCLES OF LIFE: BIORHYTHMS

One branch of emotional analysis and prediction draws on the theory that our lives are affected by three particular sets of rhythms.

Most of us are aware that, every now and then, we experience an emotional 'low'. At other times, we may feel at a peak physically, or seem to be at our best intellectually. According to the biorhythm theory, we all experience set, regular cycles, which start at birth and continue throughout life. This is how they are claimed to work.

The three cycles

The emotional cycle, lasting 28 days, affects our creativity and general moods. The physical cycle lasts only 23 days and influences the libido, feelings of well-being and immunity to disease. The intellectual cycle extends to 33 days and tempers our ability to reason, the memory and decision-making processes.

The cycles can be represented in graph form as regular waves along the path of a person's life. Unstable or 'critical' periods in each cycle have been found to occur when the cycles move from a high to a low, and vice versa, and most of us are particularly vulnerable to mishaps or illness when two or three of the 'critical' points happen to coincide. Biorhythms, it has also been claimed, can be used to assess compatibility between colleagues, or lovers, by comparing graphs.

Working it out

You can calculate your own chart, or buy a biorhythm calculator to help you. You can also buy a biorhythm calendar personally tailored to your date of birth, indicating your biorhythms for a particular year. You also need a guide to interpreting your chart on a particular day.

When reading the graph, take special note of the central horizontal or 'caution' line. Readings above the line indicate stages in a relatively positive phase, which will peak. Readings on the line show vulnerable days. Readings below the line may point to very unfavourable days.

In the example shown here, the biorhythms are shown for the last three months of 1991, for a person born on 15 October 1959.

For example, at the beginning of October the physical and intellectual cycles are both low, with the emotional cycle high. This suggests a person born on that date should be aware of the world around them: their moods will be high, but they are not likely to succeed in physical or intellectual activities.

Similarly, in mid-November, the physical and emotional cycles are low, so it's a day for brain work. On the other hand, at the end of November, both the intellectual and emotional cycles are critical, with the physical cycle high: this is an unsettling time, with plenty of energy but no emotional or creative direction.

Where does it start?

To calculate your own starting point for the same three months, start by working out the number of days old you were on 1 October 1991; remember to allow for leap years (see box, right).

For each cycle, divide the calculated number of days by the length of that cycle and note the remainder, to see how far through the cycle you would be on 1 October 1991. The cycle starts at the centre line and rises to the top of the 'high', so the remainder you have noted indicates how far through the cycle you are from that point. In the physical cycle (23 days), you reach the centre line on day 12, moving into the 'low' over days 13 – 22. In the emotional cycle you reach the centre line on day 14, with days 15 – 27 in the 'low'. And in the intellectual cycle you will be in the 'high' until day 15, and in the 'low' from days 16 – 28. The cycles repeat themselves along the length of the time scale. To plot the chart accurately, check the figures on several dates over the three-month period.

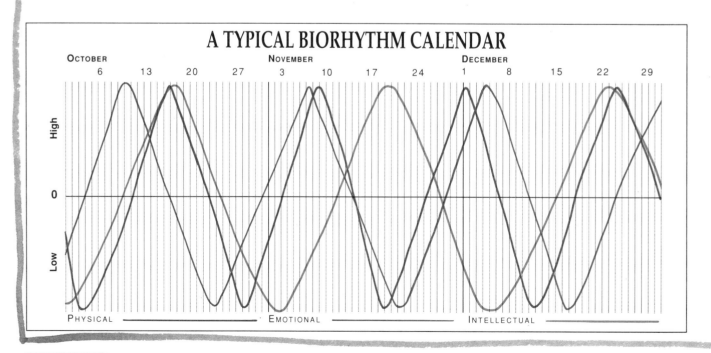

A TYPICAL BIORHYTHM CALENDAR

HOW MANY DAYS OLD ARE YOU?

Your biorhythms today hinge on the exact number of days since your birth. Here's how to do the sums.

To make a chart for a particular period, take the number of years old you will be at the start of the period you are looking at. Multiply by 365, then add on an allowance for the number of days which have elapsed since your birthday. This may help:

> 30 days has September,
> April, June and November;
> All the rest
> (January, March, May, July,
> August, October, December)
> have 31;
> Excepting February alone;
> February has 28 days clear,
> And 29 each leap year.

So add one day for each leap year. The leap years this century are: 1904; 1908; 1912; 1916; 1920; 1924; 1928; 1932; 1936; 1940; 1944; 1948; 1952; 1956; 1960; 1964; 1968; 1972; 1976; 1980; 1984; 1988; 1992; 1996.

An example

Suppose you were born on 14 January 1976, and want to calculate your chart starting on 1 October 1991. By 1 October 1991 you will be 15 years and 273 days old, plus four extra days for leap years.

Fifteen years =
15 x 365 = 4475 days
+ 273
+4
a total of 4652 days.
Divide by the number of days in each cycle, noting the remainders.

Body temperature usually goes up at sunrise, in what is thought to be an effort to stave off feelings of fatigue. There is a peak heart rate in the early afternoon, as a rule, after which it slows down. Urine production, too, rather conveniently, decreases at night. The level of testosterone — the male sex hormone — also varies in the course of a day, most frequently peaking first thing in the morning.

The body's regular rhythms are truly remarkable. We secrete the hormone cortisol on waking, and this helps us to prepare for the day. Release of adrenaline, too, is intimately linked with the daily cycle, decreasing at night as the body relaxes in preparation for sleep. There is more iron in your blood in the morning, whereas the amount of zinc in your blood falls.

At your best

When are you likely to be at your best, during the course of a day? Some of us are definitely 'morning people', feeling on top of the world early in the day, but tiring quite early. Others are more like owls, finding it hard to get going in the morning, but livening up at night. There are, of course, a very large number who fall somewhere in between, and certainly the patterns change with advancing age.

Work obligations sometimes force us to adapt our usual patterns and thereby disturb the normal daily pattern. But we also differ in the precise timings of our body clocks — it may well be that those 'morning people' among us have internal systems that run slightly more quickly than average. Nevertheless, certain tests have shown that mental performance usually peaks at around midday, and that a short dip comes just after lunch.

Using rhythms to advantage

Most of us are, however, at a very low ebb at the end of the night, shortly before daybreak. Significantly, the police may sometimes take advantage of this fact, raiding and interrogating their suspects at a very early hour.

Diurnal rhythms, it seems, can also affect how readily the slimmer will lose weight. Indeed, research has shown that if slimmers are given either a breakfast or evening meal of equal calorie content, those opting for breakfast lose more successfully.

Equally valuable advice suggests that nervous dental patients should always fix their appointments for

treatment in the afternoon. Anaesthetics are generally more effective then, and so a lower dose can be used. What is more, your teeth are likely to be less sensitive later on in the day.

The best time to revise for an exam, some claim, is just before you go to bed. Indeed, whole sleep-learning systems are based on the unproved theory that information is readily absorbed by the resting mind.

Seasonal cycles

Over extended periods, both light and darkness are known to affect diurnal rhythms and also our moods. Eskimos, for instance, have been found to suffer sometimes from a strange mental disorder (called Arctic hysteria). Their emotions are disturbed during the long, dark, winter months when the sun does not shine.

Closer to home, too, there are individuals known to suffer from seasonal affective disorder (neatly abbreviated to SAD), in which the cycle for production of the hormone melatonin changes, causing feelings of extreme depression and lethargy during the winter months.

Other forms of depression (particularly those that are worst in the early part of the day) are thought to be due to a body clock system that may be running too quickly. Some patients certainly show improvement when treated with drugs like lithium, for instance, which slow down the normal body processes.

Those Monday morning blues, meanwhile — which so many of us experience at the start of the working week — have been compared and related to jet lag in some ways. Quite simply, the body has just been through a period of adjustment to a weekend life style, full of energetic activities and late nights, when it suddenly — on Monday — finds it has to readjust itself to the

COMBATING JET LAG

Almost everyone who has experienced long-haul air travel will be only too aware of the effect that jet lag has on their body rhythms.

You get jet lag when you fly east or west across several time zones. Symptoms include headaches, insomnia, disturbed appetite, upset stomach, irritability and lack of concentration. The symptoms are more marked the older you are and the further you fly. Flying eastwards, against the sun (from America to London, from Europe to the Far East) is worse than flying with the sun.

Adjustment to new time zones undoubtedly upsets the diurnal rhythms, and causes difficulties for the body's internal clock as it tries to compensate. You could well find, for example, that whereas mental performance may be best in the morning when on home territory, on travelling to a different zone it peaks in the evening. For some, mental activity seems to be at a high at 3 am. Body temperature, heart rate and hormone rhythms can also be affected, as they will be again after the return journey, when a further period of adjustment will be needed.

Tricks of the trade

If you can't afford to give in to the symptoms of jet lag, try some of these precautions:
- Try to get used to a new time zone in advance of travel if you can, by getting up at a different time and adjusting your working day and mealtimes. (Not always possible!)
- If your stay is a short one, a business trip, for example, try to fix important meetings for times that coincide with daylight hours at home. (This will also enable you to make calls back to the office during the meetings if you need to.)

- At the start of a long flight, set your watch to the time zone you are travelling to and try to adjust your daily routine accordingly. Sleep and rest as much as possible.
- Drink plenty of water during the flight, to counteract the dehydration caused by flying. Avoid the temptation to enjoy too much duty-free – you don't want to add a hangover to the jet lag.
- Avoid taking sleeping tablets in the attempt to adjust to local time, unless they are short-acting: they may make you feel worse. If you do use them, restrict them to controlling 'in-flight' sleep, so that you rest during the night hours in the country you are travelling to.
- If you find it difficult to sleep at night after your flight, simply rest.
- Resist the temptation to cat-nap during the day after the flight: 40 winks can all too easily turn into three hours' sleep, preventing you from sleeping at night.

work schedule. Unexpected changes in diurnal patterns can sometimes provide clues to incipient illness or disease. Changes in skin temperature, for instance, are substantially different in cancerous tissue. Research is going on into changes in testosterone levels in male saliva; it is thought that such changes could indicate problems with the prostate gland.

An aid to diagnosis

Knowledge that cancer cells so often have specific and rather unique rhythms has now also enabled doctors to make particularly effective use of a number of drugs — by prescribing them for certain times of day, when normal cells are not dividing so rapidly as the cancerous cells, which are multiplying at an accelerated rate. Further understanding of the precise nature of our body rhythms could perhaps throw some light on many areas of vital medical research.

LIVING WITH SHIFT WORK

The body's clock promotes sleep at night and activity during the day. Yet as many as 20 per cent of those in employment in this country have to undertake some of their work at night. How does this affect their diurnal rhythms?

The police, hospital staff, firemen, drivers, printers, croupiers, telephone operators, factory workers, bakers – these are just some of the personnel who may regularly work for all or part of the night. Adapting to such drastic alterations in diurnal rhythms can often prove disruptive. Such workers soon adjust to the the social difficulties, but there are physical problems too.

During the first few weeks of shift work there may be marked difficulties in concentrating, or in performing exacting tasks. During daylight hours there are almost bound to be problems with sleep when everyone around is wide awake. What is more, such disturbances are generally rather greater and longer-lasting than jet lag. Changes in a shift, too, will inevitably bring additional stresses on the body's clock.

Clearly, those who are 'night people' by nature will be far more suited to working when it is dark. Diabetics on insulin, on the other hand, and those with stress-related disorders such as asthma and heart conditions, would be well-advised to avoid shift work.

It is important not to skip meals and periods of exercise or rest during shift work. Research is currently being undertaken into the effects of hormone pills containing melatonin, which may prove beneficial to night workers.

Ear Is The Key

Ear therapy, also known as auriculotherapy, is a specialised branch of acupuncture which treats disease solely by stimulating points on the outer parts of our ears. Where ordinary acupuncturists use 2000 points located along invisible meridians (energy pathways which run over our bodies), auriculotherapists use some 200 points on each ear.

Four hundred years before the birth of Christ, 'needling' a patient's ear was a well-known treatment in Mediterranean countries. It was common in ancient India and China, where full-body acupuncture has been practised for thousands of years.

The West was slow to use ear therapy until a French doctor, Paul Nogier, noticed that some of his patients had burn marks on their ears which had been made by a local lay healer. He decided to look into it further, and found out about the acupuncture points on the ears which reflex or refer to other parts of the body. To his amazement, when he joined the various points, an outline appeared of a baby in the womb. Deciding that this meant the ear was like a map of the whole body, Nogier began to treat his patients successfully with auriculotherapy and he also taught his methods to other medical practioners.

Probing through lobes

Auriculotherapists believe the ear acts as a gate into the acupuncture meridians and that treating our ears can affect every single part of our bodies. By treating points on our ear lobes they attempt to influence such things as our

The feet and tongue are often used by doctors to provide clues to health and disease. To an ear therapist, however, it's our ears that map our bodies and chart our ill health.

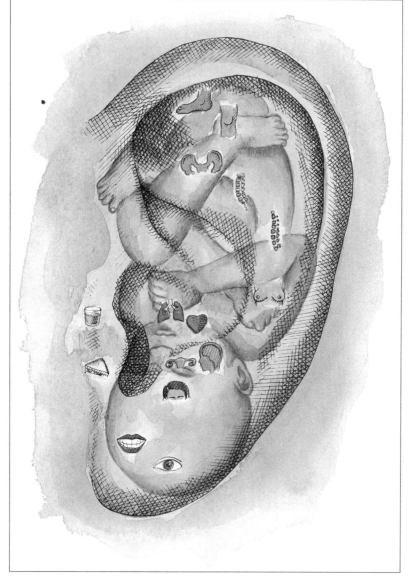

Above: this illustration shows just a few of the auriculotherapy points on the ear, and illustrates Nogier's concept of how the points reflect the shape of a foetus.

senses of taste and smell and, therefore, our appetites.

This form of acupuncture has been used for hundreds of years, especially

in the Far East. Yet even nowadays, as with whole-body acupuncture, nobody really knows how auriculotherapy works, although it is thought that stimulating the points with needles, electrical current, pressure or even lasers somehow influences the body's electrical balance. One thing, however, is certain: the treatment gets results.

Extra auricular benefits

There are several advantages for the patient who opts for ear rather than whole-body acupuncture. It is not, for example, necessary for the patient to undress which makes it quick and convenient in emergencies: even a matchstick can be used if needles are unavailable!

There is even a type of do-it-yourself ear therapy, where the patient can have what are known as 'press' needles inserted. These can be manipulated when they get home in order to relieve such conditions as the pain of arthritis or the desire to smoke. As well as being more convenient than acupuncture, ear therapy can be used to treat certain conditions and illnesses which have failed to improve through whole-body acupuncture.

When you first visit an ear therapist she will take a full case history from you, beginning with the complaint that has brought you to see her and asking the usual doctor's questions about your own medical history, your family's health, your life style, relationships, smoking, drinking, eating, and even your leisure interests. She will then examine your ears for white marks, nodules, scars or skin problems which can tell her a lot about the general state of your health and also the state of particular parts of your body and individual organs.

Next she will find the most sensitive parts of your ear by pressing with a small blunt probe. The points where you feel some discomfort often indicate which organ or part of your body's system needs treatment.

Needles, electricity and lasers

After the initial examination of your ears, the therapist can begin treatment. Therapists use one of the following four methods: needles; electricity; lasers; or press needles.

The needles used are tiny and are placed $1/8$ in (2mm) deep, which is just under the skin. The therapist then manipulates them to stimulate your acupuncture points. An alternative method of stimulation is for a tiny electric pulse to be passed down the needles instead of manipulating them by hand. This doesn't hurt and is in fact rather relaxing. Electricity can also be used to stimulate the acupuncture points without using needles, where the end of a small pen-shaped electrode is placed on the relevant acupuncture point on the ear before an electric current is passed through it.

Children and people who are afraid of needles can be treated by laser. A tiny laser light-beam is directed through the acupuncture point and stimulates it without the patient feeling a thing.

Press needles are like tiny drawing pins or small pointed studs. They are put into your ear in an operation which is just like having your ear pierced. Afterwards they are covered by a plaster to keep them clean.

The main advantage of press needles is that they can be left in place for days at a time, enabling the patient to stimulate the relevant acupuncture points by pressing the head of the needle. Press needles can be very useful for people overcoming addictions or for people who can't get along to the acupuncturist very often.

The final point to bear in mind when considering going for auriculotherapy is that the practice must be up to scratch: always check the practitioner's qualifications beforehand.

During Treatment

• Try to be very specific about the level of sensitivity you are experiencing during the initial ear examination, as this will greatly help the auriculotherapist to locate any problem areas.
• Whilst the therapist is treating the ear, you may be encouraged to exercise or massage the corresponding part of the body in a particular way.

QUESTIONS ABOUT AURICULOTHERAPY

If you are the type of person who would have second thoughts about acupuncture, you are likely to have even more doubts about the use of auriculotherapy. Here are some of the questions you might like to ask, together with some helpful answers.

Q **What type of ailments and illnesses can be treated with auriculotherapy ?**

A Auriculotherapy can treat almost all the conditions that acupuncture treats. The commonest ailments people seek treatment for include: addiction to alcohol, drugs, smoking; pre-menstrual syndrome; arthritis; frozen shoulder; asthma; indigestion; migraine; fears and phobias; cystitis. In China and Sri Lanka, auriculotherapy is widely used for complete pain relief in childbirth, dentistry and major surgical operations. Amazingly, the patients are awake throughout, seemingly relaxed and pain-free.

Q **How many needles are needed, and does it hurt?**

A Although there are 200 acupuncture points on the ear, it's unusual for an auriculotherapist to use more than four needles in each ear during one treatment. Some points on the ear may feel uncomfortable or irritable when they're pressed. But treatment – even when needles are inserted – should never be actually painful. Even having press needles inserted will be a lot less uncomfortable than the process of having your ears pierced.

Q **How many treatments will I need and what will it cost?**

A This depends on what you're being treated for. Long-standing chronic conditions like arthritis or migraine may take many treatments, but acute conditions such as a frozen shoulder or cystitis may only take one or two visits. You will probably find that the first consultation will cost quite a bit more than subsequent follow-up treatments - it will also take longer.

Q **Will it interfere with conventional treatment or drugs I'm already taking?**

A No. Auriculotherapy can be used at the same time as and alongside conventional treatments, although everyone treating you needs to know what other forms of treatment you're having.

Q **My ears are pierced. Does this mean I can't have auriculotherapy?**

A No, but if the pierced hole goes through an acupuncture point, the therapist may have difficulty treating that point.

Q **I'm scared of needles. Can I still have auriculotherapy?**

A Yes. The therapist can use pressure with a small stick, or even lasers, which are completely sensation-free.

Q **How can I tell if an auricular therapist is properly qualified - what qualifications should I look for and how can I find a therapist?**

A Telephone or write to the auriculotherapy regulatory body in your area and ask them to send you a list of members and their qualifications, together with some information describing these qualifications. Some doctors are also trained auricular therapists. Ask your friends, colleagues, or doctor for a personal recommendation.

A Touch of the Vapours

Do you find it difficult to breathe easily at night? Or do you have a cough that refuses to go away? Eucalyptus is an excellent decongestant that is commonly used to treat colds and 'flu.

Eucalyptus (*Eucalyptus globulus*) is an evergreen tree that grows in Australia and Tasmania. It is more commonly known as the gum tree. It is easy to recognise a eucalyptus tree as its bark is peeling and papery, and it grows to about 90 metres tall with small, white, petal-less flowers that grow during the summer.

Eucalyptus oil has many medicinal properties and can be obtained from the oil-bearing glands that are found on the surface of the mature bluish-green eucalyptus leaves. Because of these medicinal and therapeutic properties, the tree is now widely cultivated in many parts of the US and Europe.

Eucalyptus has always been popular with people who are ill. It was once believed that the strong fragrance of the eucalyptus tree could detoxify the air. People who were sick would move to areas where the eucalyptus trees grew, as they believed that perhaps the detoxified air would help to improve their health and cure them.

Beneficial properties

Eucalyptus is a safe, stimulating oil that is antiseptic, antiviral and even insect repellent. It has excellent decongestant properties and is commonly used to treat colds and 'flu. Eucalyptus contains volatile oils that will help to combat lung infections if they are inhaled, passed over the lungs and exhaled.

Eucalyptus is used as an expectorant in many treatments, such as throat lozenges, to help ease respiratory problems and soothe sore throats and coughs. (An expectorant helps to expel excess mucus from the lungs and so aids breathing.) Taken as a herbal tea, eucalyptus can help to ease bronchitis and asthma.

Eucalyptus can be used externally to heal cuts, burns and even ulcers as it helps the formation of new skin tissue and speeds up the healing process. It can also help to relieve muscular and rheumatic pains (see recipe below).

Eucalyptus also helps to disinfect the air, so it makes a good air freshener and is a popular ingredient in pot pourri (see recipe below).

Finally, perhaps one of eucalyptus's less important, but more interesting, uses is that it helps to remove beach tar from clothes and skin. This is a useful tip to remember if you're having a beach holiday this year!

Using your oil

Essential oils are, in fact, tiny amounts of highly scented droplets, and are found in the flowers, leaves stems, roots and barks of aromatic plants. Eucalyptus essential oil is colourless and can be obtained from the leaves of the eucalyptus trees by distillation. This is a popular and widely used process of using steam to extract the oil.

The eucalyptus leaves (far right) are placed in a deep vat and steam is passed over them. As the eucalyptus is exposed to the steam, the essence evaporates along with the water. This 'mixture' is then cooled, and the water and essential oil are separated.

Eucalyptus is toxic in large doses, so always use it with care and in moderation and never take it internally.

Before you use your eucalyptus oil, you should dilute it in a carrier oil such as almond or olive oil. Essential oils are highly concentrated, so they should therefore rarely be used undiluted (unless you're adding them to a bath or

INHALING EUCALYPTUS

One of the most popular and effective ways to ease congestion and benefit from eucalyptus is to inhale it.

BATH INHALANT

Add approximately 20 drops of undiluted eucalyptus essential oil to a bath of running hot water. The oil will evaporate and you'll breathe it in with the steam, which will help to ease congested nasal passages and aid breathing. Relax and soak in the water for about 10 minutes.

STEAMING INHALANT

Add 15 drops of eucalyptus essential oil to two pints (approximately one

a saucer of water). Add approximately six drops of the oil to 2 fl oz (60ml) of a carrier oil.

The skin on your face is particularly sensitive — so take extra care. If you are using a preparation on this area, add only four drops to the carrier oil. This is just a rough guide, as the amount of drops you add will vary, depending on what condition you're treating, so it's a good idea to read your recipe carefully.

If you're buying essential oils, it is important to note that they should always be stored in an airtight, dark glass or plastic bottle. If the oil is kept in direct sunlight, it will quickly lose its essential properties, and if not tightly lidded the oil will evaporate.

You can buy eucalyptus essential oil from aromatherapists, health-food shops, herbalists and some chemists

litre) of hot water. Drape a towel over your head and the bowl and inhale the steam for approximately 10 minutes, or as long as you find it comfortable. If you repeat this treatment three times a day – for example, first thing in the morning, around midday and last thing at night – it will help to ease your respiratory problems.

QUICK INHALANT

If you are suffering from a blocked-up nose dab two or three drops of eucalyptus essential oil on an old handkerchief. When you're feeling a little blocked up, inhale the oil from your handkerchief – it will quickly clear your nasal passages.

Did you know?

- Australian aborigines make use of the antiseptic properties of eucalyptus by tying leaves of the tree around wounds.
- Eucalpytus trees have been planted in swampy areas in North Africa in an attempt to deter mosquitoes and prevent malaria. The oil that evaporates from the leaves acts as an insect repellent and keeps mosquitoes away, and the vast roots of these massive trees - which grow to 90m (300ft) tall - act as a natural drainage system, making the ground less attractive to the insects as a breeding area. Furthermore the antiseptic properties of the oil help to strenghten immunity.

RECIPES FOR HEALTH

EUCALYPTUS MASSAGE

10 drops eucalyptus essential oil
4 fl oz (120ml) almond or olive oil

Dilute the eucalyptus essential oil with the carrier oil. Gently massage the mixture into your chest to help ease the symptoms of bronchitis, colds and 'flu. It will help you to breathe easily.

EUCALYPTUS AIR FRESHENER

2 drops eucalyptus essential oil
1 saucer of cold water

Sprinkle the drops of the eucalyptus oil into a saucer of water and place it on the top of a radiator. The heat from the radiator will evaporate the water and oil, leaving your room smelling fresh.

Oil of Evening Primrose

Evening primrose oil is said to alleviate an astonishing variety of disorders – from diabetes to schizophrenia. What's special about this oil, and what's the evidence for these remarkable claims?

Evening primrose originally came from North America, where its properties were known to the North American Indians. The seeds first came to Europe in the 17th century, where the plant soon naturalised itself. Many of the seeds were carried here accidentally in cargoes of cotton, and the docklands of Liverpool have become a natural habitat for the flowers.

In spite of its name, the evening primrose is not related to the primrose family: it is part of the willow herb family, with tall, leafy stems and papery yellow flowers, which open in the evening, giving the plant its name. The flowers only last for a day, but are produced in quick succession during the summer.

A special oil

The oil is extracted from the seeds of the plant — a complicated process. It is available as capsules (500mg or 250mg each), which you can buy over the counter, or obtain on prescription from your GP. The oil is now available in droppers, for external application. (When treating small children, the oil is rubbed into the skin.)

There are several different species of evening primrose (including *Oenothera lamarkiana* and *Oenothera biennis*) which can be used to make the oil. The most important constituent of evening primrose oil is gamma-linolenic acid (GLA). In the normal way, this acid is produced by our bodies from linoleic acid. (Linoleic acid occurs naturally in many foods, including sunflower, sesame, safflower, soya bean and corn oils, polyunsaturated margarine, green vegetables, chicken, fish and shellfish, as well as evening primrose oil itself.) After conversion from linoleic acid, GLA is itself converted into a hormone, prostaglandin E1. This is essential to us for health, helping the growth and

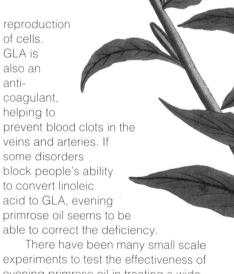

reproduction of cells. GLA is also an anti-coagulant, helping to prevent blood clots in the veins and arteries. If some disorders block people's ability to convert linoleic acid to GLA, evening primrose oil seems to be able to correct the deficiency.

There have been many small scale experiments to test the effectiveness of evening primrose oil in treating a wide range of disorders, but the two main uses are in premenstrual syndrome and atopic (allergic) eczema.

Premenstrual syndrome

The symptoms of premenstrual syndrome include irritability, anxiety, clumsiness, depression, backache, bloatedness and breast tenderness. There are standard hormonal treatments for PMS, but these do not work for everyone, and it is certainly worth trying evening primrose oil. In a controlled test, 65 women who had not responded to standard treatment were treated with evening primrose oil capsules. Over two-thirds of them reported some improvement, particularly the symptom of breast discomfort. However, the studies done so far have not been wide-ranging enough to be regarded as sound scientific evidence of the powers of evening primrose oil.

PMS also responds to treatment with vitamin B6 (pyridoxine), available

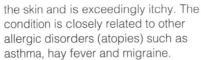
through your doctor. Vitamin B6 and evening primrose oil are combined in many of the oil capsules.

Painful breasts (due to PMS or other disorders such as benign growths) have been successfully treated under test conditions, although some patients in the trials complained of putting on weight, or an increase in breast size. **NOTE:** If you have a breast lump, consult your doctor immediately, before considering any form of treatment, since it may be malignant.

Atopic eczema

Atopic eczema is an allergic reaction which shows as patchy inflammation of

EXTERNAL APPLICATION

There is positive evidence to show that skin can benefit from evening primrose oil, and it is now used in a great many cosmetics.

● When treating children, the oil is usually rubbed into the softer parts of the skin, on the abdomen or inside of the thigh, where it is easily absorbed.
● Many people find that the oil has good moisturising properties, and it is used in many moisturisers and night creams.
● Claims that the oil has anti-ageing properties have made it popular among middle-aged people who are worried about wrinkles.

the skin and is exceedingly itchy. The condition is closely related to other allergic disorders (atopies) such as asthma, hay fever and migraine.

"Evening primrose oil is not a cure for eczema," say the British National Eczema Society, "but in clinical trials it has been shown to be effective in reducing the symptoms of eczema, particularly the itch." If you are an eczema sufferer, your doctor can refer you to a specialist who can help to find the allergen causing eczema. However, if you find it impossible to avoid the cause of the symptom, it is worth trying to alleviate the symptoms with evening primrose oil.

It is interesting to note that human breast milk contains gamma-linolenic acid, and babies do not normally develop atopic conditions when they are being breastfed. It is thought that some babies cannot use the linoleic acid in cow's milk because of a defect in the enzyme which converts it to GLA.

Research has been going on into the effects of evening primrose oil on cystic fibrosis, which is closely related to eczema and asthma. The same enzyme is involved, but the block is much worse, making cystic fibrosis sufferers extremely deficient in essential fatty acids and in prostaglandin E1.

Alcoholism and hangovers

Alcoholism is linked to the prostaglandin E1 levels in the body, in that too much alcohol lowers the level of this hormone. Doctors have found that taking evening primrose oil after heavy drinking reduces the symptoms of a hangover (by helping to boost the prostaglandin levels) and studies on animals seem to indicate that evening primrose oil helps to prevent alcohol tolerance (the need to drink more in order to get the same effect).

Other conditions

Evening primrose oil or, to be more precise, GLA, is also claimed to be useful in the treatment of other conditions. It reduces the level of cholesterol in the blood more effectively than polyunsaturated fats and is an anti-coagulant, so is thought to be useful in preventing thromboses and heart attacks. Research is also going on into its ability to reduce high blood pressure.

Evening primrose oil has also been used to treat hyperactive children: it is thought that these children are deficient in prostaglandin E1, either because they cannot convert linoleic acid to GLA, or because the final conversion to prostaglandin is blocked (by tartrazine dye, Ponceau R dye or some of the constituents of wheat and milk). The British Hyperactive Children's Support Group recommends a 'cocktail' of vitamins, minerals and evening primrose oil to alleviate the condition.

Multiple sclerosis victims have also found that evening primrose oil may alleviate their symptoms, although the treatment does not work in all cases, and research is continuing. Similarly, schizophrenia has been successfully treated in New York with evening primrose oil, combined with penicillin. Research is going on into its ability to control or prevent cancerous growths.

Further research continues into the use of evening primrose oil for treating depression, anorexia nervosa, diabetes (particularly the associated symptoms, skin lesions and eye disease), migraine, pre-eclampsia in pregnancy, mental degeneration, rheumatoid arthritis and various skin and nail disorders.

Side effects

There are some side effects from taking evening primrose, even under medical supervision. If you are considering trying it out for yourself it is advisable to consult your doctor first. It should not be taken by epileptics, as there is evidence to show that those suffering from temporal lobe epilepsy can get worse. Other side effects include nausea, headaches and some people report softer stools. There may be minor skin rashes, particular when the oil is rubbed in externally. Some women have also reported putting on weight while taking evening primrose oil, although, strangely enough tests are going on into the use of the oil for treating obesity.

Women who are considering pregnancy, or are likely to become pregnant, should consult their doctor before taking any medication, including evening primrose oil.

Other sources

The most useful ingredient of evening primrose oil is gamma-linolenic acid. This essential fatty acid is also found in other seed oils, including borage, blackcurrant, gooseberry, redcurrant hemp and hop seed oils.

FAD DIETS

Eat Until You're Thin!

Slimmers want fast results, so there has been a succession of weird and wonderful 'miracle' diets, each claiming to be the best and quickest way to lose weight. Do these fad diets really work – or are they a danger to your health?

Any doctor or nutritionist will tell you that the only way to successful and sustained weight loss is sensible, healthy eating — all the time. But we still seem to be assailed by new, gimmicky diets which claim to hold the key to 'a new you'. These fad diets usually involve excessive calorie reduction, or a limited selection of specific foods. They may advocate particular combinations of food as having a special weight-reducing effect on the body.

Fad diets play on the desire of every slimmer to lose weight quickly and easily. They are popular because people will always try something new or revolutionary — and people want to believe the claims made for the diet. 'Lose 20lb in just 14 days,' says the diet. How wonderful, you think. If you're impatient or have tried unsuccessfully to diet before, maybe this is the diet you have been waiting for. Studies have

shown that most dieters continually hop from one diet to the next, their weight constantly yo-yoing up and down. Their weight never stabilises because of the extreme eating patterns followed and because the importance of a healthy, balanced diet isn't learned and adopted along the way.

The minute they break the diet they dissolve into an eating binge, and all the benefits they may have gained from the diet are lost. Next week it's back to dieting again.

Examples of Fad Diets

Probably one of the most popular diets recently has been The Hip and Thigh Diet, based on a low-fat regime and designed to shift flab specifically in those areas which give rise to the typical British pear-shaped figure. It's highly debatable whether you can 'spot reduce' in this way (better to try exercises that concentrate on those areas), but it's a good selling point.

However, it is a sensible diet from the nutritional standpoint, cutting fat but allowing complex carbohydrates, such as wholemeal bread, brown rice and potatoes (which are high in fibre) and a moderate amount of protein. Overall, calories are cut, but to a healthy level for steady weight loss. Plenty of variety in the diet ensures good nutrition.

The F-Plan Diet was also extremely popular, and was launched around the time when the medical spotlight first focused on the merits of dietary fibre. The diet, being high in fibre and low in fat, was neither cranky nor unbalanced, yet came in for criticism. It promoted the benefits of fibre, but recommended eating large quantities of wheat bran and bran cereals (which are loaded with

YOUR HEALTH

sugar) and could lead to malabsorption of certain minerals. A straight wholefood diet is a healthier way of ensuring you eat sufficient fibre.

The Scarsdale Diet was a high-protein diet, which is now considered unhealthy. The Scarsdale Diet did not restrict fat — high-protein foods like meat, cheese and milk contain a lot of saturated fat which is known to be bad for the heart and circulatory system.

Similarly, low-carbohydrate diets have had their followers, but these, too, are considered unhealthy. We now know that carbohydrates have a high calorific value, but low-carbohydrate diets tend to lump together all types — the simple sugars and the complex starch and fibre carbohydrates — and label them as baddies.

We are now aware of the importance of dietary fibre and the need to reduce fat, particularly the saturated type, because it increases the level of cholesterol in the blood and therefore can increase the risk of heart disease. Low-carbohydrate regimes may not restrict calories too much but are nutritionally unsound and, long term, could lead to health problems.

Going to extremes

As well as the diets described so far, which have a slight imbalance, there are several true fad diets which are

DRAWBACKS AND DANGERS OF FAD DIETS

Many fad diets are worse than useless: not only do they not help you lose weight in the long run, they may be positively unhealthy.

● You're unlikely to be able to stick to a fad diet for long either because a very limited and restricted choice of foods makes it boring or because, with severe calorie reduction, your enthusiasm and willpower will soon give way to the stronger feeling of hunger.
● Fad diets are likely to be lacking in essential nutrients so you can expect to feel tired and lethargic and skin and hair will suffer too.
● If you're not eating 'normally' – the same meals and at the same times as others – dieting becomes very anti-social.
● At the beginning of any diet, you may well lose weight rapidly to start with, but this initial weight loss is just water loss (particularly with low-carbohydrate, high-protein and very low-calorie, meal-replacement diets). After dieting, the body quickly recovers its fluid content so the weight loss from water goes back on again straight away.
● If calories, particularly in the form of carbohydrates, are severely restricted, the body behaves as if it is being starved, and conserves its fat stores, allowing muscle tissue to be 'eaten up'. Taken to extremes, losing too much healthy, lean tissue is potentially dangerous and damage can be caused to vital organs, such as the heart and kidneys.
● Severe dieting simply lowers the metabolic rate, which is why you can reach a 'plateau', finding it increasingly difficult to lose weight despite eating very little – and when the diet ends the weight goes back on.

much more gimmicky. The Grapefruit Diet was based on a low-carbohydrate regime, but all the meals started with an unsweetened half grapefruit. The theory behind the diet is that special enzymes in the fruit speed up the body's fat-burning process. Pineapple, too, is rich in the same enzyme.

However, there is no scientific evidence to back it up. Weight loss is mainly due to cutting carbohydrates (which dangerously upsets the metabolism, as the liver reacts to the lack of sugar in the blood) although eating a lot of grapefruit, which are very low in calories, may replace other more calorific foods. Their sourness also helps reduce a taste for sweetness.

The Beverly Hills Diet was based on the same sort of principle, this time with exotic fruits which, it was claimed, had 'magic' weight-reducing properties. For days at a time, you're restricted to eating mangoes, pineapples, papayas and watermelon. There's severe calorie reduction so it's bound to work — just how much the fruits are responsible for any weight loss is questionable. Continued over a period of time, chronic malnutrition could result.

There have been many versions of single-food diets (you could invent one yourself) but basically they only work because ultimately, they cut calories. They are also very boring, unappetising and monotonous. Although on the one hand this makes them difficult to stick to for long, conversely they can be easier to follow because no thought has to go into shopping or meal planning. Many dieters don't want to be faced with too flexible a diet: if some freedom of choice is allowed they start going off the rails and cheating.

The calorie-counted meal-replacement is a method of dieting which plays on people who don't want to 'think' about their diet. And very low-calorie diets (VLCDs) also prescribe a regime which has a very restricted calorie intake. Such diets are easy to follow, but do nothing to improve your eating habits: the moment you revert to your previous eating pattern the weight goes back on.

The right way to diet

What's important when it comes to planning a diet is whether or not the diet is healthy, its effect on the body, where the weight loss comes from and whether it can be maintained. This is where all fad diets come in for severe criticism. Short term they may well produce the quick results the dieter is looking for but success is generally short-lived. Weight tends to pile back on and frequently becomes more difficult

FOUR FALLACIES ABOUT DIETING

1 If something is to work, it must cost you money.
Wrong. Dieting shouldn't increase your food bill or involve buying any special aids.

2 Some foods are slimming.
Wrong. All food contains calories, so no single food positively helps you to lose weight. But some foods have fewer calories, and seem to fill you up without loading the calories.

3 Dieting is a better way to lose weight than exercising.
Wrong. The best way to lose weight,

and keep muscles in good shape, is to combine the two.

4 Once you've lost weight on a diet, you'll be able to go back to your old eating habits and tuck in to chocolate again.
Wrong. If you want to keep your weight steady you'll never be able to consume a lot of 'empty' calories. Balance is vital, so you'll have to cut down on other, healthier calories for every bar of chocolate, glass of wine or whatever. Alternatively, you'll have to step up your exercise regime to burn off all those excess calories.

to lose. In the long term the weight battle isn't solved but inflated.

It would be nice to believe in miracle diets, but sadly there aren't any. Indeed, fad diets can make weight problems worse. The only way to lose weight is to eat a healthy, balanced diet which cuts calories to a safe level without sacrificing essential vitamins and minerals.

Although a short-term, crash diet may help get you started on the road to weight loss, it is not a long-term solution. What you need is a varied diet of lean meat, fish, wholegrain cereals, pulses, fruit, vegetables and low-fat dairy produce. With a good balance, you can even allow yourself an occasional treat, such as a glass of wine. Simply by eliminating all those 'empty' calories, from cakes, biscuits, crisps, puddings, sweets, chocolates and alcohol, and by limiting your intake of fats and sugars, weight loss happens virtually automatically, without having to watch calories obsessively.

Contrary to now outdated belief, starchy carbohydrates such as bread, rice, pasta and potatoes shouldn't be excluded, provided they're not loaded with fat. Not only are such foods filling and sustaining, but weight for weight they provide fewer calories than fat or protein and, if unrefined, also provide valuable fibre for a healthy digestion.

If a diet is varied, you're unlikely to go short of any essential nutrients, although it is useful to have some knowledge of nutrition, so you can check on whether your diet is adequate in all areas (see table overleaf). You can enjoy eating much the same meals as friends or family, both at home and

eating out. Results may be more gradual but weight loss will be steady and you should feel healthy and energetic. Plus, with good eating habits learned along the way, you can hope to keep that weight off permanently once you've reached your target.

Calorie requirements

Everyone is different, with different eating habits and different levels of activity. Actual body shape is largely determined by hereditary factors, but weight is basically controlled by your food intake and energy output. It comes down to a simple equation:

If food eaten (measured in calories) is equal to energy used (in calories), weight remains constant.

If food eaten provides more calories than energy used up, weight increases.

If food eaten provides fewer calories than energy used up, weight decreases.

Energy is needed for all the bodily processes, like breathing, replacing and renewing cells, regulating the body temperature and digesting food, as well as for activity. However, the rate at which calories are used up is called the metabolic rate and it varies between individuals. It is probably the amount of energy expended in everyday activities which dictates why some people have a high metabolic rate (burn up calories fast) while others have a slow one. If you are a slow burner, you will not be able to eat as many calories, without putting on weight, as your slim friends.

However, you are not necessarily stuck with a sluggish metabolism. You can help to speed it up with exercise. You can also lower it further by extreme dieting. Lean body tissue burns calories faster and more efficiently than fat tissue so you're not doing yourself any favours by losing lean tissue — as a result of excessive calorie reduction.

Balance is the key: for healthy weight loss, women should aim to reduce their food intake to about 1000 Kcal a day (about 1500 for men). Combine this reduction in eating with an increase in exercise and you will lose weight more easily, not only by burning up more calories but by increasing your metabolic rate.

YOUR HEALTH

KNOW YOUR FOODS

It's not how much you eat but what you eat that will dictate whether you win or lose the battle of the bulge. Listed here are the major nutrients and their main sources. There are many more minerals and vitamins which, although only needed in tiny amounts, are none the less essential. Only by eating a varied diet can you be sure of getting complete nourishment.

NUTRIENT	FOUND IN
Protein	Meat, fish, poultry, eggs, cheese, pulses, milk, nuts, vegetable protein products, including soya bean and quorn products. (Choose lean meat, skinned poultry, low-fat cheese and skimmed milk.)
Carbohydrates Starch and fibre (Increase)	Flour, bread, rice, pasta, cereals (preferably wholemeal), potatoes, peas, sweetcorn, baked beans, pulses.
Sugar (Reduce/cut out)	Sugar, preserves, cakes, biscuits, sweets, puddings, chocolate, fruit canned in syrup.
Fats Saturated (Reduce/cut out)	Butter, margarine, lard, suet, dairy products (cream, cheese and whole milk), unspecified vegetable oils, cakes, biscuits, pastry, chocolate.
Unsaturated (Substitute for saturated, but reduce overall)	Polyunsaturated oils and margarines, such as sunflower, soya or corn oil, olive oil, oily fish, avocados.
Low fat	Spreads and reduced-calorie salad dressings formulated for slimmers.
Vitamins/Minerals Vitamin A	Fats, sardines, liver, apricots, carrots, green vegetables.
B-Group Vitamins	Bread, pasta, cereals, green vegetables, eggs, yeast extract, meat, milk.
Vitamin C	Fruit (especially citrus fruits), green vegetables, tomatoes, potatoes.
Vitamin D	Fats, oily fish, eggs, cheese.
Calcium	Milk, cheese, yogurt, bread, flour, green vegetables, fish bones (as in canned sardines), eggs.
Iron	Red meat (particularly liver), corned beef, baked beans, eggs, dried fruit, bread, flour and other cereal products, potatoes, cabbage and spinach.

Food For Thought

Fasting is often regarded as the pastime and practice of health fanatics. However, it can sharpen up your mind, leaving you mentally and emotionally rejuvenated, as well as banishing toxins from your system.

Fasting, voluntary abstinence from food and drink, has been practised since the early days of civilisation, when it was considered a beneficial health-restoring procedure which purified the body and mind. It certainly gives the digestive system a break and the body a chance to divert its energy into eliminating toxins and metabolic waste.

By purifying the body, some people believe that fasting may actually help boost your immune system and help prevent illnesses developing. Fasting is also said to be helpful if you suffer from constipation, as it cleans out a clogged-up system.

Many people associate fasting with a crash diet, after having binged on junk foods. However, as a means of losing weight, fasting is definitely not a a good idea. Carried out in the correct manner, fasting can be a wonderfully rewarding experience. Once the body has been completely purified by the fast, your eyes should sparkle, your skin texture improve and you should find that you glow with health.

A 24-hour fast

Under exceptional circumstances, the human body can actually survive for several weeks without food, as long as water is taken. The actual length of time depends on the body's energy reserves and the amount of activity carried out during the period of abstinence. A fat, inactive person will survive longer than a thin, physically active person; and an adult will survive longer than a child.

If you decide to try fasting for health reasons, you should do it for no longer than 24 hours. It is definitely not a good idea to fast for long periods as it can result in serious medical complications. People who practise yoga seriously, for example, sometimes fast for three or four days at a time, but for the average busy woman, one day is more advisable and practical.

Don't worry about vitamin and mineral loss. You'll obviously lose some while fasting, but if you're reasonably healthy any loss will be quickly replaced when you start eating again.

You should not fast, however, if you are ill, underweight or pregnant. It's also not advisable to fast before a period. If you are in any doubt at all about whether or not to fast, or are on prescribed medication, you should consult your doctor first.

Take it easy

Fasting is not just a matter of skipping meals for a day while carrying out your normal routine, at home or at work, nor is it intended to be a way of losing weight. The purpose is to purify the body and to do so it needs to rest.

You should set aside 24 hours when you can stay quietly at home and relax. Don't be tempted to try and catch up with housework or odd jobs around the house. And, a fast day is definitely not the time to go to a strenuous aerobics class followed by the weekly trip to the supermarket. And you should never drive while fasting because you will feel light-headed.

If you have a family, try and fast midweek while they're at work or school. If you have a job and can't take a day off, fast at the weekend but try and arrange to have the house to yourself.

You will find fasting easier to cope with if you begin in the early evening after supper. This way you will be going to bed on a full stomach. If you begin a fast in the morning you will be feeling pretty hungry by bedtime, as this is the time when we normally expect to feel well-fed and relaxed. So you might find it difficult to go to bed feeling hungry. The last meal before your fast, however, should be light and easily digestible. So, don't make the mistake of 'stoking up' before a fast — you'll be giving your system more work than necessary. Try to go to bed early so you get as much rest as possible.

Some people find it helpful to reduce the amount they eat in the week preceding the fast. This begins the cleansing process and accustoms the stomach to less bulk. Once the stomach has shrunk you will feel less hungry.

The purification process

Whatever type of fast you try (see Box, Partial Fasting), it's important to drink plenty of water. It is recommended that you consume between four and eight pints during the fast. This helps flush

PARTIAL FASTING

Fasting can be total or partial. So, if you don't feel ready to go without food for a whole day, then break yourself in slowly.

The idea of a total fast can be a daunting prospect, especially if you have never done it before. So you might find it easier to limit what you eat to small quantities of one kind of food. This will still give the system a rest and allow the purification process to take place.

Types of cleansing foods are fruit and vegetable juices, whole fruit, herb or fruit teas, yoghurt or organically-grown brown rice. Eat your choice of food in small quantities, at four to five hourly intervals, at a time when you would normally eat your usual meal.

Fruit fast

A fruit fast is a good one to try because the fibre in the fruit provides bulk for the stomach and you won't feel so hungry.

Avoid citrus fruits as the acid can cause indigestion. Bananas provide carbohydrate and fill you up, but too many can cause indigestion. The secret is to vary the fruit:

Breakfast
One pear or apple

Lunch
One banana

Afternoon snack
A few grapes or slice of melon

out the system and also helps prevent headaches and hunger pangs.

At some point in your fast, usually within five hours of having missed your first meal, you'll feel that you can't go on. You are likely to suffer from headaches, bad breath, nausea, muscle cramps, irritability, as well as feeling weak and light-headed. As long as you are healthy you are in no danger.

These feelings are a normal part of the purification process and will eventually go away. When the toxins begin to move from your body tissues

and into the bloodstream you feel literally poisoned for a while. When the toxins are flushed out of your system, you'll gradually start to feel better so it's worth persevering.

When you finish fasting don't make the mistake of having a slap up meal with wine. Your system won't be able to cope with it and you'll undo the good you've done. Your stomach will have shrunk, so eat light, easily digested foods such as yoghurt, rice or soup.

OTHER REASONS FOR FASTING

Fasting is not only a means of purifying the mind and body – it is also used by many people before or during special sacred and religious times, or as a means of bringing attention to political protest.

The Islamic practice of going without food, from dawn to dusk, during the month of Ramadan usually springs to mind when we talk about fasting for religion. However, fasting has been, and in many cases still is, an important part of many of the major religions of the world.

Buddhist monks, for example, (see left) fast on certain days and confess their sins, while in India, Hindu holy men are admired for their frequent bouts of fasting. The Jews also observe several annual fast days. Some Roman Catholics fast on Ash Wednesday and Good Friday, while Protestant churches tend to look on fasting as a matter of conscience.

Fasting is also used for social or political reasons as a gesture of protest or solidarity. Famous examples are the fast conducted by Mahatma Gandhi to atone for his followers' violent behaviour, and the hunger strike and subsequent death in prison in 1981 of 10 Irish nationalists who wanted recognition for themselves and other political prisoners.

The Benefits of Biofeedback

The autonomic nervous system functions subconsciously — without any control from our brains, to control normal body functions such as blood pressure, heart rate and sweating. Until fairly recently, it seemed that only certain people, who were often renowned for their special skills — the yogis of India, for instance — could control these physical functions. Research has revealed, however, that many such abilities are within the reach of the great majority of people. What is more, they can be used with markedly beneficial medical effect. Indeed, exponents of the technique, known as biofeedback,

In a technique that can be mastered by most of us with just a little practice, there is evidence to show it is possible to control certain body processes simply by using the power of the mind.

claim that it can be used to treat — and even prevent — a whole variety of stress-related ailments.

Combating stress

We all suffer from stress — no one is immune from it. We even need a certain

amount of it — in the form of a charge of physical and mental energy — to survive. But poor skin, stomach upsets, insomnia, muscular pains, headaches and other symptoms can all quite frequently be put down to undue tension.

Doctors have long been aware that mood swings go hand in hand with physiological changes. Excessive stress can, for example, not only raise blood pressure and the level of sweating but may also affect the brain's normal electrical activity. It has been found that when yogis go into a deep state of meditation, alpha-wave (normal electrical) activities increase.

MIND OVER MATTER

If you do not have access to a biofeedback machine, it is still possible to reduce stress and thereby control certain physical symptoms by mind power.

At Harvard University it was found in experimentation with a group of students that transcendental meditation could be used effectively to lower high blood pressure and, all-importantly, to keep it under control.

Those whose blood pressure tends to be high should, of course, continue to seek a doctor's advice. But the following feedback techniques, which do not require machinery of any kind, may be of additional help.

Find a quiet spot. Sitting as comfortably as possible, but not slumping, begin to visualise idyllic, peaceful surroundings and let your mind become enveloped in the fantasy. Alternatively, you can try a simple breathing exercise. Inhale deeply without straining, and hold your breath to the count of three. Breathe out. Repeat, but this time allow the breath to escape slowly through your nose. Relax and then repeat. This sort of deep breathing can can have a valuable calming effect. Check your pulse rate both before and after these sequences to provide biofeedback.

Stress decreases the brain's alpha-wave activity, so the aim of biofeedback techniques is to learn how to be able to control this activity.

Sedatives, tranquillisers and relaxants are all very well, but are not a cure in themselves. They are merely 'chemical crutches', providing temporary relief, and may well have undesirable side effects. Learn to control the underlying processes, however, and you will almost certainly reduce the risk of stress-related

One of the simplest biofeedback machines is a skin resistance meter, which relays a low-pitched tone. The aim is to relax, so the tone goes as low as possible.

physical problems. There are various experiments which have studied the alpha-wave activity of the brain. At the University of California Medical Centre, for example, scientists have found they can train students to achieve a similar control to the yogis through biofeedback techniques. The students were encouraged to remember the sort of thoughts they generated in order to increase their alpha activity.

Taking measurements

Biofeedback — the reading of certain bodily changes of which, as a rule, we would hardly be aware — requires use of a machine that will measure such factors as electrical skin resistance, brain-wave patterns or muscle tension. Some types of machine are used in the laboratory or other experimental conditions only. In hospitals, for instance, they can be helpful to patients with various types of heart and circulatory problems. Whenever the machine shows that blood pressure is rising, the patients must try to relax. Then, when blood pressure falls, the patient has to try to remember her thoughts and feelings as it does so. Such readings can be used to control irregular heart beats or even digestive secretions. Some models, are fully portable and eminently suitable for

home use. They vary in complexity. You may have to be 'wired up', a process involving the attachment of electrodes to the hands or forehead. The machine then registers the slightest change and displays it in a number of ways: variations may show as fluctuating needles, varying colours in a visual display or low-pitched tones.

One type of machine, a so-called electromyograph, measures the activity that is generated by tense muscles. It produces a sound, as well as a reading on a meter, when electrodes are placed on the muscles of the neck or head. A skin resistance meter, meanwhile, requires electrodes that are placed on the first two fingers. It, too, produces a piercing tone when there is increased sweating. An electroencephalogram measures brain waves and pinpoints different levels of consciousness. Electrodes are placed on the head and behind the ear. The noise emitted accurately reflects the degree of alpha-wave activity in the brain.

The aim is always to relieve any tension that shows up in readings, reducing it to more acceptable levels, by using any one of a number of relaxation techniques, such as deep breathing, meditation or visualisation. There is nothing magical about these machines. Quite simply, through biofeedback training, the individual comes to recognise those sensations that occur as a more satisfactory reading shows up. Once the machine has shown you when and how to do this, patients soon learn to control these normally subconscious reactions without the use of a machine.

With the development of further technology in this area, it seems very possible that in future years we may well be able to gain much greater and more valuable control over brain function, and thus our state of mind, than we currently have.

" The mind is free, Whate'er afflict the man, A king's a King, Do Fortune what she can. "

Michael Drayton

Wind and Water

When we visit a place or enter a particular building, we very often sense that somehow the atmosphere bodes well – that it has 'good vibes' or otherwise. This, the Chinese would hold, is due to the nature of the location's Feng Shui.

The direction a building faces, the way in which you arrange your furniture and even your house number can all have a remarkable influence upon your health, well-being and prosperity, according to Chinese tradition. Indeed, in any society, architects strive to make their buildings 'work' for the future inhabitants in many ways: making the best use of the sun for extra warmth in a cold climate; building around courtyards to keep the sun out in warm climates; planning windows so that they are not only appealing but also sensible in terms of heat loss; positioning doors so that they are both practical and safe, and so on.

Adherents of Feng Shui have developed a combination of mystical philosophy, interior design and sound

logic which dictate how your home or working environment should be planned and their theories are equally meaningful in a western setting.

Literally, the two Chinese words — 'Feng' and 'Shui' — translate as 'wind' and 'water', and refer to the existence of certain currents of energy that have constant impact. Ch'i currents are said to be beneficial and follow curved paths. Sha currents, however, can be devastating, and always strike along straight lines, like 'secret arrows'.

The lie of the land

Much of the theory of Feng Shui is concerned with selection of suitable sites for buildings. Look for the Dragon, Feng Shui experts say, and you can begin to determine a site's potential.

Above: The skyscrapers of Hong Kong are situated according to the principles of Feng Shui. Inset: The escalators of the Hong Kong and Shanghai Bank are angled to catch the ch'i currents.

You may find it in nearby hills or in the skyline, where it may be represented by a prominent building. The very best or so-called 'true' Green Dragon occurs when one hill (or building) rises above others, ideally to the east, or to the north-east or south-east.

To the west of a site, you should also be able to determine the White Tiger — a lower, more gentle slope (or building perhaps). To the north and south, there should also be identifiable features. The traditional Black Tortoise of the north may be symbolised in very

LUCKY NUMBERS

Traditionally, the Chinese believe that Feng Shui principles can extend to the number given to a house or apartment, and that particular numbers will ensure happiness and well-being.

A number that has very important religious significance within Buddhism is 13. It is therefore regarded by the Chinese as being an extremely lucky number for a home. Other figures said to bring good fortune are six, which is thought to indicate wealth; and nine which closely resembles the Chinese character for 'long life' when it's written in the western way. However, the luckiest and most prized number of all is 88 which looks very much like the Chinese character denoting 'double happiness'.

many ways, as may the Red Bird of the south. (It is almost a matter of using visual imagination.) These four points correspond to the four great constellations of the Heavens. Indeed, Feng Shui and astrology are essentially complementary — astrology being concerned with the influence of the planets and Feng Shui, with matters of landscape and layout on Earth.

Watercourses, too, are said to have strong influences and will therefore affect the desirability of a plot of land. They are even believed to generate their own form of ch'i. Water found to the south of a site brings particularly good omens, as do streams that flow from east to west or west to east.

Home comforts

In days of old, the Chinese nobility would always be sure to consult a Feng Shui expert about the layout and interior design of their homes, and the practice continues today both in Hong Kong and among wealthier Chinese communities elsewhere. So what sort of advice is he likely to give when he is called in to survey a house or apartment?

At the entrance, the Feng Shui expert is certain to suggest that the path should be curved or end in steps so that the invisible 'secret arrows' of any invisible sha may be deflected. Doors should always open inwards, encouraging inflow of beneficial ch'i.

Inner and outer doors must be hung on the same side; but a rear door should never be in line with the front in case favourable ch'i escapes before exerting influence. Stairs should not face the front door, either, to prevent undue deflection of ch'i; but if they do, the simple placing of a mirror at the top of the flight is usually recommended as both a practical and aesthetically-pleasing remedy.

When it comes to deciding on the positioning of rooms, the Feng Shui man needs some personal data, for horoscopes come into play. This is particularly vital as far as the siting of the main bedroom is concerned, since it should face, if possible, the direction corresponding with the natal animal sign of the head of the household — by Chinese tradition, the man.

In the living room, ch'i must be encouraged to flow freely for the sake of family welfare. Its ideal shape will be rectangular: and the very best situation, south-facing. The wall opposite the door should be unbroken by alcoves, if possible, and a layout in which windows and the door are facing should be avoided. The Feng Shui man will also want to remind his clients that fireplaces can conduct ch'i away from a room, but that skilful placing of mirrors (above the fireplace) may avert this.

The working environment

Commercial buildings serving Chinese communities — shops, offices, financial institutions and manufacturing units alike — are always laid out in close consultation with the Feng Shui man: for even something as seemingly trivial as the position of a desk can, according to tradition, affect trade. Factors such as attracting customers, increasing productivity and ensuring good management-staff relations can all be achieved by careful attention to basic Feng Shui tenets.

A director's desk, for example, should always have its back to the wall, and not a window, and the door should be to one side of the facing wall. A reception desk should be placed at an angle to the entrance so that it will not hinder the flow of helpful currents; and the presence of water — perhaps a pool or fountain — within this area will also serve to stimulate a welcome.

Tools of the trade

Watch the Feng Shui man at work, and you will almost certainly see him using a special sort of compass, known as the

This chart, from a modern Chinese Almanac, is used by the Feng Shui man.

Lo P'an, which serves as an aid to determining siting and layout. It has at the centre of its circular Heaven Plate (surrounded by the square Earth Plate) a magnetic needle, and surrounding this are a number of concentric circles, featuring markings to aid calculations.

More complex versions of the Lo P'an will also help the Feng Shui man with other aspects of his work, for he may well be called upon, too, for advice concerning lucky days for opening a business or the most fortunate time to begin a journey. Such calculations require special expertise, rewarded not from a set scale of charges but by a fee decided upon by the satisfied client and presented, according to tradition, in a small red envelope.

> "Mid pleasures and palaces
> though we may roam,
> Be it ever so humble,
> there's
> no place like home;
> A charm from the skies
> seems to hallow us there,
> Which, seek through the world,
> is ne'er met with
> elsewhere."
>
> **J H Payne**

The Wonder Bulb

Once it became widely used, garlic became known as the 'poor man's treacle' because it was used as a cure for all types of diseases, aches and pains. People used to tie it round their necks in a piece of cloth to ward off colds!

Garlic originated in Central Asia and was transported to Europe by the Crusaders. It took on a therapeutic role among Europeans and was believed to provide protection from the plague, vampires and even possession by devils!

Garlic has been used as a therapeutic medicine for thousands of years and we would be foolish not to use it simply because we sometimes find its strong, effusive smell overpowering. Primitive people were fascinated by this pungent odour and believed that it was this that gave the plant its magical healing powers.

The Ancient Egyptians believed that garlic held the secret to eternal youth. They even gave it to labourers building the pyramids to keep the workforce

healthy and vigorous. The Greeks and Romans also held garlic in high esteem because of its medicinal properties; the Greek philosopher Hippocrates once proclaimed that it was a 'hot, laxative and diuretic' remedy.

The Ayurvedic system of medicine (an ancient Indian form of holistic medicine still practised today) classifies garlic as a preventative for arthritis and nervous disorders. It's also used to relieve bronchitis, pneumonia, asthma, 'flu and other lung conditions; to expel gas and parasites; and as an effective inhalant to relieve the symptoms of whooping cough in children.

Although garlic has been used medicinally for thousands of years, its chemical structure and the reasons why and how it works as a remedy are only

just beginning to be understood. Pharmacological investigations and clinical trials have now confirmed the medicinal claims attributed to it.

Fresh garlic contains an amino acid called alliin. When the bulb is cut or broken, alliin comes in contact with an enzyme called allinase which converts alliin to allicin, a powerful antibacterial agent with the characteristic garlicky odour. This in turn is broken down into several therapeutic compounds which are antifungal, antithrombotic (they help to prevent thromboses because they inhibit blood clotting by making the platelets less sticky) and may also help to reduce high blood pressure.

Because of these properties, there is particular interest in the way garlic may be of use in the prevention of

RECIPE FOR HEALTH

CHICKEN ROASTED WITH GARLIC

Don't be put off by the amount of garlic. Prepared like this it takes on a mild, almost sweet, flavour.

Serves 4

1 x 1.5kg chicken
salt and pepper
juice of one lemon
1kg plump garlic cloves, half
of them peeled
1 bayleaf
thyme
olive oil
glass of white wine

Pre-heat oven to 220°C (425°F, Gas mark 7). Season chicken with salt, pepper and lemon juice. Stuff with the peeled garlic cloves, bayleaf and thyme. Rub with olive oil and place breast down in a roasting pan. Roast for 30 minutes or until chicken begins to brown. Reduce heat to 170°C. (325°F, Gas mark 3). Add remaining garlic cloves and 2 tbsp olive oil. Turn the chicken on its back and continue roasting, basting occasionally, for about an hour or until the juices run clear. Transfer to a warm serving dish and surround with the roasted unpeeled garlic cloves. Add white wine to juices in pan. Bubble over a medium heat for a few minutes, then season and strain over the chicken.

IN THE RAW

If you want to use garlic for medicinal purposes, it must be eaten raw because cooking destroys its medicinal properties.

The best way of eating raw garlic is to chop or slice two or three cloves and add them to a salad. Another way of increasing raw garlic intake is to crush several cloves and to mix the liquid with other vegetable juices or even to take it by itself in small amounts.

However, as we all know, the unfortunate side effect of eating garlic, especially when raw, is the pungent reminder on your breath and even in your skin, which many people find unpleasant. A good way of cleansing the breath after eating garlic is to chew raw parsley, mint or celery.

Another way to avoid wafting garlic fumes over everybody is to take garlic capsules or tablets. Used in this form, alliin and allinase are kept separate and the transformation to the odour-producing allicin occurs only during digestion in the stomach and intestine.

coronary heart disease and strokes. Experiments have shown that garlic oil given to rabbits decreases blood levels of low-density lipoprotein (LDL), the 'bad' cholesterol which sticks to artery walls and increases the risk of coronary heart disease. At the same time a corresponding increase occurs in blood levels of high-density lipoprotein (HDL), the 'good' cholesterol which doesn't stick to your artery walls.

Clinical studies in which patients with heart disease were given ten cloves of garlic a day for a month, showed an increase in the anti-clotting substances in their blood.

Additionally, laboratory experiments show that garlic juice inhibits the growth of a broad range of potentially harmful bacteria, yeasts and fungi. As such, garlic is believed to have a powerful effect on wound healing. Enormous quantities were in fact used for this purpose during the First and Second World Wars.

Garlic has been used successfully to treat intestinal disorders such as persistent diarrhoea and amoebic dysentery. It has been found to improve the quality of the bacteria which are naturally present in the gut and which aid the digestion of food.

If you're prepared to eat enough of it, garlic is a good source of nutrients.

It's high in carbohydrates and contains some protein, fibre and very little fat. It also contains plenty of health-giving vitamins and minerals, especially vitamin C, iron and potassium.

It is also one of the best sources of germanium, a mineral trace element which is believed to help in boosting the body's immune system; and of selenium, another trace element with anti-oxidant properties which are similar to those of vitamin E.

WHAT'S IN A CLOVE?

Nutrient Content (per 100g)
(1 clove = 3g approx.)

kcal	117.0
Protein	3.5g
Fat	0.3g
Carbohydrate	26.7g
Sodium	18.0mg
Potassium	373.0mg
Calcium	18.0mg
Magnesium	8.0mg
Iron	1.5mg
Zinc	0.9mg
Vit A	0.0
Vit B complex	0.69mg
Vit C	10.0mg

Rumphii
Jin-Som
Medici Siner
sis Zau
quii.
Jap:

Jap:

人 gy
参 Sei

A Root Of Goodness

Ginseng has only recently become a fashionable health product in Western countries, but it has been used in the Far East for thousands of years.

Two thousand years ago the Chinese believed ginseng had the spiritual power to quieten the animal spirit, establish the soul, benefit an individual's understanding and allay fears. Its physical effects were said to include invigorating the body, opening up the heart and expelling evil effluvia.

Today, the Chinese still regard ginseng as a kind of omnipotent herb and use it not only as a remedy for a wide range of complaints and illnesses but also as an aphrodisiac.

In the West, ginseng is without doubt the 'health food' of all health foods with its seemingly magical powers widely promoted by its users. They claim that it will not only increase a person's lifespan and transform their sex life but will improve their stamina, energy levels and immunity to disease. Ginseng is also said to have been used

successfully to treat rheumatic pains, thinning hair, depression and stress-related illnesses.

Ginseng's geographical roots

Ginseng is a small shrub with a sweetly aromatic flavour which originally grew wild in the mountainous forests of North America and Asia. The plant needs five to seven years to mature before the root is large enough to harvest. After harvesting, the root is ground up and used to make powders, teas, tablets extracts and cosmetics.

Asian ginseng is known as Panax schinseng and is a member of the Araliaceae family of plants. North American ginseng is called Panax

Right: Panax quinquefolius or wild ginseng has an abundance of leaves and spherically-shaped white flowers.

quinquefolius. The generic name Panax comes from Panacea, the Greek goddess who was able to 'heal all'.

Although difficult and expensive to grow, it's now widely cultivated commercially and is one of South

Korea's major exports. Most ginseng grown in North America is exported to Hong Kong. However, the American type is said to be less effective than the Asian type.

There is also on the market a cheaper ginseng 'substitute' called Eleutherococcus senticosus, sometimes called Siberian ginseng. It comes from the same family as Asian ginseng and is said to have similar properties. It's very popular in the USSR where doctors often prescribe it for the elderly, convalescents and in the treatment of anaemia and stress.

The name of the type of ginseng used in various products is usually stated on the label, but the 'Rolls Royce' of ginsengs is Panax schinseng.

Analysing the chemistry

Ginseng has been the subject of many clinical and laboratory investigations, the purpose being to establish whether or not it is a safe over-the-counter product. However, there isn't much evidence on the chemical effects and the results of experiments are hard to interpret because of the different types and doses of ginseng used.

The ginseng root is made up of a large number of chemicals, which include a group called saponins or ginsenosides, as well as a volatile oil, a fatty acid, vitamins B1 and B2 and phosphates. The chemical effect of ginseng is generally thought to be a result of the action of the ginsenosides, but as the levels vary depending on the type of ginseng, the age of the root and where and how it was grown, the effects are hard to predict.

One study showed improved carbohydrate

A ROOT OF TROUBLE?

There have been a few disturbing reports of unwanted side effects from ginseng. One elderly woman developed swollen, lumpy breasts after taking ginseng powder for three weeks, although she did have an all-round feeling of well-being. The symptoms disappeared when she stopped taking the herb. Another elderly woman experienced vaginal bleeding after taking ginseng tablets.

Both these side effects were thought to be the result of hormonal imbalance which had been caused by substances in the plant which have a similar structure to female hormones.

There are other reports of what is called Ginseng Abuse Syndrome. In order to intensify the sense of well-being and stimulation, many people were taking up to 15g per day. However, doses as low as 3g have produced side effects which include insomnia, nervousness, depression, skin eruptions and diarrhoea.

One of the problems is that ginseng preparations are classified as a food. As such there is no legal requirement for labels to warn people whether they should avoid the product. Dosage instructions also tend to be vague. Some labels suggest an intake of 600mg daily as being the ideal dose but others suggest taking 'more if required'.

Some doctors and herbalists advise people not to take ginseng if they are suffering from anxiety disorders, asthma, high blood pressure, menstrual irregularities or heart disease. Another drawback for ginseng-takers is that they should avoid coffee and alcohol.

---

tolerance in diabetics treated with ginseng. Several reports on the reaction of elderly people given ginseng demonstrate positive improvement of complaints such as headaches, loss of mental and physical capacity and cardiovascular conditions.

An earthy explanation

The nutritional benefits of ginseng are often promoted on the grounds that the plant extracts from the soil so many minerals and essential trace elements that nothing can be grown in the used soil for 10 years; and the plant, therefore, must be richer in these nutrients than any other plant. However, there is no real scientific evidence to back this claim. Some scientists have referred to ginseng as an

'adaptogen' — a substance that increases resistance to stress and disease but one that doesn't produce harmful side effects. Adaptogens are said to help stimulate metabolic processes in the body to create a state of homeostasis (physiological balance).

Is it safe?

Most laboratory studies indicate that ginseng is safe; and the US Food and Drug Administration classify it as a GRAS (Generally Recognised as Safe) ingredient for herbal teas.

The evidence does seem to show that ginseng acts as a general tonic and a mild stimulant, so you may find it useful as a short term remedy for improving stamina and concentration or for overcoming stress and fatigue. This may also explain the plant's reputation as an aphrodisiac — it boosts your energy so that you will probably feel like making love more often.

Ginseng is available in a variety of forms. From left to right: extract of ginseng, ginseng root, ginseng tea, ginseng capsules, ginseng elixir and tablets.

Whole Goodness

YOUR HEALTH

Grains, or cereals (from Ceres, the Roman goddess of agriculture), are the seeds of cultivated grasses. They contain the plant's embryo and with it a package of concentrated nutrients to support the new plant's growth. Because these nutrients can be stored for long periods, grains form the staple diet for most of the world's population.

Grains brought about a radical change in our evolution. Ten thousand years ago, man was a nomadic hunter-gatherer, continually in search of new food supplies. The discovery of grains and their subsequent cultivation gave rise to a more settled way of life as primitive tribes were now able to store food for long periods.

In descending order of world production, grains consist of wheat, rice, corn (maize), millet, sorghum, barley, oats and rye. There are also less well-known but highly nutritious grains such as amaranth and quinoa. Buckwheat is not a true grain, but as it is used in the same way it is usually classified as one.

A typical cereal grain (shown on the right) consists of four main parts:

1 The germ, which is the actual seed or embryo from which new growth starts.
2 The endosperm, a white starchy part which forms the bulk of the grain. Most of the carbohydrate and protein is stored here ready to provide the new plant with food when it starts to grow.
3 Bran, the protective outer layer.
4 The aleurone layer, a thin protective outer layer between the endosperm and the bran, which is a concentrated store of nutrients.

Barley, oats and rice are covered with an indigestible hull or husk, which has to be removed before these grains can be used as food. Wheat, rye and maize do not have a husk and are known as naked or free-threshing grains.

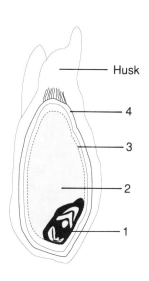

Husk

4

3

2

1

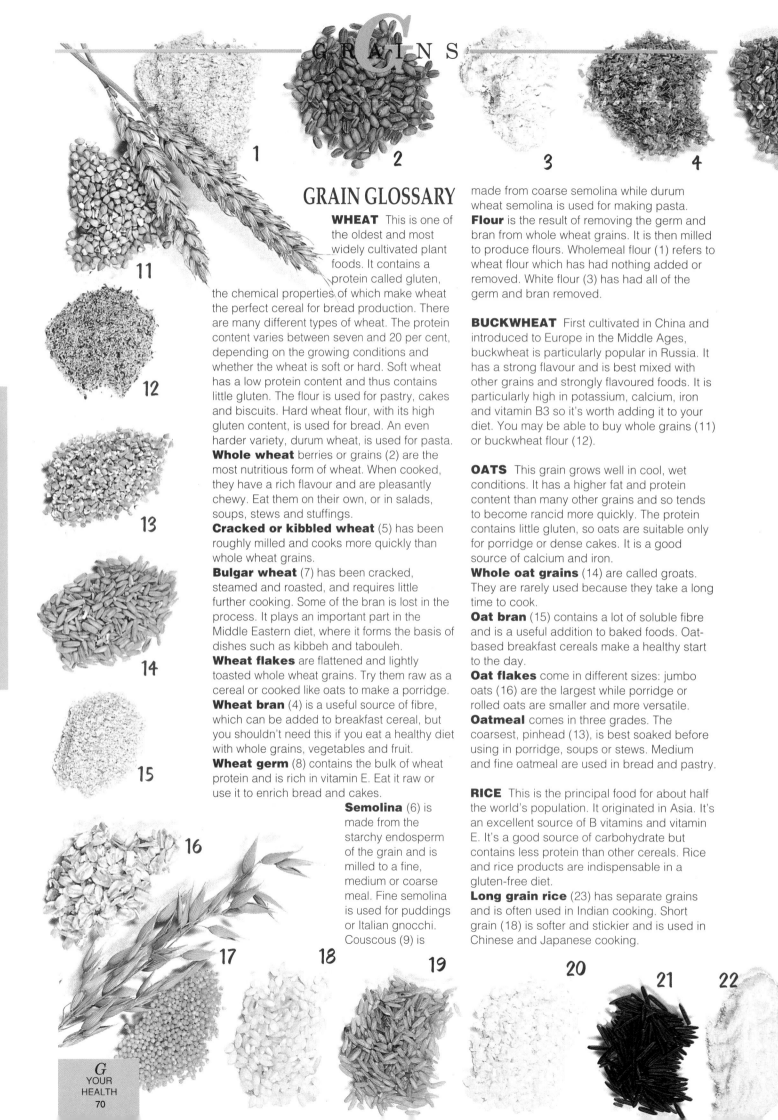

1

2

3

4

11

12

13

14

15

16

17

18

19

20

21

22

GRAIN GLOSSARY

WHEAT This is one of the oldest and most widely cultivated plant foods. It contains a protein called gluten, the chemical properties of which make wheat the perfect cereal for bread production. There are many different types of wheat. The protein content varies between seven and 20 per cent, depending on the growing conditions and whether the wheat is soft or hard. Soft wheat has a low protein content and thus contains little gluten. The flour is used for pastry, cakes and biscuits. Hard wheat flour, with its high gluten content, is used for bread. An even harder variety, durum wheat, is used for pasta.

Whole wheat berries or grains (2) are the most nutritious form of wheat. When cooked, they have a rich flavour and are pleasantly chewy. Eat them on their own, or in salads, soups, stews and stuffings.

Cracked or kibbled wheat (5) has been roughly milled and cooks more quickly than whole wheat grains.

Bulgar wheat (7) has been cracked, steamed and roasted, and requires little further cooking. Some of the bran is lost in the process. It plays an important part in the Middle Eastern diet, where it forms the basis of dishes such as kibbeh and tabouleh.

Wheat flakes are flattened and lightly toasted whole wheat grains. Try them raw as a cereal or cooked like oats to make a porridge.

Wheat bran (4) is a useful source of fibre, which can be added to breakfast cereal, but you shouldn't need this if you eat a healthy diet with whole grains, vegetables and fruit.

Wheat germ (8) contains the bulk of wheat protein and is rich in vitamin E. Eat it raw or use it to enrich bread and cakes.

Semolina (6) is made from the starchy endosperm of the grain and is milled to a fine, medium or coarse meal. Fine semolina is used for puddings or Italian gnocchi. Couscous (9) is made from coarse semolina while durum wheat semolina is used for making pasta.

Flour is the result of removing the germ and bran from whole wheat grains. It is then milled to produce flours. Wholemeal flour (1) refers to wheat flour which has had nothing added or removed. White flour (3) has had all of the germ and bran removed.

BUCKWHEAT First cultivated in China and introduced to Europe in the Middle Ages, buckwheat is particularly popular in Russia. It has a strong flavour and is best mixed with other grains and strongly flavoured foods. It is particularly high in potassium, calcium, iron and vitamin B3 so it's worth adding it to your diet. You may be able to buy whole grains (11) or buckwheat flour (12).

OATS This grain grows well in cool, wet conditions. It has a higher fat and protein content than many other grains and so tends to become rancid more quickly. The protein contains little gluten, so oats are suitable only for porridge or dense cakes. It is a good source of calcium and iron.

Whole oat grains (14) are called groats. They are rarely used because they take a long time to cook.

Oat bran (15) contains a lot of soluble fibre and is a useful addition to baked foods. Oat-based breakfast cereals make a healthy start to the day.

Oat flakes come in different sizes: jumbo oats (16) are the largest while porridge or rolled oats are smaller and more versatile.

Oatmeal comes in three grades. The coarsest, pinhead (13), is best soaked before using in porridge, soups or stews. Medium and fine oatmeal are used in bread and pastry.

RICE This is the principal food for about half the world's population. It originated in Asia. It's an excellent source of B vitamins and vitamin E. It's a good source of carbohydrate but contains less protein than other cereals. Rice and rice products are indispensable in a gluten-free diet.

Long grain rice (23) has separate grains and is often used in Indian cooking. Short grain (18) is softer and stickier and is used in Chinese and Japanese cooking.

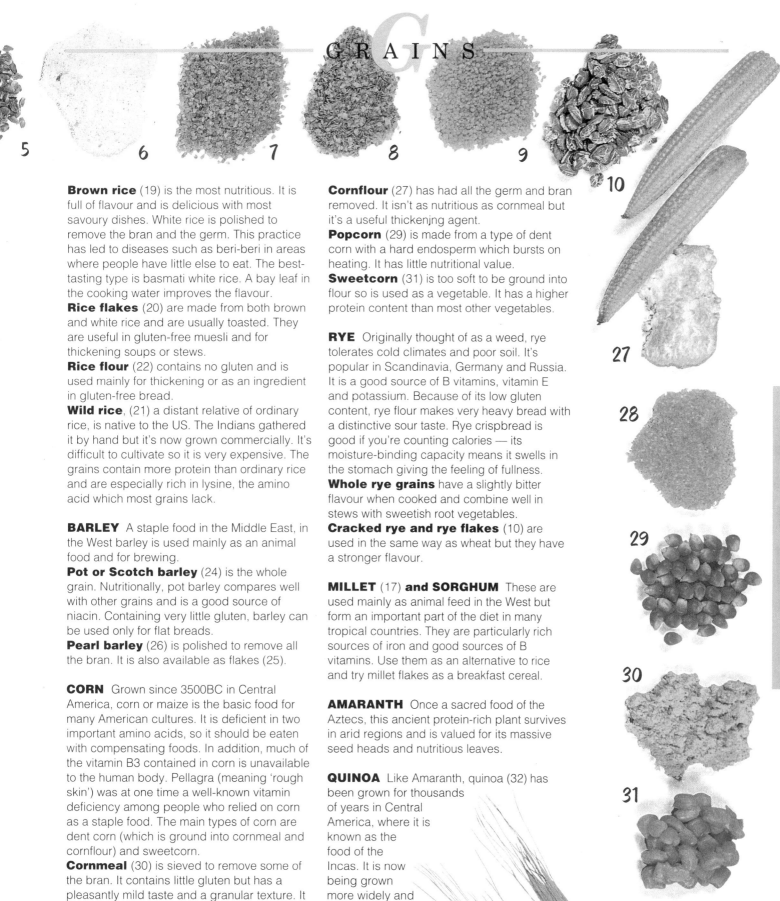

5   6   7   8   9   10

27

28

29

30

31

32

YOUR HEALTH

Brown rice (19) is the most nutritious. It is full of flavour and is delicious with most savoury dishes. White rice is polished to remove the bran and the germ. This practice has led to diseases such as beri-beri in areas where people have little else to eat. The best-tasting type is basmati white rice. A bay leaf in the cooking water improves the flavour.

Rice flakes (20) are made from both brown and white rice and are usually toasted. They are useful in gluten-free muesli and for thickening soups or stews.

Rice flour (22) contains no gluten and is used mainly for thickening or as an ingredient in gluten-free bread.

Wild rice, (21) a distant relative of ordinary rice, is native to the US. The Indians gathered it by hand but it's now grown commercially. It's difficult to cultivate so it is very expensive. The grains contain more protein than ordinary rice and are especially rich in lysine, the amino acid which most grains lack.

BARLEY A staple food in the Middle East, in the West barley is used mainly as an animal food and for brewing.

Pot or Scotch barley (24) is the whole grain. Nutritionally, pot barley compares well with other grains and is a good source of niacin. Containing very little gluten, barley can be used only for flat breads.

Pearl barley (26) is polished to remove all the bran. It is also available as flakes (25).

CORN Grown since 3500BC in Central America, corn or maize is the basic food for many American cultures. It is deficient in two important amino acids, so it should be eaten with compensating foods. In addition, much of the vitamin B3 contained in corn is unavailable to the human body. Pellagra (meaning 'rough skin') was at one time a well-known vitamin deficiency among people who relied on corn as a staple food. The main types of corn are dent corn (which is ground into cornmeal and cornflour) and sweetcorn.

Cornmeal (30) is sieved to remove some of the bran. It contains little gluten but has a pleasantly mild taste and a granular texture. It can be used in cakes or puddings, boiled and served with a sauce, or fried in strips. Polenta (28) is similar to cornmeal and is used in Italy.

Cornflour (27) has had all the germ and bran removed. It isn't as nutritious as cornmeal but it's a useful thickening agent.

Popcorn (29) is made from a type of dent corn with a hard endosperm which bursts on heating. It has little nutritional value.

Sweetcorn (31) is too soft to be ground into flour so is used as a vegetable. It has a higher protein content than most other vegetables.

RYE Originally thought of as a weed, rye tolerates cold climates and poor soil. It's popular in Scandinavia, Germany and Russia. It is a good source of B vitamins, vitamin E and potassium. Because of its low gluten content, rye flour makes very heavy bread with a distinctive sour taste. Rye crispbread is good if you're counting calories — its moisture-binding capacity means it swells in the stomach giving the feeling of fullness.

Whole rye grains have a slightly bitter flavour when cooked and combine well in stews with sweetish root vegetables.

Cracked rye and rye flakes (10) are used in the same way as wheat but they have a stronger flavour.

MILLET (17) **and SORGHUM** These are used mainly as animal feed in the West but form an important part of the diet in many tropical countries. They are particularly rich sources of iron and good sources of B vitamins. Use them as an alternative to rice and try millet flakes as a breakfast cereal.

AMARANTH Once a sacred food of the Aztecs, this ancient protein-rich plant survives in arid regions and is valued for its massive seed heads and nutritious leaves.

QUINOA Like Amaranth, quinoa (32) has been grown for thousands of years in Central America, where it is known as the food of the Incas. It is now being grown more widely and is available in health food shops. Use it like rice.

23   24   25   26

The benefits of grains

Grains are a rich source of carbo-hydrate, which our bodies need for energy. Grains also contain important amounts of protein, fibre, B-group vitamins, vitamin E and essential minerals. But the presence of phytic acid in some grains may interfere with the absorption of these minerals.

Although grains are an important source of protein, they have one drawback. Unlike protein from animal sources, the protein in grains (and other seeds such as pulses) is 'incomplete' — it is deficient in one or more of the essential amino acids which make up 'complete' protein. However, we can balance our plant protein intake by combining in the diet different types of seeds. For instance, by eating a grain with a pulse the amino acids deficient in the grain are provided by those present in the pulse. The Mexican diet of corn and beans, Indian dishes based on rice and dhal (split peas) or even baked beans on toast are all examples of this.

Grains which are used whole have the greatest nutritional value, because they retain all the nutrients from the bran and the germ.

Wheat flour

For most of us, the majority of the grain we eat is in foods made from flour. Cakes, biscuits, bread, pastry — most are made from milled wheat grains. Wholemeal flour still has much of the bran and germ (and nutrients) left in it, while white flour has had all the bran and germ removed. Some manufacturers used to bleach white flour to make it look 'cleaner' but now most millers leave it unbleached.

By law, manufacturers must enrich white flours with vitamin B1 (thiamin), B3 (niacin) and iron. They must also add calcium to all flours except wholemeal and certain self-raising flours.

Self-raising flour is white flour with raising agents (monocalcium phosphate, sodium bicarbonate) added. Strong flour is white flour milled from hard wheat, which is better for baking bread.

Storage

Whole grains contain the germ and so have a higher proportion of oil than refined grains. The oil can become rancid if the grains are incorrectly stored. Kept in a sealed container away from heat, light and moisture, they should stay fresh for a year or two. However, grains that have been

GLUTEN INTOLERANCE

Although wheat is our basic staple food, some people are sensitive to gluten and suffer from a condition known as coeliac disease. It causes damage to the intestinal villi.

People who suffer from coeliac disease are unable to digest certain foods properly, particularly fat. This results in frequent and copious bowel movements and, in children, failure to grow and thrive. The condition can also lead to anaemia, rickets and osteomalacia. Some babies are born with this sensitivity although they usually lose it after a few months or years. For this reason many baby foods are free of gluten-containing items.

The condition improves if a gluten-free diet is followed. This means avoiding the obvious sources of gluten such as breakfast cereals, bread and pasta but also homemade and manufactured food items to which flour is often added. These include sauces, pie fillings, cakes, stock cubes, cheap chocolate, mustard and salad dressings. Fortunately, gluten-free products are now labelled and the number of such products is increasing.

processed begin to lose their nutrients and flavour much sooner. Use them within three to six months.

Using grains in cooking

Food made with grains doesn't have to be heavy and boring. Grains provide plenty of different tastes and textures and there is a huge variety of ways to serve them. Widen your range by using the less well-known grains and flours.

Grains are simple to prepare. Just rinse in several changes of water to get rid of surface starch and impurities, then put in boiling water and simmer until tender and chewy but not mushy. They'll be tastier if the cooking water has flavour — add some herbs or use meat or vegetable stocks. Serve them as a vegetable, in place of potatoes, with casseroles, or allow them to cool and add freshly chopped tomatoes, peppers and cucumber to make a satisfying and unusual salad dish.

Store grains in airtight jars in a cool, dark place, where they will be ready to use.

Striking A Balance

Over 100 years ago, an American doctor developed a dietary theory which, he claimed, would ensure health and happiness. How true were his claims, and how relevant is his diet to today's life styles?

Born in 1866 in Pennsylvania, USA, Doctor William Hay was one of the first doctors to recognise the link between nutrition and health.

During a period of serious ill-health, Dr Hay became deeply dissatisfied with contemporary medicine and the orthodox treatment he was offered. He went for help to a group called the Natural Hygiene Practitioners. They didn't prescribe drugs but recommended instead a change of diet to one high in whole grains, fruits and vegetables — much in line with current nutritional thinking. They also taught the theory of 'food combining' in which animal protein foods (meat, fish, cheese) and starchy carbohydrate foods (bread, rice, pasta, potatoes) are not mixed in the same meal, and acid fruits are not eaten at the same time as carbohydrates.

Within three months of changing his diet, Dr Hay felt healthier and fitter than ever before.

Chemical balance

Dr Hay's treatment was based on the belief that most diseases are a result of a disruption to the acid-alkaline balance in the body. This is brought about by an overload of the acid residue from digestion and metabolism, which the body is unable to eliminate adequately. The causes of the imbalance are thought to be eating too many 'acid-promoting' foods such as meat and refined carbohydrates (white flour products and sugar), constipation and a lack of understanding of the way our bodies digest food.

The Hay theory is that protein foods need an acid medium for digestion and carbohydrates need an alkaline medium. When food enters the stomach, gastric juices are secreted. They contain very concentrated hydrochloric acid and an enzyme called pepsin. This enzyme starts the process of protein digestion. Dr Hay believed that starches and sugars are alkaline-forming. So if they are present in the stomach with protein foods they neutralise the acid medium and protein is incompletely digested.

In the case of carbohydrate digestion, the food is broken down as you chew by the enzyme ptyalin in your saliva. The process carries on in the stomach. If no other foods are present, starchy foods can pass through to the more alkaline medium of the small intestine where the digestive process continues. However, Dr Hay thought the presence of meat or acid fruits slowed down the passage of starchy foods, causing fermentation and incomplete digestion.

The Hay theory, therefore, is that foods containing a high proportion of carbohydrate are incompatible with acid fruits (apples, pears, citrus fruits) and with foods containing a lot of protein. They should not be eaten at the same meal.

Other considerations

In addition, the Hay system recommends that:
● We should wait at least four hours before eating a meal from another group of foods.

WHAT CAN YOU EAT?

The Hay system promotes the idea that for optimum health our diet should consist of 80% alkali-forming foods and 20% acid-forming foods.

Start the day with a fruit meal to promote alkalinity. Eat most fruits on their own or as part of a protein meal; but you can eat 'sweet' fruit with a starch meal. Some foods are 'neutral' and can be eaten with either protein or starch meals.

Foods for a protein meal	Neutral foods	Foods for a starch meal
Proteins Meat, poultry, game, fish, shell-fish, eggs, cheese, milk, yogurt	*Nuts* All except peanuts	*Cereals* Whole grains, bread (100% wholewheat), flour (100% or 85% wholewheat)
Fruits Apples, apricots, blackberries, black currants, blueberries, cherries, gooseberries (ripe), grapefruit, grapes, guavas, kiwis, lemons, limes, lychees, mangoes, melons (best eaten alone), nectarines, oranges, passion fruit, pears, pineapples, raspberries, redcurrants, strawberries, tangerines (cranberries, plums and rhubarb are not recommended as they are too acid)	*Fats* (use in moderation) Butter, cream, egg yolk, olive oil, sunflower seed oil, sesame seed oil (all cold pressed) *Vegetables* All except Jerusalem artichokes, potatoes, pumpkin and sweet potatoes	*Sweet fruits* Bananas (ripe), dried fruit, grapes (very sweet), papaya (very ripe), pears (very ripe) *Vegetables* Jerusalem artichokes, potatoes, pumpkin, sweet potatoes
Salad dressings Oil, lemon juice, cider vinegar, mayonnaise (home-made)	*Salads* All leaves, herbs, seeds and sprouted seeds, avocado, chicory, cucumber, fennel, garlic, peppers, radishes, spring onions, tomatoes (raw)	*Dairy products* Milk and yogurt (in moderation) *Salad dressings* Soured cream, olive oil or cold pressed seed oils, tomato juice with oil and seasoning
Pulses and soya products (vegetarians to use sparingly) Butter beans, chick peas, kidney beans, lentils, dried peas, soya beans, tofu	*Miscellaneous* Wheat or oat bran, wheat or oat germ, raisins, raisin juice, honey, maple syrup, grated orange and lemon rind (organically grown)	*Sugars* Barbados sugar, honey (use sparingly)
Alcohol Dry red and white wine, dry cider	*Alcohol* Whisky, gin	*Alcohol* Beer

FOODS TO AVOID

All refined carbohydrates (white sugar, white flour, white rice and foods made with them), fizzy soft drinks, fruit-flavoured squashes, muesli and high-fibre cereals with added sugar, foods containing additives, tinned foods, battery eggs and chickens, rhubarb and plums, instant coffee, fried foods, artificial sweeteners

● Vegetables, salads and fruit should form the major part of the diet.
● Protein, starches and fats should be eaten in small quantities.
● Only whole grains and unprocessed flours should be used — white flour and sugars should be excluded.
● Highly processed fats such as margarine should not be eaten.

Does it work?
Alkali-forming foods are fresh fruits, all vegetables, salads, almonds and milk. Acid-forming foods are meat, poultry, fish, shell-fish, eggs, cheese, nuts (except almonds), grains, cereal products and sugars.

The classification of acid-tasting fruit (eg berries, citrus fruit) as alkali-forming is sometimes confusing. But the classification refers to the residue from digestion and not to the alkalinity or acidity of the foods themselves or of the medium needed for digestion to occur.

Many doctors and nutritionists insist that the theory is nonsense, and that digestive problems cannot arise from eating protein and carbohydrate at the same time or from mixing acid fruits and carbohydrate.

Whether the theory is right or wrong, thousands of people claim to have benefited from following it. They feel more clear-headed and energetic, they lose weight without noticing, the temptation to snack between meals disappears and digestive problems become a thing of the past. The system is also said to improve conditions such as arthritis, asthma and hay fever.

The Healing Touch

Throughout history, the 'laying on of hands' has been claimed to heal the sick. Today, with a growing distrust in the side effects of drugs and the dangers of surgery, such age-old methods of healing are seeing a surge of popularity. But are we being deluded – is healing at best 'all in the mind' and at worst a dangerous con?

Healers claim that healing works, that it isn't just a matter of faith after all. In support of their belief they quote several experiments carried out in the USA that suggest people can be healed even if they had no knowledge that it was happening.

In one Californian test case in 1990, only the healer and the chief experimenter knew the real nature of their work — all the others involved believed they were taking part in an experiment to test a new time-lapse camera. Forty four volunteers had a deep incision made in their arms, and for 16 days they spent five minutes each with their arms shoved through a curtain into another room. They could see and hear nothing — as far as they knew only the experimental camera was in that next-door room. But completely unknown to the volunteers, a healer in the next room was silently concentrating on half of them, while ignoring the remaining 22. At the end of the 16-day period, the arm wound of every one of the 'healees' — the healers' word for their patients — showed a measurable improvement. A high percentage were completely healed but those who had not received the healing were much slower at recovering.

GOING TO A HEALER

Should you go to a healer? That depends on whether you believe their claims to be able to do more than orthodox medicine.

You probably should not consider going to a healer unless you have found the treatment your doctor prescribes to be a failure. If you do eventually decide to see what a healer can offer, make sure you have found out something about them before you go; get a first hand recommendation from somebody who has been treated by them so that you know the healer is both reputable and honest.

Here is a short checklist of what to expect when you go to a healer.

● A good healer will promise you nothing, but everything about them will be calm and positive.
● Expect to pay something. Some healers work free of charge, but some work full-time and need to pay the mortgage like anyone else! Often there is a sliding scale for people with different abilities to pay.
● Healing should take place in an atmosphere so calm it is almost meditative. Your breathing should synchronise with the healer's quite naturally.
● There's no right or wrong way to feel during a healing session. Many people report localised sensations of extreme heat where the healer touches them, whereas some feel cool spots or tingling.
● Instant miracles are rare. Most people experience a distinct improvement in their condition after one session, plus an enormous sense of release and relaxation. Some patients discover an improvement a few hours after the session – or a day or two.
● Give your healer a proper chance. If he or she suggests you need a course of treatment, then go back for it.
● A good healer will *never* suggest that you stop your medical treatment. Always carry on with whatever your doctor has ordered even if you are receiving healing, with the obvious exception of those people who get completely better and have no further need of pills or surgery.
● Often a change of life style will be suggested. A large part of the healing process is the realisation that your health is your own responsibility.

Healing has always been seen as either a miracle or a confidence trick played on the gullible. But some healers defy such scepticism – Cambridgeshire-based healer Matthew Manning (above) has established a worldwide reputation for what many regard as miracle cures. He claims that his patients do not need faith to be healed. Other famous centres of healing, such as Lourdes in France, (left) have always attracted the sick from the world's Christian community, who believe that miracles occur due to their faith.

Using cosmic energy

So what is this mysterious power that healers claim to exploit? Do you have to be a saint to be a healer, or can anyone learn the technique?

Most people know about the miracles of the Bible — Jesus healed the sick and even raised the dead, and he passed on this power to the disciples. Today, the 'living Hindu saint', Sai Baba, is reputed to have similar gifts. But healers believe that there are literally thousands of ordinary men and women who are born with the gift of healing — or who learn how to discover it for themselves.

Opinions vary slightly about the nature of the healing power, but healers generally agrree that there is a great flow of universal or cosmic energy that can be tapped into for healing

Some people believe that we're surrounded by an invisible, multicoloured forcefield known as the aura. Psychics claim they can see it, and use its variations in colour and intensity to determine the state of our health.

purposes. It isn't the healer who makes the sick well, but this force — which some call God — and the healees themselves.

Cambridgeshire healer, Matthew Manning, says: "I give people permission to heal themselves," and although it may sound arrogant, this is a view shared by almost all top healers in the world. The idea behind it is that every individual has the capacity to cure themselves of almost any affliction, but that negative feelings, such as guilt or low self-esteem, prevent this natural healing process from happening. The healer opens them up to the cosmic energy, and, in doing so, triggers their own inner powers.

Healers believe that almost anyone can learn to heal, although, as with anything else in life, some people show more of a talent for it than others. Techniques that open up the potential healer vary, but essentially they concentrate on quelling the busy thinking part of the brain — the left half — and letting the intuitive right brain begin to operate on all cylinders. Meditation and visualisation help to achieve the inner calmness necessary for this to happen.

Healing the whole person

Healing operates holistically — that is, on all levels of being at once. Healers see the physical body as only one part of the individual; the mind, the emotions, and the spirit must also be considered. True and lasting healing works positively on all these levels, because one affects the other. Orthodox medicine, healers say, fails us in trying to cure only the physical level, and then often only the symptoms, rarely the cause. If, however, you discover the cause of an illness, you can cure it and prevent it emerging elsewhere in the body in another form.

Healers often find that their patients are in great distress emotionally, and they believe that it is this inner turmoil that causes the illness, not the other way round. The laying on of hands can be a very effective way of putting a person in touch with those half-buried emotional traumas and letting them out.

Although some healers do not actually touch a patient's body, claiming instead to be working with their 'aura', or the invisible electrical forcefield of colour that is said to surround us all, most of them do touch. This in itself is claimed to be effective in reducing

THE THOUGHT THAT COUNTS?

How can just thinking of someone make them better? it seems odd, yet there is some evidence to suggest that 'absent healing' may actually work.

In the 1970s, Joyce Goodrich, a New York psychologist, ran an experiment to test whether healees could tell when distant healers were working on them. She told them to expect absent healing on certain days – but little did they know that the healing was only 'sent' to them on an irregular basis. Yet independent judges recorded that almost all of the healees reported knowing that they were being healed at exactly the moment it was really happening.

In other American experiments, similar groups of healees proved that they knew when they were being prayed for, or even simply being thought about intensely by distant healers. As one healer, Dr Daniel Benor, put it, "Absence can make the heart grow stronger..."

HEALING HANDS

A healing session with 44-year-old Geoff Boltwood often ends up like a cross between laying on of hands and an aromatherapy session – for fragrant gooey oil has been seen to ooze from his fingertips as he lays his hands on the sick.

No one knows how or why it happens, but what matters is that it seems to help the sick get well. Geoff shrugs: "It's a gift from out there, something that happens when people need it." Initial analysis of this mysterious oil shows that it contains fatty globules of lipids and is of organic origin. These days Geoff bottles it for use in the aromatherapy work of a colleague – an unusual collaboration in the world of healing!

One four-year-old had this substance rubbed on her forehead. She'd been taken to see Geoff by her mother because her appetite had gone and she was troubled by constant coughs and colds. Immediately after her first session, she said she was hungry. In all, she visited him three times and was completely cured after the last visit.

Geoff has no particular religious beliefs, but is eager to encourage us to reassess our ideas of reality. He says: "When you are diagnosed as ill, all you can see is illness, not the possibility of recovery. All reality is malleable. The oil, the crackling noise that some people hear when I touch them... are just ways of demonstrating that reality can be changed. It's a question of perception and expectation. After all, we expect cuts to heal themselves, broken bones to knit, colds to clear up. You have the power to change your illness if you really believe you can. It must come from inside you – then it becomes real in the outside world of your body."

stress and encouraging a healthier immune system.

The healing touch

Dolores Krieger, an American teacher of nursing, was a pioneer in 'touch therapy', having discovered in the 1970s that patients who were touched recovered more quickly than those who were just given their medication and left alone. Follow-up experiments have shown that even among bereaved people — whose immune systems are measurably depleted during the grieving process — touch therapy actually increases the healthy cell count in their blood. Again, it's not all in the mind — but in the mind *and* the body!

Despite widespread scepticism, and some active opposition from the medical profession, thousands of people from all walks of life have turned to healers. Student healers flock to learn how to tap into the cosmic energy and put it to good use. As London healer, Lynn Picknett says: "In the end, it's all about love. I tell people who come to my group that we can't promise miracles, but we can promise love. And often the two things are the same."

Today, healers can feel a cautious optimism about their future. Although some doctors remain sceptical, many more are beginning to welcome healers into clinics and even hospitals as a complementary service alongside orthodox treatment. Some doctors, and some members of the nursing profession, are themselves learning a variety of healing techniques.

" It [healing] is spiritual in the sense that it reaches down to the spiritual roots of the personality. The aim of spiritual healing is that there should be total healing."

Canon Christopher Pilkington

"Miracles do not happen in contradiction to Nature, but only in contradiction to that which is known to us in Nature."

TAKE A BREAK

Most health farms offer very comfortable - even luxurious - accommodation, in beautiful surroundings. You will be invited to relax, probably to follow a fairly strict dietary regime, to exercise a little and to enjoy a number of highly enjoyable treatments ranging from facials and saunas to massage and reflexology.

Individual health farms actually vary enormously. Some establishments regard the health benefits as paramount and expect their guests (whom they'll actually call patients) to have the same attitude. Others place the accent on beauty rather than health and offer nothing more rigorous than gentle pampering. The health farm you choose will depend largely on what you hope to gain from it.

How long?

A stay at a health farm can last as long as your money does, but many spas have a minimum stay of at least four or even seven days. This is particularly true of the more serious places, who believe that you need to stay that long before you can begin to benefit from the rest and the healthy diet that you'll have enjoyed.

In fact, you can almost judge how serious a place is by the length of time it suggests you stay there. The more frivolous, short-stay places — which sometimes offer bargain breaks, or relaxing weekend breaks — tend to concentrate heavily on the beauty side rather than on health.

Health farms are certainly not cheap and it's important to choose one that will meet your particular needs. The choice is yours, after all, and you should spend time researching the best one for you.

The different approaches

Health farms vary considerably both in their attitude towards health and in the kind of treatments they offer. Many health farms adhere to one particular form of alternative medicine. This may be naturopathy, for example, which relies on natural methods, such as meditation, hot baths, massage and organically grown health foods, to promote fitness and well-being. Or it may be osteopathy or chiropractic, where the basic treatment is the manipulation of the spine in order to remove pressure from the nerves.

But they also vary a lot in the attitude with which they approach their chosen discipline. Some spas take it very seriously indeed, and run their timetables along much the same lines as a nursing home. But, even so, the atmosphere is more informal and the surroundings generally more luxurious. And, when all's said and done, you have the final choice to take it or leave it, and, in that knowledge, the routine — however assiduously it's run — becomes a welcome, voluntarily chosen discipline, not an irksome and unpleasant one.

At the best clinics, the aim is not to treat one particular aspect of a person but rather to follow a holistic approach — which means to treat the whole person and all aspects of that person's general health, which includes emotional and psychological factors as well as physical ones.

On arrival

At any health farm, you will probably be asked what you would like to do during your stay and what you hope to gain from it. If weight loss and improvement in body shape are your priorities, you will certainly be weighed and measured.

At some of the more serious clinics, you will have a fairly detailed consultation with one of the medical staff, during which you will be asked about your reasons for coming to the clinic, your past medical history, and any current medical complaints, and your weight and blood pressure will be measured. The consultation is modelled on an orthodox medical interview, though a full medical is rare.

If your clinic specialises in any particular therapy, such as osteopathy or chiropractic, you will also have a full osteopathic or chiropractic examination to determine the health of your spine, muscles and joints, and any abnormalities will be noted.

Once your consultant is in full possession of all the facts, he or she

Health farms offer many rejuvenative facilities. You can treat yourself to a facial (top), a relaxing swim (centre, the pool at Chewton Glen) or use the time to slim (above, a patient is weighed).

A TYPICAL DIET FOR THE FIRST THREE DAYS

No diet is compulsory and you can eat other things, as long as they are available at the health farm. Some people, after all, need to gain not lose weight, and their needs are taken into consideration. Refined or processed foods are off the menu.

DAY 1

Breakfast
Hot water and lemon
Lightly stewed fruit
Yoghurt with Bran and Honey

Lunch
Home-made vegetable soup
Fresh fruit
Hot water and lemon

Dinner
Fresh fruit
Yoghurt, Wheatgerm, Honey
Hot water and
lemon

DAY 2

Breakfast
Hot water and lemon
Fresh fruit
Yoghurt, Bran, Honey

Lunch
Fresh salad
Lightly stewed fruit
Yoghurt, Wheatgerm, Honey
Hot water and lemon

Dinner
Home-made vegetable soup
Fresh fruit
Yoghurt, Wheatgerm, Honey
Hot water and lemon

DAY 3

Breakfast
Hot water and lemon
Lightly stewed fruit
Yoghurt, Bran, Honey

Lunch
Home-made vegetable soup
Baked potato & knob of butter
Fresh fruit
Hot water and lemon

Dinner
Grilled lean meat, chicken or fish
Lightly cooked fresh vegetables
Lightly stewed fruit
Yoghurt, Wheatgerm, Honey

and you will, together, work out a mutually acceptable programme, which you will then follow for the duration of your stay at the health farm.

Diet

Health farms generally offer a fairly strict diet. There may be different reasons for this: at a naturopathic clinic, it will be founded on a firm belief both in the need to rid the body of assimilated toxins and in the importance of sound nutrition; at a more frivolous health farm, it may simply be viewed as a first step to weight loss.

Is is not uncommon for a person at a health clinic to begin by spending two or three days fasting, or semi-fasting. On a fast, you are allowed only water and lemon juice; on a semi-fast, you are also allowed fruit.

Many people experience unpleasant side effects during a fast, such as headaches, feelings of weakness and dizziness, and slight nausea. These feelings do no lasting harm and usually disappear after 48 hours.

After fasting, you usually follow a gentle diet of fresh, simple foods, such as fruit, vegetables, honey, yoghurt, wheatgerm, and

small amounts of lean meat, chicken or fish. A lot of health farms grow their own organic vegetables.

Massage

Most health farms include massage as an essential part of their treatment programme. It is especially recommended for releasing tension — particularly valuable if you are prone to stress — stimulating the circulation and encouraging the elimination of toxins through the skin.

There are various methods of massage that may be on offer during your stay at a health farm. These include:

● A Jacuzzi is a strong, deep type of massage taken in a special bath, during which the body is bombarded with jets of water. Specially recommended for those with arthritis and rheumatism.
● A Neuromuscular massage is a deep fingertip massage, aimed at specific motor points of the muscles, to relieve muscular tension.
● Shiatsu is similar to neuromuscular massage, except that pressure is applied to points running along energy channels, or meridians, rather than to muscles. The aim of the Shiatsu massage is to restore the flow of energy along the meridians.
● Swedish massage consists of forceful, heavy stroking, slapping and beating movements over the large muscle masses of the legs and back. It works well to relieve tension and stimulate the circulation.

Heat treatments

Most health farms offer a range of heat treatments, including

One of the highlights of a health farm visit can be a relaxing Jacuzzi massage. The jets of water give a tingly sensation all over!

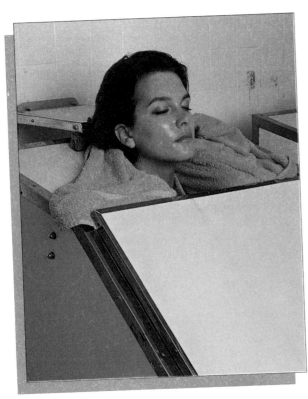

Purifying your body in a sweat box is one of the best ways of expelling harmful toxins from the system.

both generalised and localised treatments.

Generalised heat treatments include saunas, steam cabinets and hot body wraps. The idea is that they increase the temperature of the body, thereby improving the circulation and encouraging the elimination of toxins from the body. They also make the body sweat profusely, which is also believed to eliminate harmful toxins through the skin.

Other gentler generalised heat treatments include special baths, such as moor, oatmeal, peat and seaweed baths, which promote relaxation in a person who is tired and tense, but are not strong enough to withstand the much more intense heat of a sauna, a steam cabinet or a hot body wrap.

Localised heat treatments include poultices, which are used primarily for arthritis, sprains, strains and muscle injuries, and Sitz baths, which help tone up the muscles and organs in the abdominal and pelvic cavities and are therefore said to be very good for illnesses affecting the lower body.

Physiotherapy

The physiotherapy offered in some of the more modern clinics compares favourably with hospital physiotherapy departments. Treatment needs, obviously, to be tailored to the individual needs of the patient.

Treatments include:
● Exercise programmes, both to tone up healthy but out of condition patients, and to strengthen damaged muscles, weakened perhaps by injury or by arthritis.
● Localised heat therapy, perhaps by infra-red radiation or wax baths, to treat sore and damaged parts of the body.
● Ultraviolet therapy to treat deeper layers of injured

A TYPICAL DAY

The following is a typical day at a health farm.

7.00 am **Breakfast**
8.00 am **Check on progress**
  with a member of staff
8.15-11.30 am **Treatments:**
  ● Sauna
  ● Massage
  ● Slendertone
  ● Facial
11.30 am **Osteopathy**
12.15 pm **Lunch**
1.30 pm **Physiotherapy**
3.00 pm **Bracing walk**
4.00 pm **Tea**
4.30 pm **Relaxation exercises**
5.30 pm **Rest**
7.00 pm **Dinner**
8.00 pm **Lecture on yoga**

You will find that practically every moment of your day is occupied and that you are always doing – or about to do – something on your busy schedule. And any free time you do have you can always spend exploring the surrounding countryside or on some optional sporting activity.

Forget any worry that you might be bored – you certainly won't.

Many health farms offer a range of sporting activities for active visitors (left, an aerobics class at Springs Hydro Limited). Sport can be a useful way of releasing aggression (above, mixed doubles at Chewton Glen).

muscles and joints.
● Inhalation therapy for patients with chest complaints.
● Electrical stimulation to promote healing of inflamed muscles and joints, and — as in Slendertone — to tone up flaccid muscles.
● Ultrasound therapy to treat such obstinate sprains and strains as frozen shoulder and tennis elbow.

Relaxation
The peace and quiet you'll get at a health farm will usually go a long way to helping you rest and relax. In addition, most health farms hold optional afternoon classes, run by a member of staff or a visiting specialist, which you can attend to learn more about relaxation, yoga and meditation.

Is it worth it?
Health farms are certainly not cheap, but they are highly enjoyable and there are undoubted benefits.

The best way of summarising these is in relaxation and rest, both of which will do much to improve both your health and your looks. Someone who feels and appears rested looks a million times better than someone who looks tense. You'll also feel pampered, which gives the morale a terrific boost.

You can't even expect to lose a lot of weight, because although you probably eat a lot less than you would in a week at home, your level of activity is probably also much less than during a working week. The most valuable thing you can do is to view your stay as a holiday. Learn new habits in diet, exercise and relaxation, and you'll also be taking something valuable with you.

Useful Addresses

Tel: 008 044 944
This spa resort offers body wraps, a float tank, shiatsu and massage.

ENGLAND
Chewton Glen (left)
New Milton
Hampshire
BH25 6QS
Tel: 0425 275 341
A health club has been added to a stylish hotel, with the emphasis on holistic health care.

Grayshott Hall (below)
Headley Road
Grayshott
nr Hindhead

Surrey GU26 6JJ
Tel: 0428 606189
Enjoy a full range of health and beauty treatments in blissful surroundings.

Henlow Grange
Henlow
Bedfordshire
SG16 6DB
Tel: 0426 811111
An extensive range of health and beauty treatments and fitness facilities.

UNITED STATES
Arlington Resort Spa
Central Avenue
Hot Springs
Arkansas 71901
Tel: 501 623 7771
Try the mountainside thermal jacuzzi and swim in the mineral water pools.

AUSTRALIA
Camp Eden
Currumbin Creek Rd
Currumbin Valley
Queensland 4233
Tel: 075 33 0333
A holistic approach. Stress control, exercise, and massage.

Hopewood Health Centre
Greendale Road
Wallacia
New South Wales 2745
Tel 047 73 8401
The emphasis is on relaxation and healing. Health talks and naturopathy.

Solar Springs Health Retreat
96 Osborne Avenue
Bundanoon

Aveda Spa Osceola
1015 Cascade St
Rte 3, Box 72
Osceola
Wisconsin 54020
Tel: 715 294 4465
Flower remedies, yoga, massage and stress relieving exercises.

Greenbriar Spa
White Sulphur Springs
West Virginia 24986
Tel: 304 536 1110
Enjoy hydrotherapy baths and thalasso treatments at this elegant spa resort.

Herbs For Health

Cast into the shade for decades by modern wonderdrugs, the ancient practice of using herbs for healing is now making a gentle comeback.

Medical herbalism is a system of healing that uses selected plants from around the world to cure all kinds of sickness. Every major culture has used herbalism at some time as its main or only source of medicine. Indian, Ayurvedic, Chinese, and North American Indian medicines are all based on herbal healing. Although plants in different parts of the world may look completely unalike, their medicinal effects are often very similar. Thus, in places as far apart as Wales, Southern India and the North American plains, plants of different species but with similar healing properties are found. This may explain why herbalism is so widespread and so ancient: the Celts, the Greeks and the ancient Egyptians all had herbal systems of medicine. In fact as long ago as 3000 BC — five thousand years ago — Egypt had well-established schools for training herbalists. In Tudor England, herbal prescribing by the common folk was so widespread that Henry VIII's

HERBS AND HEALTH WARNINGS

There have been several scares recently over the use of herbal teas. Are they safe to drink?

Concern has been expressed by the medical establishment about the safety of some herbs, especially comfrey. Generally, herbal teas are very mild and quite safe, but it's always as well to remember that they can have a medicinal effect, and to respect their power. Drinking gallons of any particular herbal tea is as unbalanced as drinking gallons of coffee or Coke; as a general rule, change the type of medicinal herbal teas you drink once a month or so, and don't drink more than three cups of the same tea in any one day.

Herbal remedies have played an important part in Chinese medicine for thousands of years.

MODERN DRUGS DERIVED FROM PLANTS

Many modern drugs are derived from plants, and are made more powerful by isolating and concentrating the main active ingredients.

Aspirin, for example, comes from several different plants, including meadowsweet and black willow; steroids are synthesised from the wild yam; morphine comes from the opium poppy; and amphetamines and some anti-asthmatic drugs may be derived from the Chinese herb known as Ma Huang.

Herbal preparations do not have the side effects often experienced with the drugs made from the same plant, because many ingredients of a plant which science would consider inactive actually act to prevent the side effects of the main ingredient.

This was shown very clearly with the anti-asthmatic drug ephedrine, made from the plant *Ephedra sinica*. The plant has been used herbally in China for thousands of years with no ill effects, but when scientists extracted its medicinal alkaloid, ephedrine, and used it to treat asthmatics, it was found to raise blood pressure to dangerous levels. The drug was dropped from general use.

Herbalists know that *Ephedra sinica* contains another alkaloid, pseudo-ephedrine, which actually reduces the heart rate and lowers the blood pressure. So when the whole plant is used in herbal medicine it is quite safe and the patient's health improves overall.

Opium poppy

Knapweed

court doctors persuaded him to outlaw the practice by anyone but a chosen few. The outcry was so great that he had to change his mind and decree a law — the Herbalist's Charter — which allowed anyone to practise healing with herbs. This law still stands today. However, as modern medicine, based on drugs and surgery, became more powerful, herbalism was forced into the sidelines, sometimes by law. A famous 19th-century American herbalist, Samuel Thomson, who blended British herbal lore with that of the North American Indians, was forbidden to treat people for any ailment by the New Hampshire legislature.

Today herbalism is enjoying a revival as people increasingly look for a gentle, safe way of healing without any of the side effects which are often associated with modern drugs.

Conventional drugs often begin life as extracts of medicinal plants. Many medicinal plants contain substances which appear to have no function for the plant, but when extracted and given to humans, they affect us both physically and mentally. These 'plant by-products' include:

● Alkaloids, such as nicotine, caffeine, morphine, and amphetamines.
● Cardiac glycosides (found in golden rod, chickweed, and wild yam).
● Antibiotic, antifungal or sedative 'bitter principles' found in many bitter-tasting plants such as valerian and white horehound.

Plants used by herbalists, on the other hand, are left whole: it is the combination of different chemicals within the plant that gives each its particular healing properties.

How herbalists work

Herbalists use their deep knowledge of these plants to treat specific complaints and to rebalance, support and boost a patient's vital energy so that their body does the necessary healing. Whether their training is Eastern or Western most herbalists prefer this holistic approach. They believe that our bodies act together with our minds and emotions, always trying to produce good health for us, and that physical, mental and emotional symptoms must be respected as the body's attempt to heal itself.

Until the 18th century, this was how most physicians worked, seeing the body as a self-regulating balance of energies or 'humours'. Chinese herbalists still use the four elements of earth, air, fire and water to categorise their remedies and diagnose illness. Modern medicine, on the other hand, has tended to see our minds and bodies as separate, with the body acting like a machine. When something goes wrong with a part, it and its unwelcome symptoms are treated in isolation. So, where a doctor might lower fever artificially, or block nerve pathways with drugs to reduce pain, a herbalist would often encourage a fever, seeing it as the body's way of burning out bacteria or viruses, and would look to the underlying cause of pain and treat that, rather than simply blocking the pain. Herbalists believe the body always does its best to achieve health, and they try to work with it.

Strictly speaking, herbalists don't treat named diseases, they treat people as a whole, whatever their particular complaint may be. Even when a disease is 'incurable', like Parkinson's disease or multiple sclerosis, herbalism can still help to ease pain, relieve anxiety and improve the person's quality of life.

Common complaints

Some of the common complaints that herbalism claims to treat very successfully include:

- Colds, coughs, tonsillitis
- Children's ailments
- Indigestion, stomach ulcers, irritable bowel syndrome
- Varicose veins, angina, high and low blood pressure
- Headaches, migraine, insomnia
- Eczema, psoriasis, acne
- Pre-menstrual syndrome, period problems, menopausal problems, infertility, post-natal depression
- Cystitis, kidney infections, thrush
- Arthritis and rheumatism
- Allergies, asthma, hay fever.

Herbalists agree with doctors that surgery or drug treatment is necessary in certain cases — for example, in advanced cancer or in emergency accident cases. But in general, their view is that drugs and surgery don't act to boost the body's vitality or immunity, and should be rarely used. They consider that when overused, drugs become less effective and can even cause unnecessary stress to a sick person's body.

Herbalists usually practise from a Natural Health Centre, their own premises, or from home. In the consultation room, instead of a prescription pad you'll find shelves of herbal mixtures in dark glass bottles. Your first appointment will last about an hour, as the herbalist needs to find out as much as she can about you in order to find the successful remedies. She'll ask what the specific problem is, and then question you about diet, life style, your medical history,

DIFFERENT HERBAL PREPARATIONS

Herbal remedies may be given in several different ways, depending on which is most appropriate for the patient and the herb being used.

- Tinctures are made by mashing the whole plant and steeping it in alcohol for a month. The resulting mixture then has to be diluted before being taken.
- Decoctions are made by boiling the herb for several minutes, then straining the mixture, and drinking the liquid.
- Infusions are like teas: the herb is immersed in hot water for a few minutes, and the liquid drunk.
- Capsules are powdered herbs enclosed in a gelatine capsule like many ordinary drugs, so that they can be swallowed.
- Lozenges are a mixture of herbs and non-toxic filler material which allow you to suck the herb slowly.
- Ointments are made by mixing the herb with an oil-based carrier to spread easily on the skin.

YOUR HEALTH

and your family's health. Even the tone of your voice and your handshake — warm and moist or dry and firm — can help build up a complete picture of your health. As when visiting your doctor, it may be necessary to examine you or take your blood pressure, and the herbalist will need to know what medication you're taking, the results of any clinical test or the doctor's diagnosis of your condition. The consultation is, of course, in strict confidence.

Treatment and advice

Once the picture is clear, the herbalist can prescribe a remedy or a number of different remedies, carefully tailored to you as a whole person.

The herbs she selects will be designed not just to treat your specific complaint, but also to boost your immune system and enhance your vitality, so helping you to ward off some future illnesses. All herbalists follow

Hippocrates' advice: "Let foods be your medicine". So as well as prescribing herbal remedies for you, they will also advise you about which foods to eat and which to avoid to aid your recovery. For instance, people with a lot of catarrh or a sluggish bowel may be advised to avoid dairy foods for a while, as these may be exacerbating their problem.

Most herbalists prefer to work with your doctor, especially if you are already receiving ordinary medical treatment. Orthodox and herbal treatment often work well together.

A first consultation may cost from £20-£30, with follow-up visits costing less. There may be special rates for senior citizens, children and people on low incomes.

How long treatment takes really depends on how serious your illness is. A simple case of constipation may clear up in a couple of weeks, whereas long-standing osteoarthritis or acne will take much longer. You should allow two or

three weeks before you see a major improvement, and with long-standing illnesses a rough guide is to allow a month for every year that you've had the condition. Your herbalist will discuss with you how long the treatment might take, but even if the complete treatment takes months, you should begin to feel a sense of well-being in a few weeks.

Finding a practitioner

Most people find a herbalist by recommendation from a friend or colleague, or by visiting their local Natural Health Centre. The recognised body of herbalists is the National Institute of Medical Herbalists — members will have the intials MNIMH after their name. To get a list of qualified practitioners, send an sae to the National Institute of Medical Herbalists, 9 Palace Gate, Exeter, Devon EX1 1JA. Tel: 0392 426022.

HOME HERBAL REMEDIES

Many herbal remedies are simple enough to make in the kitchen. It's fine to treat simple ailments at home, but any condition which lingers or seems more serious should be taken to a qualified herbalist.

Colds At the first hint of a cold, make a decoction from:

- 30g sliced fresh ginger root
- 1-2 broken cinnamon sticks
- 2-5g coriander seeds
- 4 cloves
- 600 ml water

Bring to the boil, cover and simmer for 20 minutes. Add a slice of lemon in the last five minutes. Strain and sweeten with organic honey to taste. Drink a cupful, hot, every two to three hours.

Sore throat Make a gargle with:

- 1 handful dried or fresh sage leaves
- $1/2$ dessertspoon cider vinegar
- 500 ml boiling water

Pour the boiling water on to the herb and cover. Leave to stand until cool, then add the cider vinegar. Gargle every four hours.

Coughs Take one large onion and some organic honey. Slice the onion into rings and place in a deep bowl. Cover it with honey and leave for eight hours. Strain off the liquid, discard the onion and take a dessertspoon of the liquid every two to four hours.

Tired and sore eyes Make an infusion by placing a tea-bag of fennel or camomile herb tea in a cup of boiling water for five minutes. Strain and cool, then bathe the eye with a sterile eye-bath, using fresh infusions for each eye. Alternatively, use the cooled teabags to cover eyelids (left).

Travel sickness Chew a small piece of fresh ginger root or stem before setting out.

Insomnia and anxiety Before bed, drink one of these herbal teas: limeflower, camomile, passion flower, valerian, hops. You'll soon find which one helps you the most.

Burns Apply a drop of lavender oil to the burn or alternatively, try applying a small

amount of comfrey ointment.

Bruises Apply ointment made from the roots and seeds of the greater knapweed plant.

Treating Like With Like

Homeopathy is becoming increasingly popular among both doctors and patients. It is a safe, natural form of holistic medicine that's cheap to prescribe and works equally well for adults, children – and even animals.

The word homeopathy (pronounced home-ee-oppathy) is the Greek term for 'similar suffering'. Homeopathy itself is a system of medicine based on the Greek physician Hippocrates' idea that 'like cures like'. If a healthy person takes a homeopathic remedy, it will actually produce the symptoms of the illness it is prescribed to cure in the sick person.

So, for example, if you have a streaming cold, whereas your doctor might give you something to dry the symptoms up, a homeopath could give you a remedy like Allium Cepe, made from onions, which make our eyes stream and our noses run!

Homeopathy is a holistic medicine — it takes into account the whole person including their mind, body, emotions, life style, diet, relationships and family history.

Homeopathy vs vaccination

Homeopathy has often been compared with vaccination, but this is misleading. Vaccination gives you a mild dose of the disease you haven't had. Homeopathy, however, gives you a remedy which is capable of producing

WHAT WILL HOMEOPATHY TREAT?

The aim of homeopathy is to cure ailments by stimulating the body's own healing powers, or life force. The idea is to help the body heal itself. Disease is perceived as a natural process – we only fall ill when there is a disturbance in our vital force. The homeopath sees symptoms like eczema, 'flu, depression or cystitis as the body's way of expressing and discharging such a disturbance.

Although strictly speaking, a homeopath only treats a person, not their illness, there are some ailments which respond particularly well to homeopathy. These include:

- premenstrual syndrome (PMS)
- myalgic encephalomyelitis (ME)
- depression
- behavioural difficulties in children
- cystitis and thrush

- migraine
- menstrual and menopausal problems
- eating disorders
- glue ear
- sinusitis
- irritable bowel syndrome
- continual coughs and colds
- hay fever
- asthma
- eczema.

symptoms similar to the ones you already have. The remedy does not give you the actual disease.

Another difference is that vaccination assumes we are all equally susceptible to the same diseases, so we all need vaccinating against a particular range of infectious diseases. Homeopathy treats each person as an individual with their own strengths and weaknesses, knowing that where one person might get every bug going, another will naturally resist them and doesn't need blanket protection.

But perhaps the most interesting thing about homeopathic remedies is the way in which they are prepared.

The history of homeopathy
Although the idea of like curing like is very old, homeopathy was discovered only 200 years ago, by an eminent German doctor and chemist, Samuel Hahnemann. He experimented on himself by taking infusions of cinchona bark, the source of quinine.

In Hahnemann's time, the bark was a popular remedy for marsh fever, and to his amazement he discovered that he began to develop the symptoms of a classic attack of marsh fever. Many experiments later, he became convinced that Hippocrates was right: a

substance which can create illness in a healthy person, can cure the same illness in a sick person. Hahnemann spent the rest of his life developing his ideas, finding out the best way to prepare remedies, testing his theories and trying out new remedies on himself, friends and patients, until he was satisfied that his new system worked.

Since Hahnemann's time, homeopathy has spread all over the world. The British Royal Family have been using homeopathy for six generations; most Indian hospitals use it where appropriate, and it is popular in Mexico and in Europe, where by law only medically-qualified doctors are permitted to practise. In the UK, where once only qualified doctors practised, and a few GPs are homeopaths, there are now many excellent 'lay' homeopaths who have studied for four years to qualify as practitioners.

Powerful remedies
There are remedies for many different ailments, many of which particularly

affect children or women. Homeopathic remedies are mainly derived from plants and minerals, although some of the most successful remedies come from animals, such as Lachesis (a snake venom) and Apis (from the bee). Although the original material might be poisonous, the beauty of homeopathic remedies is that they are very safe and non-toxic — this is due to the way the remedies are made.

The original substance — a natural tincture — is alternately diluted with alcohol and shaken up (a process called succussion). A drop of the tincture is diluted either 1:10 or 1:100 and shaken, then drops of the diluted tincture are diluted and shaken again. This may be repeated hundreds of times, so that in some cases it would be physically impossible for the final medication to contain a single molecule of the original tincture. The resulting dilutions are used to make the tablets, powders or liquids prescribed by the homeopath.

The extraordinary fact which Hahnemann found was that the more dilute the remedy, the more powerfully it acts. No one knows why this principle holds, or why homeopathic remedies work at all. It may be that dilution and succussion somehow release the holding energy of the substance, leaving an imprint of itself in the alcohol but rendering the original remedy harmless. Meanwhile, scientists are continuing to investigate homeopathy, but so far they haven't proved or disproved any of homeopathy's claims.

Labelling the remedies
Repeated dilution and succussion 'potentises' a remedy: the longer the process continues, the more powerful the remedy becomes. Remedies available from the chemist are usually in one of the lowest potencies, called a 6c, but homeopaths get higher potencies, from 30c to 50M, for example. These are only available from specialised homeopathic pharmacies. The numbers refer to the number of times the tincture has been diluted: 6c indicates it has been through the dilution and succussion process six times, 30c has been through the process 30 times, while 50M means that it has been

diluted and shaken 50 thousand times. As with any medicine, you must respect the power of remedies, as a badly-chosen one may simply make your condition worse.

How the homeopath works

As we all tend to respond to illnesses in our own way, and are susceptible to particular illnesses, the homeopath treats each person as a special case. Whereas a doctor might give five people with rheumatism the same drug, a homeopath could give each of them a different remedy.

The way the homeopath works is based on what is known as the Homeopathic Law of Cure. This states that when a person is getting better, their symptoms should move from above downwards, from the inside to the outside, from the most important to the least important organs, and in the reverse order of their original appearance. So someone suffering from asthma might find that as their asthma attacks lessen, they experience a brief return of the eczema they suffered as a

child, which then goes, leaving them free of illness. Some people experience a brief aggravation of their symptoms after taking a remedy: this is nothing to worry about, but means that the remedy is working well. Obviously, the homeopath tries to make these aggravations as slight as possible, or avoid them altogether, which is done by selecting the correct potency of the given remedy very carefully.

The homeopathic consultation

The first consultation with a homeopath will take up to two hours. The homeopath's aim will be to build up a complete picture of your health, and to do that, they will ask you in great detail, all about yourself. The homeopath will observe you from the moment you step in the door, noticing the way you walk,

your skin colour, the way you express yourself, if you're nervous or confident, happy or sad, whether you bite your nails and so on. They will take copious notes about everything you say, asking about your complaint, your previous social history, your family's health, what you dream about, what kind of weather suits you, your favourite and least favourite foods, the position you sleep in and whether you have any strong fears or anxieties.

They will quiz you on the exact symptoms you are suffering from. For example, if you have headaches, they'll want to know which side the pain is on, what makes it better or worse, when it starts and when it goes away. You may find this great attention to detail a little confusing but it all adds up to a complete symptom picture that the

---

HOMEOPATHIC REMEDIES IN THE HOME

A few homeopathic remedies in your first-aid cupboard may help to speed recovery from many of life's little scrapes and bumps.

Remember all remedies should be handled with respect. Bear the following points in mind before taking a remedy.
● If symptoms persist, or for more serious accidents or illnesses, you should consult your homeopath or doctor.
● Use the 6c potency of tablets, available from your chemist or health-food store.
● Take up to three tablets a day for not more than three days in a row.
● Tablets given to children or animals can be crushed between two spoons first to make them easier to swallow.
● Avoid food, drink, toothpaste and tobacco for 20 minutes before and after taking a remedy.
● Avoid handling the tablets. Tip them into the container lid and drop them under your tongue to dissolve. Do not crunch or swallow them.

Choosing a remedy

ARNICA Heals physical trauma, such as shock, bumps and bruises, sprains or aching muscles after a too-strenuous workout. Lessens jet lag and aids recovery after childbirth or surgical operation.
ACONITE The first remedy to take for fear and shock, for example, after a car accident. Also helps feverish colds and chills and travel sickness.
LEDUM Treats puncture wounds, bee or wasp stings, swollen insect bites, dog bites or accidents with nails.
HYPERICUM For very painful cuts and lacerations,

crushed toes or fingers squashed in car doors, and for falls which affect the base of the spine.
NUX VOMICA Treats indigestion and hangovers when the cause is overindulgence in too-rich food and drink.
CHAMOMILLA Teething granules. Calms very fractious teething babies.
URTICA Soothes minor burns and hot, smarting sunburn. Available in ointment form.
CALENDULA This is an antiseptic healer for grazes, small cuts and septic wounds. Dilute three drops of the lotion in a cup of water to use.

A homeopathic remedy is diluted, then shaken to potentise it. This process is known as 'succussion'. The more dilute the remedy, the more powerful it is.

homeopath can then use to find the correct remedy. They will look for the pattern that is characteristic for you as a person, and match this with one or more remedies individually tailored to you. Don't be surprised if your homeopath consults reference books as you talk — they aren't panicking, just checking which of the 2000 or so remedies in use most closely match your symptoms.

When they have decided on a remedy, you will be given one or more white pills to swallow, or a liquid remedy, then and there, or given a course of tablets to take home. Your next appointment — usually an hour in length — will be from a fortnight to six weeks later when the homeopath will check on how the remedy has helped.

Homeopaths do not prescribe more than one remedy at a time, in an effort to ensure that all the symptoms are matched. Since Hahnemann's original research only 'proved' the effect of one remedy at a time, there is no rigorous testing that shows whether combin-ations of remedies would work or would interact in a quite different way. .

How long does treatment take?
In acute situations like a child's fever or an accident, homeopathy can work

extremely fast — even in minutes. For longer-standing complaints, treatment may take weeks or months, depending on how you respond to the remedies. Even if you experience a brief aggravation of your symptoms, you should soon experience an increased sense of well-being and a freedom from minor ailments like coughs and colds.

Working together
Homeopaths like to work closely with your doctor if you are taking medication or receiving other treatment. They will want to know the results of tests and the doctor's diagnosis so that they can work with them, not against them.

Conventional drugs, especially steroids, HRT and the Pill, often mask or remove symptoms so that it is difficult for the homeopath to see a clear picture of your health. Treatment is always easier if you are not taking other medication. However, many homeopaths are willing to work with people taking conventional medicines, and with your doctor's consent, you may be able to discontinue drugs after some homeopathic treatment. This will always be done at your request and in consultation with your doctor.

Increasing numbers of doctors are becoming trained homeopaths so first

ask your doctor if he practises himself, or he can recommend a therapist. You could also ask for an appointment at a homeopathic hospital, although this may involve travelling some distance. As with many other alternative therapies, you will probably need more than one appointment. Children are sometimes charged less than adults, and some homeopaths offer special rates for people on low incomes. The cost of the remedies is usually included in the consultation fee, but check this when you book your first appointment.

Homeopathy for animals
Because of the mysterious way in which homeopathy works, critics have suggested that psychological forces come in to play: positive thinking produces positive health. However, this idea is disproved by the fact that the system works just as well for animals as people. There are only a few homeopathic vets in the UK, but they are working enthusiastically with farmers and pet owners to improve their animals' health.

One homeopathic vet, Christopher Day, has shown that homeopathy does work (to his fiercest critics — his farmers). In one instance, he treated half a herd of cattle with homeopathic remedies to prevent mastitis (an infection of the udder), while the other half acted as a control group. The homeopathic group remained almost totally healthy, while the untreated group developed the same amount of mastitis as usual.

> " The highest ideal of therapy is to restore health rapidly, gently, permanently; to remove and destroy the whole disease in the shortest, surest, least harmful way, according to clearly comprehensible principles. "
>
> *Samuel Hahnemann*

> "By opposites, opposites are cured."
>
> *Hippocrates*

A Gift From The Bees

Throughout history, honey has been regarded as a source of goodness and nowadays no health-food shop would look complete without several varieties of honey on its shelves. Yet its reputation owes more to its appearance and taste than to health-giving properties.

The most ancient and delightful of all sweeteners, honey has been used since prehistoric times not only as a food, but also as an offering to the gods and as a healing substance. The Egyptians even used it as an embalming material. Its origins were a mystery to early civilisations and this gave honey a kind of magical status. The ancient Greeks thought it was dew fallen from the skies, while Pliny, the Roman historian, wondered rather unappealingly whether honey was "the perspiration of the sky or a sort of saliva of the stars".

Honey was thought of as a miraculous substance which symbolized wealth and happiness. The Old Testament refers to the Promised Land as "flowing with milk and honey" and honey is widely praised in ancient Egyptian and Babylonian writings. Honey has always been endowed with unique properties — as an aphrodisiac, for prolonging youthfulness and as a promoter of health and well-being. Even today, many people firmly believe that honey is a kind of cure-all and that it is the most 'natural' of all natural foods.

The work of the bees

But what exactly is honey and does it live up to the claims made about it?

Honey is made from nectar, a thin watery fluid which worker bees suck from the nectaries in the flowers of certain plants. The most common plant is clover but also used are nectars from acacia, alfalfa, orange blossom, sage, rosemary, eucalyptus, blackberries, willowherb, heather, sycamore, lime, oilseed rape, mustard, and others.

Almost all nectars are edible but a very few are toxic to humans, although harmless to bees, and therefore create poisonous honeys; and honey made from opium poppy nectar is narcotic. A notorious poisonous honey once produced in eastern Turkey was made with nectar from rhododendrons.

A hive of activity

Bees suck the nectar through a narrow tube called the proboscis into a special honey sac located near their intestines. Here enzymes begin the process of breaking down the sucrose into smaller glucose and fructose molecules. The worker bees deposit the nectar in the hive, where the 'house' bees pump the nectar in and out of themselves until it is sufficiently concentrated to resist spoilage from bacteria and moulds.

TYPES OF HONEY

Honey is classified according to the plants the bees visit. These are just some of the many types available.

all-purpose honey. English clover honey is expensive.

Eucalyptus
Powerfully-flavoured, brownish honey from Australia and the Mediterranean.

Heather
Buttery, reddish-brown soft honey with an intense flavour.

Hymettus
From Greece, an expensive, dark brown, thyme-flavoured honey.

Lavender
From Provence, golden and thick with a perfumed flavour.

Leatherwood
Amber-coloured Australian honey with a mild flavour.

Lime flower
Greenish-gold honey with a full flavour.

Orange blossom
Delicately-perfumed, pale gold, liquid honey.

Rosemary
Pale and clear with a medium flavour.

Acacia
Delicately-flavoured clear honey which does not crystallize with age. Good for sweetening herbal teas.

Clover
Pale, thick and full-flavoured. A useful

COMPOSITION OF HONEY

Water	18%
Glucose	35%
Fructose	40%
Other sugars	4%
Other substances	3%

Over 200 different substances have been identified as 'other substances': pollen, small amounts of some of the B vitamins; traces of vitamin C; several minerals including potassium, calcium, chlorine, phosphorus and iron; and a little protein.

This concentrated nectar is dropped into the hexagonal cells in the honeycomb, a multi-layered structure made from the waxy secretions of young worker bees. It then ripens for about three weeks during which time the flavour and colour develop.

A spectrum of colours

Honeys vary in colour, aroma and flavour depending on the type and location of the flowers from which the bees collect the nectar. The colour ranges from creamy white to almost black. There is even an exotic greenish honey in red combs found in Africa.

The lighter the colour, the more mild and subtle the flavour. As the colour darkens the amount of minerals present, and possibly protein, increase the intensity of flavour. The best flavoured honey is that freshly taken from the hive in the comb — after harvesting the flavour gradually disappears. Heating honey also accelerates loss of flavour.

The main producers of honey are the USSR, China, USA, Mexico, Canada and Argentina. Honey may be a blend from different countries or the product of a single country or region. Most commercial honeys are a blend of several flowers. Single flower honey is available but it is more expensive as it is harder to produce.

Commercial honey is extracted centrifugally from the combs, then filtered and purified. This is called 'cast' honey. A rarer type of honey, made from crushed honeycombs, is called 'pressed' honey. It does not keep so well as cast honey.

Royal jelly

Sometimes called 'bees' milk', royal jelly is the substance that turns the larva of a worker bee into a queen bee. The larva floats in a cell of royal jelly, which it eats to its fill all the time.

The substance undoubtedly has special properties for the bees but it is unlikely that humans derive the same benefits. We would have to consume about 700,000 times more in order to take in an amount equivalent to that of a bee larva's intake. Many claims are made for royal jelly's rejuvenating properties and nutritional benefits. While it's true that royal jelly contains vitamin B5 (pantothenic acid) and B6 (pyridoxine), we get plenty of both vitamins in our ordinary food, so taking royal jelly is an expensive way of topping up your vitamin intake.

Although claims are often made in literature from health-food shops that honey helps to cure a range of ailments from coughs and sore throats to anaemia, kidney disease, peptic ulcers

and other digestive complaints, there is no scientific evidence to demonstrate that this is so.

Honey is not a miracle food. The vitamin and mineral content of honey is minimal — you would have to eat about 25kg of honey to give the body a day's requirement of riboflavin (vitamin B2). And, although pollen and royal jelly are great for bees, there is no evidence that they do anything special for humans.

However, honey is a highly concentrated source of energy. The sugars it contains are already broken down into monosaccharides, so honey is easily digested and can be used quickly by the body. It is therefore a useful food for athletes, invalids, children and the elderly. It's also the traditional sweetening agent used in national delicacies such as nougat and halva; and in some liqueurs.

Because of its special water-attracting characteristics, honey keeps bread and cakes more moist than sugar and so improves their keeping quality. Try substituting sugar with honey — four teaspoons of honey are roughly the equivalent of five teaspoons of sugar.

Taking The Waters

Any treatment involving the use of water, either internally, as with 'taking the waters at Bath', or externally, as with blitz showers and special baths, is known as hydrotherapy.

There is currently a revival of interest in hydrotherapy, a form of health treatment which was an integral part of the life style of classical Greeks and Romans. They constructed aqueducts to transport pure mountain water into their towns to drink and use in steam baths.

The first modern hydrotherapy establishment was founded in Bohemia in the early 19th century by a formidable man called Vincent Priessnitz who insisted that his patients followed a strict regime of ice-cold baths, sluices and douches. They also had to submit to being wrapped in damp sheets and drinking huge amounts of the local water. Nowadays health farms and hydros offer less Spartan treatments but hydrotherapy and thalassotherapy are still practised for the purpose of de-toxifying the body.

Saunas

Once regarded as an eccentric Finnish habit, saunas have taken over from Turkish baths in popularity. The principle is to sit in a room heated to a minimum temperature of 38°C although the temperature may be kept considerably higher for those who can stand it. Beginners should stay in the sauna for five minute periods initially, and then take a swim or shower. The time spent in the sauna may be increased as the individual builds up tolerance to the heat but it will always be important to douse yourself in cold water after each stint in the sauna.

HOME TREATMENTS

Most of us would find it difficult to stretch to the expense of having a sauna or jacuzzi installed in our home. There are however, several useful water treatments that can be performed in a normal household shower or bath.

Water under normal pressure can be used to invigorate and stimulate circulation in the facial area.

First, remove the nozzle from a hand shower. Then, with the neck supported on a towel over a bath or handbasin, direct cold water in a circling movement all over your face for a couple of minutes. Apart from waking you up, blood is brought to the face and a healthy glow results.

Sufferers from insomnia could try water treading in a few inches of cold water – the rest of the body should be kept warm.

A commonly used home water therapy is to direct cold water all over the body for a minute at the end of a shower. This is practised by many athletes and greatly increases vitality.

Through this treatment the body becomes accustomed to changes in temperature, often the cause of chills which precipitate colds.

Another cold-water cure is the sitz bath. You sit in a bath of waist-high cold water for no longer than a few seconds with the result, it is claimed, that your body's immune function will be boosted and constipation alleviated.

More mundane hydrotherapy treatments include mustard baths for aching feet and steam inhalations for head colds. Compresses for sprains, bruises, swellings and inflammations are also a form of hydrotherapy. And drinking six to eight glasses of water a day is said to purify the system and promote health.

enjoying a revival of interest with its proponents claiming that seaweed and water treatments have the effect of balancing the body, stabilising adverse skin conditions and hydrating connective tissue. Treatments are designed to relax you thoroughly, both physically and mentally, and restore a feeling of total well-being.

It is claimed that many of these treatments reduce body weight as well as eliminating fat deposits and excess fluids. For this reason a course of five or six sessions is recommended. However, although 'inch loss' can be measured and seen after treatments it is arguable whether it can be maintained without a change in diet and personal fitness. Such treatments are also ineffective in those people who are more than two stones (12.7kg) overweight.

Most hydrotherapy treatments, such as blitz showers and body wraps, usually last for about an hour and involve a process of exfoliation (rubbing off the dead skin), and massage. Before undertaking a treatment, however, a client should be asked about their health as there are certain conditions, such as pregnancy and low or high blood pressure, which should not be exposed to these therapies.

While saunas are not recommended for people with heart conditions, they are of benefit to those with aches and pains, respiratory troubles and indigestion. Taking a sauna can be extremely invigorating and an excellent way of deep cleansing the skin, and it is also a wonderful way to recover from a hangover.

Those who don't enjoy breathing in the hot air can use individual steam cabinets which engulf the body from the neck downwards and offer similar benefits to a sauna.

Jacuzzis

Jacuzzis are heated to normal bath temperature and can usually accommodate as many as six to eight people at a time. Underwater showers and jets massage the body, producing a healthy all-

People flocked to the Pump Room in Bath for hydrotherapy treatment during the 18th century (near right). Nowadays, high pressure water treatment centres are within the reach of most women (far right).

over glow, easing tired and sore muscles, toning and revitalising the skin and stimulating the internal organs. An immersion of about five to 10 minutes ought to relax the mind and body and should then be followed by a rest period.

Thalassotherapy

The Greek word 'thalassa' means 'the sea' and thalassotherapy involves treatments using salt water. The salts in our blood serum are known to be closely linked to those in the sea and are therefore thought to have many therapeutic properties. Thalassotherapy is currently

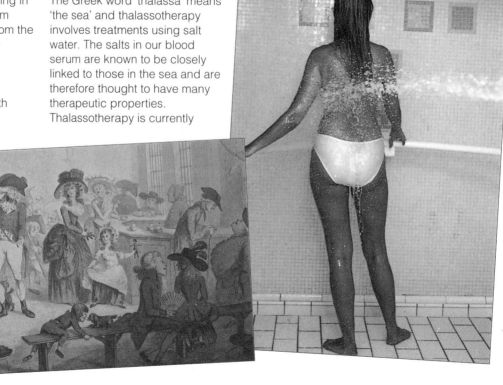

ALTERED STATE OF CONSCIOUSNESS

Is hypnosis really about swinging a watch in front of somebody's face and bewitching them into doing anything you say? Could this really happen? Just what is hypnosis?

In the past, hypnotists have been known to use their skills as a form of music-hall entertainment — getting their unwitting subjects to quack like a duck or leap from their seat believing it to be red-hot. It's all very funny if you're the audience, and humiliating if you're the subject, and it does hypnosis in general no favours. People go away from such shows in secret terror of being hypnotised and made to look an idiot in public. But hypnosis needn't be like that at all.

Hypnosis in history

There is evidence that hypnosis has been used the world over for centuries. The ancient Egyptians had their 'sleep temples' in which people with spiritual or psychological problems were put to sleep in order to be healed naturally. Sometimes they were drugged, at other times they were put into a trance to make them sleep for days on end — very likely this was a hypnotic trance.

In the eighteenth century the Austrian doctor Franz Anton Mesmer

developed a method of throwing sick people into an altered state of consciousness through a combination of induced convulsions and hypnosis, which came to be known as mesmerism. Often highly dramatic, this treatment was said to be very effective for a host of ailments, but because of its bizarre theatricality, it was soon outlawed in many European countries.

In the nineteenth century there were several attempts by doctors in various parts of the British Empire — such as Dr

James Braid in India — to be allowed to use hypnosis to anaesthetise patients during surgical operations, but to no avail. The medical establishment refused to acknowledge the validity of this technique — and thousands of patients continued to endure the appalling tortures of surgery without anaesthetic, until chloroform came to be used. It was only when Sigmund Freud's teacher Charcot used hypnosis to demonstrate the power of mind over body in hysterical patients that some doctors began to accept hypnosis as a useful clinical tool.

What is hypnosis?

Hypnosis is an altered state of consciousness, which feels like something between sleeping and waking, and has qualities of both those states. In general, hypnotised subjects find that their body is deeply relaxed, almost in a state of sleep, while their subconscious mind becomes very alert. This state of consciousness is what makes hypnosis an excellent tool for unlocking buried memories, or for discovering hidden motives.

When you're hypnotised you're very suggestible — you will believe what the hypnotherapist suggests to your mind. Historical experiments have shown that deeply hypnotised subjects will not react even to a cut or burn if they are told they are not being hurt — the really amazing thing is that their bodies will believe this too. No burn mark or wound will appear on their skin!

It is possible to hypnotise someone so that they feel no pain even during major surgery, although they remain fully awake during the operation. On a lesser level, post-operative hypnotic suggestion has been used to heal scars more quickly and speed up recovery.

In the 1950s one trial demonstrated that a range of skin diseases could be eliminated through the use of hypnosis — the subconscious mind of the sufferer was contacted while she was in a trance and told that it would make first an arm, then a leg and so on, clear of the skin disorder.

Can anyone be hypnotised?

Many people believe that it would be impossible to hypnotise them because they have a strong will, or are sceptical about the whole thing, or they feel that they would fight it. In fact, there are very, very few people who cannot be hypnotised — estimates vary between four and nought per cent of the population! If you ever lose yourself in a book, or become distracted, or find your are able to do something automatically, such as driving or typing, while you are thinking about something else, then you can be hypnotised.

The depth of trance may be different; deep trance subjects are relatively hard to find, but most people can reach a light to medium trance with little difficulty. There seems to be a secret willingness on the part of most people to go in to the state of relaxation that is hypnosis. Sceptics are often easy subjects — perhaps because their scepticism is just a defence against their potential for total surrender!

Putting it to use

Hypnosis is used for a variety of purposes. Used together with psychological techniques to help eliminate unwanted habits, fears, phobias and certain illnesses, it becomes hypnotherapy. This is used increasingly by doctors, psychiatrists and dentists in the UK.

As an aid for memory retrieval it is sometimes used on behalf of the police, especially where vital witnesses to a crime cannot recall some of the details in their normal conscious state. Hypnosis, it is claimed, will take them back to the event and enable them to 'see' all the details quite clearly. There is some controversy about this, as people under hypnosis tend to show a great willingness to please the hypnotist by coming out with colourful stories that may or may not be based on the truth.

The trance state is also used experimentally by New Age practitioners in order to 'recall' alleged past lives to release present day traumas (see below).

Looking Back At Other Lives

Taking hypnotic subjects back to their childhood is known as hypnotic regression. It can be taken further, enabling the therapist to find emotional triggers in people's reputed past lives.

The idea that hypnotic regression can access past lives – experiences of living as other people, in other times in history – is controversial.

Many critics suggest hypnosis is notorious for making subjects keen to please the hypnotist by inventing colourful material – so any alleged past lives they may describe could well be fantasy. Indeed, some classic cases of regression have been proved to be merely versions of historical novels the subject read a long time ago and consciously forgot. But the subconscious mind – the part that speaks when the subject is hypnotised – never forgets anything. It is this facility for dressing up the storyline of novels and films as past

lives that makes regression an uncertain tool for proving the idea of reincarnation.

Yet certain questions remain. Some subjects return time and time again to the same alleged past life – perhaps a boring, uneventful life as a nobody in the back of beyond. You can't prove that the person they claimed to be ever lived, but you can't prove that they didn't. And why should their subconscious mind choose to describe such a tedious existence if there was no truth in it, and all they really wanted to do was please the hypnotherapist?

Left and above: from Elizabethan noblewomen to Indian dancing girls – some people find themselves acting the roles of many different characters under hypnosis.

'Wide Awake At The Count of Ten'

A hypnotherapist treats phobias, psychosomatic aches and pains, and addictions such as overeating or smoking. What will happen to us when we get on the hypnotherapist's couch and is it safe to do so?

Hypnotherapy uses hypnosis to overcome undesirable mental states or habits. Used by Freud, this therapy has been shown to be a highly successful method of treating patients for a variety of ailments and psychological problems, such as certain skin disorders, insomnia, anxiety attacks and phobias.

Many people are attracted by the success rate of hypnotherapy, but are worried by the image of hypnosis. Among the many questions they ask are: 'Will I lose my self control and babble stupidly or do something humiliating while under hypnosis?'; 'Can the hypnotist make me do something against my will?'; 'What happens if I'm hypnotised and the building starts to burn down?'

Facts and fallacies

Hypnosis is an altered state of consciousness in which we become deeply relaxed and therefore 'highly suggestible'. This means that we are open to receive and process new ideas and positive suggestions without our normal suspicious or critical response. A hypnotherapist will use her hypnotic skills to reach your mental problem and reprogramme your thinking about it.

There is no real mystique involved: all reputable hypnotherapists will have trained either as psychiatrists or as psychotherapists, and will treat the patient in a warm and compassionate way. Remember, they're not entertainers and have absolutely no wish to humiliate you!

At the beginning of a session with a hypnotherapist, it will be explained to you what a session involves, and what being hypnotised is likely to entail. While it is true that under exceptional circumstances, a hypnotic subject could do something against his or her will, this is highly unlikely. Scientific research shows hypnosis is a wakeful state — subjects are not asleep. Everything that happens in a hypnotherapy session will be perfectly ethical and agreed by both subject and therapist (also known as the 'operator').

If an emergency happens, your subconscious mind will allow you to respond in a normal way. Alarm bells, people screaming for help, and your own child's voice are all triggers that will bring you back — very sharply — to normal functioning.

Being hypnotised

The actual process of being hypnotised is usually considerably less dramatic than most people imagine it to be.

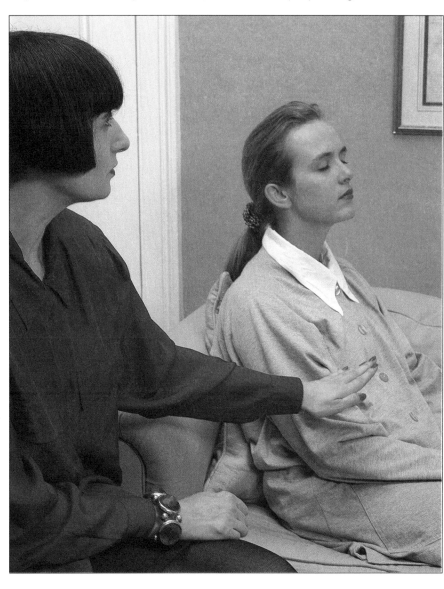

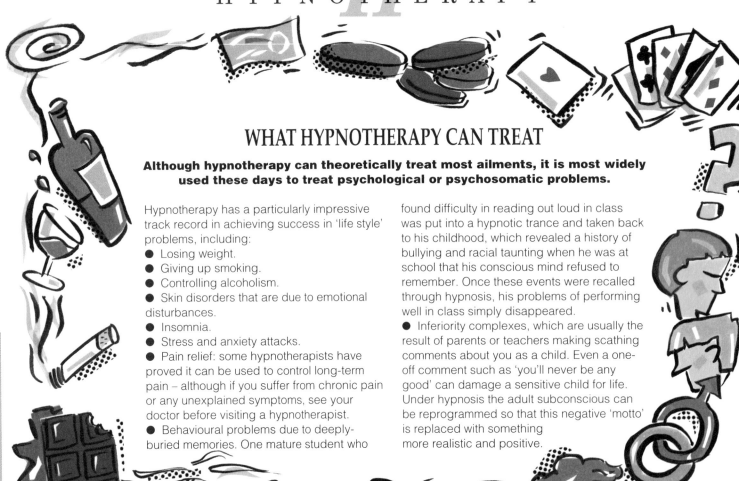

WHAT HYPNOTHERAPY CAN TREAT

Although hypnotherapy can theoretically treat most ailments, it is most widely used these days to treat psychological or psychosomatic problems.

Hypnotherapy has a particularly impressive track record in achieving success in 'life style' problems, including:
● Losing weight.
● Giving up smoking.
● Controlling alcoholism.
● Skin disorders that are due to emotional disturbances.
● Insomnia.
● Stress and anxiety attacks.
● Pain relief: some hypnotherapists have proved it can be used to control long-term pain – although if you suffer from chronic pain or any unexplained symptoms, see your doctor before visiting a hypnotherapist.
● Behavioural problems due to deeply-buried memories. One mature student who

found difficulty in reading out loud in class was put into a hypnotic trance and taken back to his childhood, which revealed a history of bullying and racial taunting when he was at school that his conscious mind refused to remember. Once these events were recalled through hypnosis, his problems of performing well in class simply disappeared.
● Inferiority complexes, which are usually the result of parents or teachers making scathing comments about you as a child. Even a one-off comment such as 'you'll never be any good' can damage a sensitive child for life. Under hypnosis the adult subconscious can be reprogrammed so that this negative 'motto' is replaced with something more realistic and positive.

Some subjects actually leave their first session fully believing that they were never even hypnotised!

One woman who visited a hypnotherapist in order to stop smoking said: "I thought all I'd done was sit in the chair with my eyes closed, listening to his voice. After a while, I started to feel a bit embarrassed because I didn't feel hypnotised. I thought, 'Don't let on, pay the man and don't come back again. It obviously hasn't worked.' That was in the morning. By the evening I was telling everyone about my failure to be hypnotised — then suddenly I realised that I hadn't had a cigarette all day. That was six years ago. I still haven't had one."

Hypnosis is very much a relaxation technique, and by all accounts it feels wonderful! If you're tense or stressed, being hypnotised is a particularly pleasant experience, like sliding into the most blissful sleep, while at the same time being able to concentrate without much effort on the hypnotherapist's voice. It's a gentle, pleasant sensation — so much so that often new subjects feel reluctant to 'come back'! The

operator will begin by making you comfortable in a chair or on a couch. The induction — the method used to put you into a hypnotic trance — varies, but it usually involves counting you into a state of deep relaxation in a quiet, monotonous voice, interspersed with suggestions that you are becoming sleepy, your eyelids are heavy, and so on. Sometimes you may be asked to look at a spot on the wall or ceiling while the induction goes on, until you finally close your eyes.

Once you're relaxed

Once you're deeply relaxed, the suggestions can be made. You will have agreed what form they will take beforehand — perhaps the therapist will suggest that you no longer want or need to eat cream cakes at all hours of the day and night, or that you feel disgusted by the sight of a cigarette. she may want to 'unlock' the reason for some of you phobias or psychological problems by helping you to talk about your past experiences.

Taking you back to your childhood may not be a happy experience for

many, but this technique can often reveal traumas that have left otherwise unexplained scars in adults. Sometimes you may be required to answer a question or two to clarify an issue for the therapist — and you may find it strangely difficult to speak. Often this is the first proof you have that you are truly hypnotised! In many cases, however, you simply lie there listening to the therapist's voice. At the end of the session you will be brought out of the trance. The therapist may well say, 'When I reach the count of ten you will be wide awake, alert, relaxed, happy and feeling positive.'

Some people need more than one session of hypnotherapy, although many find their condition improves after just one visit to a therapist. Expect to pay around £35, although some therapists do cost more.

Hypnotherapy will not turn you into Superwoman. It can't put there what isn't there. But what it can do is remove unnecessary pain and suffering, and help adults take responsibility for their own lives and potential.

Positive Negatives

Most of us tend to feel invigorated after a storm or when we are by the sea. According to scientists, this feeling of being refreshed is brought about by an abundance of electrically charged particles known as negative ions, which are present in the air.

At the other extreme, when positive ions prevail to a substantial degree, people often suffer more frequently than usual from headaches and depression.

It has also been noted that at times when there are a great deal of positive ions in the atmosphere there is an increased rate of accidents, domestic disturbances, murders and suicides. Interestingly, there definitely seem to exist weather-sensitive individuals who begin to suffer up to two days before these unpleasant weather conditions, when there is an increase in the body of a chemical messenger known as serotonin. When these people are given air to inhale that is rich in negative ions, however, their general health and mood improve markedly.

Positive ions predominate in areas of the world when hot, dry winds are found, such as the Foehn of Switzerland or the Sharav of Israel, to take two extreme examples. In certain legal cases, these winds have been used as an acceptable 'excuse' for what would normally be regarded as major crimes.

The presence of ions in our air was not discovered until the end of the 19th century. Electro-magnetic waves, the sun and storms, as well as other natural

sources, all provide the sources of energy which produce this presence. What is more, in certain climactic and geographical conditions, the ratio of positive to negative ions will alter. In cities, for example, the concentration of beneficial negative ions will drop dramatically, and in air-conditioned buildings it may drop even further.

It is now possible to create a favourable, negative ion environment at home, at work and even when driving, through the use of a simple machine called an ioniser.

Better health
Research has shown that negative ions have a beneficial effect on the body, reducing blood pressure and improving the natural rhythms of the brain. They also help improve the performance of the cleansing cells in the respiratory system, and reverse the effects of positive ions in the air. Studies have even pointed to the fact that as many as 75 per cent of those with respiratory ailments such as hay fever, sinusitis, bronchitis and asthma have all benefited, while 45 per cent of those suffering from debilitating headaches reported relief.

Burns and scalds have even been found to heal more quickly in the

Headaches, asthma, bronchitis, eczema and general well-being can all, it seems, be alleviated to a remarkable degree by using an ioniser that will charge air particles negatively.

presence of an ioniser and severe anxiety, due to stress factors, can be substantially alleviated. Negative ions may also reduce the risk of cross-infection, when, for instance, one of the family or a work colleague is suffering from 'flu or a cold.

An ioniser by the bed may also provide night relief for those having trouble with breathing and the machine should also reduce the harmful effects of passive smoking. Some ioniser manufacturers claim that the machines can be beneficial to animals and plants. Crop yields in greenhouses are said to increase substantially with the help of negative ions, and milk production has also been found to improve when ionisers are provided for cattle.

Aid to alertness

As part of his research into the effect of negative ions, Professor L H Hawkins of the University of Surrey carried out a 12-week study at the headquarters of a well-known insurance company. Staff were informed that a new air-conditioning system was being installed, but the machines which were put in place around the offices were actually negative ion generators.

The results were astonishing. There was a reduction in the number of staff suffering from headaches from 26 per cent to between five and six per cent. Staff were more pleasant to one another and felt more comfortable. Hawkins also found in a further study that people's

eyesight and hearing were improved under the effect of negative ions.

In the United States, meanwhile, research at Rockefeller University, New York, has shown that an increase in positive ions will affect ion-sensitive people adversely, slowing down their reactions considerably. So it seems that not only will an ioniser help many people who have respiratory complaints but it will also help them to concentrate.

Improving the environment

Inadequate ventilation, smoke, artificial fibres and electrical equipment are all, it is claimed, causes of the Sick Building Syndrome. The theory is that photo-copiers, fluorescent lighting, VDUs, synthetic fibres, cigarettes, smoke and ducted air-conditioning can all play havoc with a person's well-being by decreasing the level of negative ions in the surrounding atmosphere. Indeed, in many instances, it could well be that the work environment itself is capable of making staff sick. Ionisers are said to reverse this effect.

In the car, too, ionisers may have a place, increasing the alertness of the driver by charging the air negatively and removing unwanted particles such as dust, smoke and even bacteria. Open the car window and you are immediately exposed to polluted air. The ioniser, however, plugs into the cigarette lighter socket and provides invigorating negative ions instantly. This can be of

particular value on a tiring journey and lorry drivers travelling long distances may benefit greatly.

In the past, critics have tried to dismiss the apparent benefits of the ioniser as a mere placebo effect. However, studies such as those referred to here, certainly indicate impressive results. Some ionisers will effectively treat an area within a 20 ft (6m) radius with negatively charged pollutants moving to earthed surfaces.

Many manufacturers emphasise the complete safety of their equipment, and they also stress how inexpensive ionisers are to run, as they only cost a few pence each month, even when left on for long periods for maximum effect. You cannot, they say, breathe in too many negative ions, as there is no maximum dose.

THE IONISER IN OPERATION

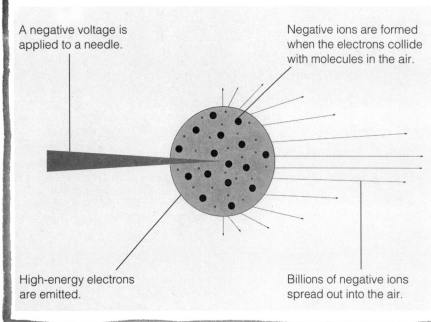

A negative voltage is applied to a needle.

Negative ions are formed when the electrons collide with molecules in the air.

High-energy electrons are emitted.

Billions of negative ions spread out into the air.

Negative ions are known to improve the quality of the air we breathe, but how does an ioniser work?

When switched on, the machine inside an ioniser applies a negative voltage to a series of needles, causing high-energy electrons to be emitted. As these collide with molecules in the air, billions of negative ions are formed and spread out into the environment, revitalising the atmosphere and cleansing it of pollutants.

An ioniser should be left on for long periods to have the maximum benefit. The discharge, known as the 'ion-wind', can be felt against the skin. It may also sometimes be heard as a very faint noise.

Insights To Your Health?

The eyes are sometimes described as being the windows to the soul, but can they also be used as the windows to your health?

Iridology is the study of the iris (the coloured part of the eye) in order to determine a person's state of health and their predisposition towards illness. It is strictly a diagnostic tool and is not a type of healing or therapy.

It is one of the least-known forms of complementary medicine currently being practised in the UK. For all its low profile, however, iridologists claim to be able to predict and detect illness just from the study of the iris of the eye. However, it has not yet been established that this can really work.

How it began

Although an iridology society was only offici-ally founded in the UK in 1983, it has actually been available in several other countries for at least a century. It originated in Germany, and the founder was a man called Ignaz Peczely.

As a boy, Ignaz came across an injured owl, and when he tried to capture it, the bird's leg was broken in the tussle that followed. It was an unfortunate accident, and Ignaz then took the bird home to look after it while its leg was healing.

As he was bandaging the injured limb, he noticed a small black dot beginning to form within the owl's iris. By the next day the dot had become a black line running from the pupil to the edge of the iris.

Eventually, the owl's leg healed properly, and the bird remained as a pet for several months. Ignaz noted that once the bird had made a complete recovery, the black line in the iris changed to a white one. He was fascinated by his discovery and it spurred him on to train to be a doctor and to carry on researching his findings on iridology.

Other pioneers of iridology research came from parts of Germany and Switzerland. Over the years, more and more accurate and detailed maps of the iris have been developed and these maps are the iridologist's most important tools (see overpage).

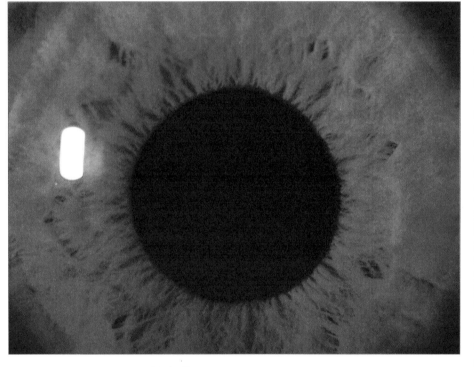

Health indicators

Illness is depicted by marks, lines or flecks within the iris. Iridologists also claim that they can see details of past illnesses within the iris, as well as current ones and predispositions towards future ill health.

Iridologists believe this information is mirrored within the iris because the iris is connected, through the third cranial nerve, to the nervous system. As the nervous system connects all the organs of the body with one another, all such information is shown in the iris.

What iridology can diagnose

Iridologists claim to be able to diagnose most forms of illness. Iridology is most useful for picking up strengths and weaknesses within the body, particularly any inherited tendencies towards illness. If you are worried about developing diabetes because of a family trait, then an iris examination may show whether or not it is actually in the process of happening.

Iridology is also used by some people as a form of preventive medicine and they will go to their iridologist even when they are feeling well just to check up on their state of health. Not surprisingly, iridologists are also good at picking up any disease of the eye. However, an iridologist cannot detect whether you have a viral infection such as measles or a cold, or whether you are pregnant or are suffering from mental illnesses such as schizophrenia, unless there is some other physical disturbance accompanying the symptoms.

Whether iridology actually works is debatable. Although many people, even non-iridologists, claim to be able to discern a great deal about a person simply by looking in their eyes, there is no foundation for this belief in iridology.

There have been a number of studies by scientists proving that it is useless as a diagnostic tool and a few others which seem to indicate that it might be a helpful one. Certainly no one is quite sure of its standing at present. The medical profession views it sceptically, partly because, according to James Colton, of the Society of Iridologists: "It isn't a specific tool of

OUR HEALTH IN OUR EYES

By looking into a patient's eyes, an iridologist should be able to spot the signs of illness anywhere in the body without having to perform a physical examination.

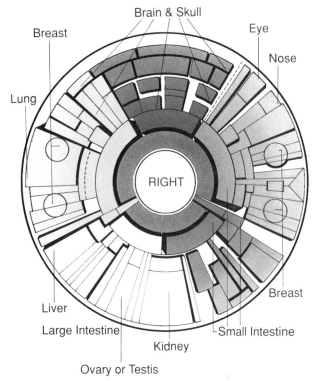
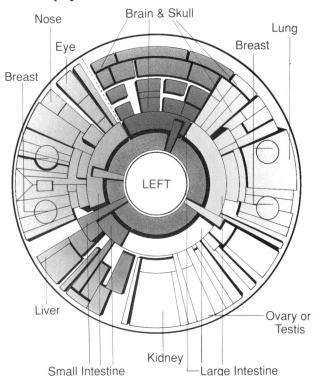

There are two maps, one for each eye, and on each map the iris is divided into sections which relate to parts of the body. So, at the top of the chart are organs such as the brain, while the feet are shown towards the bottom. Each person has a unique iris pattern, rather like a fingerprint, and within that pattern will be indicators of that person's state of health. Colour is the first indicator the iridologist takes into account when she examines the eyes. The yellow pigmentation in a green eye, for example, might be an indicator of liver or gallbladder problems.

diagnosis. Doctors want to have a diagnostic tool which will cover everything, and iridology doesn't claim to do that."

The consultation

In an iridology consultation, which lasts between one and two hours, the irises of both eyes are examined. Some iridologists will take a photograph of the iris, in which case you would be asked to return a second time for the analysis of the developed picture.

Others will examine the eye by shining a torch into it — by all accounts this isn't too uncomfortable. They won't ask you for any details of your illness until they have made their examination and compared your irises to the charts. Then they will tell you what is indicated within your eyes to see if it matches up to your own version of your health.

The iridologist will then perform one of five simple tests, depending on the outcome of the diagnosis. Your blood pressure might be tested, for instance,

if there is an indication that it is too high or too low. Iridologists aren't medically trained, but will refer people to doctors if they can't deal with a patient's illness.

Many iridologists are trained in various other forms of alternative treatment, and it is useful to consult an iridologist who has some knowledge of health and nutrition, so that your initial diagnosis can then be followed up by some practical, positive advice. In Germany, most medically trained homeopaths have iridology training. In the UK, many iridologists have a background in herbal medicine, homeopathy or osteopathy.

A new development in iridology is regularisation of treatments for specific illnesses and conditions which are indicated through iris diagnosis. This is bioiridology, and the prescribed remedies are herbal or nutritional.

Finding an iridologist

There are very few trained iridologists, so you may find that you have to travel

to see one. Telephone or write to the regulatory body for iridologists in your area, and ask them to give you a list of the names and addresses of practitioners local to you with their qualifications. Also ask for details describing the various qualifications - the training for iridologists varies from one country to another

> " This life's five windows of
> the soul
> Distorts the Heavens from
> pole to pole,
> And leads you to believe
> a lie
> When you see with, not thro'
> the eye."
>
> William Blake

YOUR HEALTH

Muscle Matters

Kinesiology is both a therapy in itself and also a diagnostic tool, used by complementary therapists to assess the health of their patients. Kinesiologists believe that ill health shows up in the muscles of the body. A particular illness, they claim, corresponds to an imbalance in the body's energy flow, which can be detected as a weakening of certain muscle groups.

Therefore, by testing the strength of muscles, the kinesiologist can make an assessment about a person's state of health. Having located a problem, the kinesiologist then tries to resolve it by giving light finger-tip massage to pressure points on the body or head. Kinesiologists share the same belief as acupuncturists — that the body's energy flows around the body along

Kinesiology is a form of complementary medicine which aims to improve the health of a person by rebalancing muscles. What does treatment involve, and what can it do for you?

energy lines or meridians. However, kinesiology's system of pressure points is unique to the therapy.

How it started

In the early 1960s an American chiropractor called Dr George Goodheart discovered that muscle testing could reveal information about a patient that could not be learned by any

other method of investigation. His research led him to combine muscle testing with pressure point massage which is particularly effective in aiding lymph drainage.

Later, Goodheart completed the development of the technique called Applied Kinesiology by making the link between western medical science and ancient Chinese principles of natural energy flow in the body, and how it may be assessed and monitored by the use of simple muscle tests.

What is confusing about kinesiology is that it can be used both as a diagnostic tool and as a therapy in its own right. You may come across herbalists or acupuncturists using kinesiology as a diagnostic tool with their patients. However, there are also practitioners of pure kinesiology, who

WHAT IT CAN HELP

Kinesiology is perhaps best known for diagnosing allergies, but it has a wide range of other applications too.

Kinesiological balancing can help with many common health problems, such as immune dysfunction, back pain, learning difficulties, anxiety and phobia states, nutritional deficiencies and food sensitivity, sports fitness and injury, plus enhancing general wellbeing.

Kinesiology is perhaps best known for showing up sensitivity or allergy to certain foods. The body is thought to recognise and react instantly to foods and chemicals, which in turn affect the way muscles work. Practitioners use the response of muscles to indicate a sensitivity or allergy. Symptoms of a food sensitivity can include headaches, digestive disturbances, joint pains, frequent colds and catarrh, depression and tiredness.

Kinesiologists also aim to locate and correct vitamin and mineral deficiencies as well as digestive disorders such as constipation and imbalances in gastric juices and digestive enzymes that can inhibit proper absorption of vital ingredients.

EMOTIONAL STRESS RELEASE

This is a simple, but powerful self-help tool which kinesiologists recommend to relieve tension and fear. You can do this to yourself, or get a friend to do it, which may be more effective.

● Make yourself comfortable. Place the tips of your fingers on the two mounds, about halfway between the eyebrows and the person's hairline, above the iris. The contact should be very light. Once you have made contact, stretch the skin up towards the hairline just one or two millimetres. Maintain steady, light pressure until there is relief from discomfort.

● The person who is looking for stress relief must concentrate on the nature of the problem that is causing the tension, so the tension can disappear. As long as the fingertips are kept on the front of the forehead, the pain, distress and hurt should melt away within minutes.

believe that their system of knowledge can help all forms of illness.

Consulting a practitioner

Before consulting a practitioner of kinesiology, check to see what kind of expertise and qualifications the person has. At present, the recognised form of kinesiology is Systematic Kinesiology, which is basically the same as the original form discovered by Goodheart. Make sure your therapist is qualified to give you advice in whatever other branch of complementary therapy they profess to know about.

At your first kinesiology session, the practitioner will start by taking your full health profile to assess if you have any major health problems. The first consultation takes about one and a half hours, and should cost around £30. Subsequent sessions last from half an hour to one hour, and should cost a little less — probably about £20.

A thorough examination is carried out by using a series of systematic tests on particular muscle groups. Some practitioners work with clothed clients, while others require you to strip to your underwear.

In the therapy session you are shown how to put an arm or leg in a particular position. You are asked to hold it steady and gentle pressure is applied for a few

seconds. Your ability to exert an equal and opposite pressure is assessed, then a series of touch tests are made to find out why any particular muscle is not 'firing' properly. More tests will reveal which imbalance needs correction first.

The practitioner then works on the appropriate corrective pressure points. Sometimes you may be asked to suck a vitamin or mineral supplement, or to concentrate on a particular anxiety or fear, while the practitioner works on the points. This is to enable the correction to be effective on physical, chemical, emotional and energetic planes so as to create a holistic balance. If a pressure point is sore, this is because of congestion caused by toxins building up in the tissues and impeding the flow of nervous or electrical impulses to and from the muscles to the brain.

Self help

The practitioner may suggest ways in which a person can help their own wellbeing. This may include dietary advice, ways of reducing levels of stress and tension, gentle exercises to practise at home or showing you how a partner or friend can massage the relevant pressure points.

Chronic problems may take several sessions before they begin to improve, but often an improvement in the main discomfort and in wellbeing can be felt almost immediately. The most common feeling patients experience after a 'balance', as kinesiology sessions are known, is that of lightness, as if a great weight has been lifted.

Useful Addresses

The Association of Systematic Kinesiology
39 Browns Road
Surbiton
Surrey KT5 8ST

The Association keeps a register of practitioners in the United Kingdom and Ireland. Members of the Association may also be qualified in other fields. Most of these practitioners have completed at least 200 hours practising kinesiology, and they may use kinesiology on its own or with other professional skills in natural therapies. Information and a list of practitioners in your area are available on request.

Energy Control

Macrobiotics is a philosophy based on the idea that every aspect of our lives involves a continuous balancing of two energies: yin and yang. Living according to these natural rhythms is said to create a deep sense of physical and mental well-being.

Macrobiotics is all about living in harmony with your environment, which means being in balance with it. The eastern idea of energy, that there is yin energy (which has qualities of coldness, expansion, softness) and yang energy (with qualities of warmth, contraction, hardness) underpins macrobiotics. The diet is based on balancing the yin and yang qualities in food, and you choose a diet which is suited to your personal requirements.

A macrobiotic counsellor sees diet as a vital way of helping the body return to full health. The founder, George Ohsawa, is said to have cured himself of tuberculosis by applying the ideas of ancient oriental medicine to his own diet and health. In terms of energy intake, the diet is very much along the lines of the current World Health Organisation recommendations of 55-75 per cent complex carbohydrate (grains, pulses, starchy vegetables and so on), 15-30 per cent fat and 10-15 per cent protein.

There are three broad categories of food: 'more yang' animal foods, 'more yin' plant foods and some plant foods which fall between the two. The main categories are listed below. Dairy foods are both yin and yang. Yin food is characterised by acidity, potassium, sugar and fruits; yang food by alkalinity and sodium.

Getting the right balance

A diet consisting mainly of yin foods is said to cause 'expansion' and 'weakening' in the body. A diet consisting mainly of yang foods is said to cause parts of the body to become 'hard' and 'contracted'. So the principle of the macrobiotic diet is to eat foods mainly from the group which falls in between the more extreme yin and yang foods (see below). They are thought to be more balanced and conducive to good health.

Disadvantages of the diet

Early macrobiotic teachings promoted brown rice as the most perfectly balanced food — a concept severely at odds with western nutritional thinking. Brown rice may do wonders for your yin-yang balance, but it cannot supply complete proteins and it is deficient in a number of vital vitamins and minerals. In their enthusiasm for macrobiotics, many people went overboard with the brown rice. This led to an outbreak of cases of malnutrition, resulting in scurvy, anaemia, and there were even a few deaths.

In the early days, the macrobiotic diet excluded animal foods because they are very yang. Dairy products were, and still are, considered unhealthy and 'mucus making', even though they are an important source of protein and concentrated energy in an otherwise meat-free diet. If the protein

THE MACROBIOTIC BALANCE

Most versions of the macrobiotic diet contain the same proportions of the main nutrients. The charts show where to find the yin and yang.

The standard macrobiotic diet

40-60% whole grains
25-40% vegetables
5-10% pulses (beans)
5% soup
5% fish, nuts, seeds, seasonings
3-4% sea vegetables

More yin foods	Balanced foods	More yang foods
alcohol	beans	eggs
coffee, tea	vegetables	meat
milk, cream	grains	fish
fruit and juices	nuts	poultry
herbs, spices	seeds	hard cheese
honey, sugar		
molasses		
vitamin C		
yoghurt		

and energy are to be adequately supplied by plant foods alone, the amount of grains or pulses which needs to be eaten may be too bulky. This can lead to nutritional deficiencies, particularly in babies and children.

It may be difficult to get enough vitamin B12 when following the diet. It is only available in food from animals, or specially treated food supplements. Deficiencies cause anaemia and, in severe cases, neurological disorder.

Changes in the diet

The brown-rice-only diet is no longer the ultimate goal of the macrobiotic diet. There now exists a standard macrobiotic diet based on the more balanced foods in the yin-yang scale and more in tune with western tastes. Unlike the early version of the diet, it includes a small amount of fish, which makes the protein content less bulky and ensures a supply of vitamin B12.

On a practical level, macrobiotics does create problems because it takes a lot of time and effort to prepare the food correctly. It is also quite an expensive diet to follow, as it advocates organic foods as well as expensive imported products from Japan. However, some people claim it gives them a renewed sense of life and improves their health.

> "Tao produced the One,
> The One produced the two.
> The two produced the three.
> And the three produced the tenthousand things.
> The ten thousand things carry the Yinand embrace the Yang
> And through the blending of the Ki
> They achieve harmony."

FOODS USED IN MACROBIOTICS

Once you have looked at the proportions of the main categories of food in the diet, it is necessary to look in detail at how they are cooked and prepared.

● **Whole grains and grain products** These are eaten at every meal and include rice, barley, wheat, millet, corn, buckwheat, wholewheat noodles, rolled oats, cous-cous, bulgar wheat. The milling process is thought to deprive grains of some of their vital energy, so products such as noodles, rolled oats etc should be eaten in smaller quantities than whole grains.

● **Vegetables** As wide as possible a variety of leafy greens, round and root vegetables should be used, preferably organically-grown. 75 per cent to be cooked, 25 per cent pickled or raw.

● **Sea vegetables** Dulse, hiziki, kelp, nori (laver), carageen (Irish moss) and wakame are available dried or fresh. They are sprinkled in soups, stews or salads or used like vine leaves. Carageen is a thickening agent.

● **Pulses and pulse products** These include chick peas, aduki beans, lentils, kidney beans, split peas and soya beans – eat about two tablespoons a day. Foods made from soya beans are miso (a fermented paste), tofu (a curd), tempeh (cakes of fermented beans) and soya milk.

● **Soups** Eaten daily with a variety of grains, pulses, sea vegetables and ordinary vegetables.

● **Seeds and nuts** Sesame, pumpkin and sunflower seeds, almonds, peanuts, brazil nuts, walnuts and hazelnuts – these are eaten as a snack or added to grain dishes, salads, vegetables and desserts. Can be roasted, ground and used as a seasoning. Sunflower butter, tahini (sesame seed paste) and peanut butter are used as a spread.

● **Fruit** Used dried or fresh, fruit is extremely yin so is eaten only two or three times a week. Choose fruit grown in the climate in which you live – anything else is thought to have a weakening effect.

● **Fish** This is eaten once or twice a week and provides protein in a more digestible form than meat or dairy foods. A yang food, but white-fleshed varieties are preferred as they are more yin. Shellfish is more yang and eaten only occasionally.

● **Seasonings** A small amount of sea salt is used in cooking but not added at table. Over-use makes you more yang, under-use more yin. Tamari, shoyu soy sauce and miso can be used instead of sea salt to season soups, salad dressings, gravies and sauces. Umeboshi are pickled green plums with a refreshingly sour taste. Highly alkaline, they are said to counteract overacidity and are used to flavour sauces and salad dressings. Rice vinegar is milder than other types so is more balanced. Used on vegetables and salads. Ginger, mustard and horseradish add heat and pungency to bland dishes.

● **Beverages** Coffee, tea, herb teas and fruit juice are very yin. Drinks used on a daily basis are bancha (twig tea), barleycup (grain coffee), dandelion coffee and spring water. Mu tea, apple juice, vegetable juices, camomile and lime blossom teas are used occasionally. Alcohol is yin but will be more yang if made from a grain rather than a fruit. Therefore wine is avoided and traditionally brewed beer, saki (rice wine) or whisky may be drunk occasionally.

Untreated rice forms an important part of the macrobiotic diet. Once polished, it loses much of its vital energy.

The Lingering Illness

ME or myalgic encephalomyelitis, to give it its full name, is a highly controversial disease which still puzzles both patients and doctors.

ME is a syndrome that can develop when a patient fails to make her expected recovery after viral infections such as influenza or gastroenteritis. The patient usually remembers one particular infection, which she believes to have been the starting point of the whole problem,

though sometimes it has a slow, insidious onset and it is not possible to pinpoint any one specific trigger. The initial infection may actually have been something rather trivial and may not even have been noticed.

Those who are particularly susceptible to ME tend to be active,

successful people in their late 20s and early 30s, which may go some way towards explaining its dismissal by the media when it was first discovered during the 1980s as 'yuppie 'flu'. It can also affect even younger people, including children.

ME is a fluctuating disease, characterised by setbacks and improvements that cannot easily be explained. Most sufferers do, in time, recover — many after several months, some even after several years. A small number of sufferers remain chronically ill, but this is rare.

It is important that ME should not be confused with post-viral debility, when a person simply feels rather 'low' or below par for a while after they have suffered a viral infection. ME is something far more serious.

What causes it?

ME is probably caused by damage to the immune system following a viral infection. Medical researchers have detected a number of abnormalities in sufferers from ME — particularly changes in the immune system and in the muscle cells — but have, as yet, been unable to point the finger at any one particular cause. The cause may also be a genetic defect in the victim's immune system.

There used to be a lot of sceptics who were reluctant to believe that ME really existed at all. When someone showed the symptoms of the disease, these critics were quick to say that the victim was just malingering in order to get a few days off work.

However, this sort of dismissive cynicism has largely evaporated in the light of increasingly strong medical advice. Although there are some doctors who remain sceptical, ME is now widely recognised as a debilitating and distressing illness.

ME used to be known as post-viral fatigue syndrome and, in many cases, this is probably a rather more appropriate name. Myalgic encephalomyelitis literally means inflammation of the brain and spinal cord, which is quite wrong and — were

DEALING WITH THE DISEASE

If you are suffering from ME, it is all too easy to sit back and let the illness take over. Many people have found ways of coping with the illness, and you may find some or all of the following courses of action helpful.

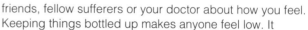

● Start by finding out all you can about ME. Contact the ME Association and read as much as you can about the illness. Make it your friend – no matter how much you hate it – and become familiar with its pattern of ups and downs. Reading about the subject may help you to work out what seems to bring these about.

● Don't overdo things. Learn to recognise when your body is telling you that enough is enough. Avoid the temptation to catch up on things when you're feeling a little better because that could be just enough to push you back downhill.

● Learn to pace yourself and find a healthy balance – for you – between rest and activity.

● Keep a diary, to note down details of the course of the illness. Include a record of your diet, activities and symptoms. This may help you to identify a pattern. Only you can really know what alleviates or worsens your condition.

● Try to develop a particular interest which, while not too taxing, will help you to fill your time and so stave off the danger of depression and loneliness. Take up knitting, develop an interest in music through the radio or records, become the world's leading Scrabble expert, or start a scrapbook.

● If you get depressed, talk to family,

friends, fellow sufferers or your doctor about how you feel. Keeping things bottled up makes anyone feel low. It always helps to know that there are other people with the same problem.

● Avoid alcohol and coffee, which seem to make the symptoms worse for many sufferers.

● If you suspect that you have developed a sensitivity to certain foods (which you may be able to identify from your diary), it is sensible to cut them out. But continue to eat a balanced diet, eat fresh rather than processed foods, and avoid additives. This is good nutritional advice for everyone, whether they suffer from ME or not.

● Keep in touch with your doctor and the ME Association, who may be able to keep you informed about new research into diet. If there's anything in particular that worries you about your diet, discuss it with your doctor.

● Try to avoid catching infections, by all means, but don't wrap yourself in cotton wool and cut yourself off from other people more than is absolutely necessary. Isolation will do nothing to relieve any symptoms of depression. You must aim to live as normal a life as possible while you have the illness.

● Avoid, as far as you can, certain medications such as antibiotics, vaccinations and anaesthetics, which have been known to make some people with ME feel worse.

● Finally, although it may sound trite, it's actually very important that you keep your pecker up! Stay hopeful and remember that you will get better.

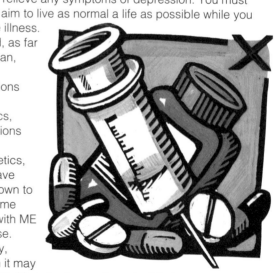

SYMPTOMS OF ME

The symptoms of ME are many and varied, and are shared by many other illnesses, which means that ME may be hard to diagnose. Common symptoms include:

- Extreme exhaustion
- Muscle fatigue/muscle weakness/muscle pains, particularly after exercise/muscle twitches
- Lethargy
- Dizziness/headaches
- Nausea
- Upset bowel
- Visual disturbances
- Ringing in the ears
- Swollen glands
- Frequent need to pass urine
- Disturbed sleep
- Chest pains
- Localised sweating
- Pins and needles
- Cold limbs/shivering fits/low body temperature
- Persistent, itchy skin rash
- Noticeable difficulty in concentrating/confused thoughts/memory problems
- Fragile emotions/panic states/changeable moods

British yachtswoman Clare Francis has suffered from ME for several years and is president of the ME Action Campaign which she helped found in 1987.

people to understand it — totally misleading. It has also been called Iceland disease, epidemic neuromyasthenia and Royal Free Disease (after an outbreak of a mysterious disease at the Royal Free Hospital in London in the 1950s). Dr Elizabeth Dowsett, who is a consultant microbiologist and Vice President of the ME Association, told a conference on ME in Cambridge in 1990 that it is estimated that there may be as many as 150,000 sufferers in the UK. Women are said to be three times more likely to suffer from the disease than men.

Treatment
There is, as yet, no evidence that any particular treatment is effective in combating ME. That doesn't mean you won't get better — you will — and there's a lot to be said for that age-old friend we have all learned to know and love: Time, the Great Healer.

Diagnosis is difficult, because tests have to be done to rule out other causes of the many disparate symptoms associated with ME.

However, early diagnosis is an important step. This not only reduces the stress involved for both sufferer and family, but also makes it possible to manage the disease in an appropriate and positive way.

Misdiagnosis can lead to the wrong advice, and this can have a negative effect. Referral for active physiotherapy, for example, or an attempt to 'snap out of it' or exercise your way to better health will probably only make you feel worse. Setbacks are often brought on by a sufferer doing too much too soon.

This can greatly prolong the patient's recovery period. It is a great deal more appropriate to ensure that there is better management of the disease than to search for its 'cure'. There simply isn't one.

The management of ME
The best way of managing ME is to ensure that the sufferer gets sufficient rest, particularly during the early stages and at those times when the sufferer has a setback. Sufficient rest does not, however, necessarily mean a period of prolonged bed rest.

Bed rest may help during the initial, acute stage, but — beyond that — the danger of prolonged bed rest is that the sufferer may become trapped in a vicious circle of immobility and weakness: the longer the sufferer stays in bed, the weaker they are likely to feel, and so on.

Within these very general guidelines, the sufferer will have to find the particular level of combined rest and activity which is most effective for

YOUR HEALTH

COMPLEMENTARY MEDICINE

Alternative treatments that have been found to have some success with ME include:

- Acupuncture, which is used generally to stimulate the immune system and to produce increased energy and strength.
- Aromatherapy, which relaxes, alleviates tiredness and helps to promote sleep.

- Hydrotherapy, which stimulates the circulation, promotes relaxation and is particularly beneficial to anyone suffering from insomnia.
- Herbalism, which can promote rest and increase strength.
- Homeopathy, which is said to have offered great relief to many sufferers. However, be sure to consult an experienced homeopath before starting homeopathic treatment.

ADVICE FOR CARERS

ME can be an extremely debilitating disease and, when looking after a sufferer, you need to exercise great patience, sensitivity and understanding. You may find the following helpful:

● Be sensitive to the distress the sufferer feels in becoming dependent on you. Avoid being patronising.

● Never tell the sufferer to 'get a grip' or 'pull herself together'. This is never helpful and can only worsen matters.

● Be careful not to add to the sufferer's loss of self-confidence. Encourage her to keep up appearances – to dress well, apply make-up, look after her hair and so on.

● Do not leave the sufferer out of any family discussions and decisions. Make sure she is always involved, just as much as before the illness.

● Try not to be impatient. Accept any sudden changes in mood or unexpected alterations to plans for what they are: an integral part of the illness and quite beyond the sufferer's control. Do not get irritated – or at least don't allow your irritation to show!

● Keep the sufferer's surroundings as pleasant and cheerful as possible but be careful about this – there's a difference between trying to be cheerful and being insensitively cheery. Avoid the intrusion of any great stress or loud noise.

● Encourage the sufferer to have some fresh air. This may mean nothing more than sitting in the garden – weather permitting, of course – in the early days, with short walks further afield as strength and stamina return. Such outings can bring a sense of achievement which, in turn, can be a great morale booster.

● Without seeming to intrude, make sure the sufferer keeps in touch with her doctor. If you see any persistent or worsening depression, you may need to step in and seek medical advice for them.

● Help the sufferer to talk about her illness so that she can get some of the depression off her chest. Don't

only talk about this, though, and try to enlarge your sphere of conversation and interest.

● Encourage visitors – they can lessen a sufferer's all too understandable sense of isolation.

● Do not be dismissive about anything the sufferer may wish to try – complementary medicine, perhaps, or a change in diet. It is important for the sufferer to do something positive, and any attempt, however silly it may seem to you, should be encouraged.

● Be particularly observant as you watch the course of the illness on a day-to-day basis. Try to notice anything that seems to make the sufferer feel either better or worse – be it food, drinks, household chemicals – and take appropriate action.

herself, and this level can only be discovered through a process of experiment and experience.

Self-help

A lot of people feel better if they take some sort of responsibility for their own health and contribute positively to their own health care. There is nothing more depressing for many people than giving in to illness and abandoning themselves to the care — excellent though this may be — of other people. In general, people do not like feeling dependent on others and, in some cases, this can lead to a serious loss of self-confidence.

> " Blessings on him who invented sleep,
> the mantle that covers
> All human thoughts,
> The food that satisfies hunger,
> The drink that slakes thirst,
> The fire that warms cold,
> The cold that moderates heat,
> and, lastly,
> The common currency that buys all things,
> The balance and weight that equalises
> The shepherd and the king,
> The simpleton and the sage."
>
> *Miguel de Cervantes*

Overdoses of Goodness

People who undergo megavitamin therapy believe that a greatly increased intake of certain vitamins will help them to resist disease and will slow down the ageing process.

Our bodies need the correct balance of vitamins and minerals in order to function smoothly. Because of this, the theory was put forward that an imbalance of nutrients could be the cause of reduced lifespan, and any number of diseases ranging from the common cold to cancer. Proponents of the theory went on to suggest that if the tissues are flooded with very large amounts of a vitamin, or combination of vitamins, the balance will be restored and this will cure any disease that has occurred previously, as well as preventing future diseases and slowing down the ageing process.

The idea is an attractive one — especially as vitamins are generally perceived as being beneficial and without the nasty side effects of conventional drugs. They are also currently available without prescription. So what better way of perking yourself up without having to go to the doctor and, even if you're not actually ill, becoming 'superhealthy'? It all sounds like a good idea but the trend for megadosing on vitamins has actually caused alarm among the medical community and resulted in a number of cases of toxicity.

Unique results

Megavitamin therapy was first developed in the United States in the 1950s, when it was noticed that some of the symptoms of schizophrenia resembled those of pellagra, a disease caused by severe deficiency of nicotinamide (a constituent of vitamin B3).

Treatment of a group of schizophrenics with massive doses of this vitamin produced encouraging results. Unfortunately no one has ever been able to repeat the results in subsequent tests. Nevertheless, claims were still made that megavitamin therapy could cure a wide range of psychiatric illnesses and the treatment continued to gain in popularity.

Enthusiastic support also came from Dr Linus Pauling, a distinguished American scientist and Nobel Prize winner. He called the therapy 'orthomolecular' medicine, from 'ortho' meaning optimum or best. It was Dr Pauling who promoted the idea that massive doses of vitamin C were an effective treatment for the common cold. Even though research work provides little conclusive evidence to support the theory, vitamin C sales continue to rocket in winter.

Despite the fact that the American Psychiatric Association later repudiated many of the earlier claims, megadoses of vitamins were hailed as the cure-all for a whole range of conditions, including alcoholism, hyperactivity in children and depression. The trend continued into the 1970s and 80s, boosted by health clubs, gyms and fitness magazines.

A tempting idea

The idea that there might be a relatively easy way out of unpleasant diseases is a very tempting one, as is being able to delay signs of ageing and enjoying an increase in your energy levels, libido and general well-being. The idea of 'self-help' is also very attractive and is preferable to long waits in the doctor's surgery for treatment of fairly mild complaints.

What is a megadose?

It's important not to confuse normal vitamin supplementation with megadosing. In megavitamin therapy, the quantities taken are extremely high. For instance, Dr Pauling suggested that the daily requirement of vitamin C to achieve perfect health should be a minimum of 3g per day — over a hundred times the Estimated Average Requirement in Britain. (The Estimated Average Requirement (EAR) and the Reference Nutrient Intake (RNI) have replaced the Recommended Daily Intake values for nutrients which were previously recommended by the Department of Health.)

Megavitamin therapy enthusiasts have recommended daily doses of up to 50,000 micrograms of vitamin A (over 100 times the EAR) to help cure colds, cystitis, diabetes and varicose veins. Amounts varying from 50mg to 7g per day of vitamin B6 have been recommended to help counter pre-menstrual tension and the undesirable side effects of the Pill.

However, in reality, megadoses of vitamins are necessary only in very specialised situations, for example when the body is unable to absorb enough vitamins from the stomach or in certain diseases where vitamins are not functioning in the body as they should. In such cases, vitamin levels are carefully monitored and any vitamins needed should be prescribed only by qualified medical personnel.

Vitamin pills may seem harmless but taking megadoses in an arbitrary manner without medical or dietetic advice can lead to trouble. Many essential nutrients are toxic if we take them in excess. Moreover, because vitamins and minerals often combine to work as a team it's important to maintain a balance within each team. For example, taking excess vitamin B6 can cause an imbalance within the B group as a whole.

Withdrawal symptoms

One of the problems with prolonged vitamin overdosing is that the body develops a way of destroying and eliminating the excess. It continues to do so for some time after the megadosing has stopped and then real deficiencies arise. For example, cases of scurvy have been reported in some people after they have stopped megadosing on vitamin C. A similar effect occurred in the case of several babies who had seizures caused by vitamin B6 deficiency — a result of their mothers taking 5-300g per day during pregnancy.

It's likely that most of us will benefit from short periods of normal, as opposed to mega, vitamin supplementation at some point in our lives. The very young, the elderly, pregnant women and those breastfeeding are likely to need supplementation, as are alcoholics and the chronically ill. You may be at risk of deficiency if you're slimming, or following a vegetarian diet. On the whole, however, if you eat a healthy and varied diet containing a good range of nutrients, you will be getting all the vitamins you will need from your food.

POTENTIAL DANGER OF MEGADOSES

With each vitamin there is a different level of consumption at which a megadose can become dangerous, depending on the vitamin's function in the body.

Vitamin A (EAR per day for a female adult: 400mcg) A fat-soluble vitamin which becomes highly toxic once the capacity of the liver to store it has been exceeded. Symptoms of toxicity include fatigue, irritability, loss of appetite and weight, nausea, cracked lips, dry skin. Severe toxicity causes swellings in the liver and pains in the joints. Overdosing during pregnancy is a possible cause of birth defects.

Thiamin (vitamin B1) (EAR 0.8mg) Prolonged intake in excess of 3g per day will often cause headaches, irritability, insomnia, a rapid pulse rate, weakness, dermatitis and pruritus.

Riboflavin (vitamin B2) (EAR 0.9mg) This vitamin has a very low solubility rate which prevents its absorption in the amounts which would be likely to cause toxicity.

Niacin (vitamin B3) (EAR 13mg) 3-6g per day can cause changes in liver function, carbohydrate tolerance and in uric acid metabolism, resulting in toxicity. Doses in excess of 200mg per day can cause flushing, dilation of blood vessels and a fall in blood pressure.

Vitamin B6 (EAR 1.2mg) Doses of 2-7g per day have caused impaired function of sensory nerves in fingertips.

Vitamin B12 (EAR 1.25mcg) Very low toxicity. High doses appear to have no harmful effect.

Vitamin C (EAR 25mg) Doses in excess of 600g per day have caused diarrhoea and an increased risk of developing kidney stones.

Vitamin D (no EAR for adults as we get enough from sunlight) Supplements are toxic when taken in excess. The difference between a toxic dose (50mcg per day) and a therapeutic dose (10mcg per day) is small, so always stick to the recommended dose for children.

Vitamin E (EAR none, as widely available in food) Vitamin E supplements are safer than other fat-soluble vitamins but high doses have caused gastrointestinal problems. High doses also cause excessive bleeding in people taking anticoagulants (blood thinning tablets).

Naturopathy is one of the oldest forms of complementary medicine — the principles it uses go right back to antiquity, when the Greeks and Romans advocated simple nature cures to combat disease. In many respects, naturopathy is based on common sense — if we all ate sensibly, exercised in fresh air, rested adequately and relaxed properly, then there would be considerably less illness in the world. There is nothing new or complex about naturopathy at all, but often the oldest and simplest ideas are the best.

When did it begin?

The basis of modern naturopathic theory started over 150 years ago in a small village, Grafenberg, in the Silesian mountains. A farmer called Vincent Priessnitz advocated the use of fresh air, applications of cold water and a diet of wholesome food such as black bread, vegetables and fresh cow's milk to cure his family and friends. Another farmer evolved a system of treating rheumatic sufferers with a strict dietary regime, combined with water treatments known as hydrotherapy.

From then on, naturopathy developed, with further refinement of the major principles, until it reached its present-day definition. According to The General Council and Register of Naturopaths it is "a system of primary care medicine which seeks to facilitate and promote the body's inherent physiological self-healing mechanisms".

A natural 'life force'

Fundamental to naturopathy is the belief in the existence of the 'life force' — that elusive and indefinable energy within humans which is said to keep us alive and healthy. Naturopathic theory promotes the belief that it is our natural healing abilities that can cure us of any ailments, rather than drugs or other external agents. The naturopath aims to

Nature's Cure

Using only natural elements such as food, rest, water, sunlight and relaxation, the naturopath tries to stimulate the body into healing itself. But can such simple measures really work?

stimulate the natural life force within the patient, using equally natural means.

The naturopath tries to view the patient as a whole, assessing their general life style and ascertaining what treatments or special requirements would suit the individual. The first meeting with a naturopath takes over an hour or so, during which a detailed case history of the patient is drawn up. There is a physical examination, including readings of your blood pressure and

pulse rate, and a look at your posture, as well as the condition of your hair, skin, nails and tongue.

It might then be necessary to progress to blood tests, urine analysis and x-rays. Naturopaths tend to have their own specific backgrounds in other complementary therapies, so some might be keen to have a mineral analysis done on a sample of your hair, for example, or to measure various pulses throughout your body with a view

Drinking plenty of spa water helps flush toxins from our bodies which are passed on from pollution in the atmosphere and food additives.

to using acupuncture. Some use iridology — the study of the iris of the eye — as a diagnostic tool.

The treatments

Naturopathic treatments are designed to restore the body's homeostasis, or balance. Therapists aren't tied down to specific formulae for illness, so the treatment is different for each patient. Basically though, there are two approaches. If a patient's body is weak and needs building up with supplements, then they will be advised to follow a good wholesome diet with lots of rest,

relaxation, gentle manipulation, and counselling to ensure a positive mental attitude. If a patient is diagnosed as having an excess of toxins (poisons) in their body, which means that it needs purifying, they would be required to follow a strict diet or fasting and a course of internal and external hydrotherapy, stimulating exercises and manipulative therapy.

Does it work?

Naturopathy appears to have been successful for many years. How successful it is in each case depends on the level of motivation of the patient and how serious the conditions or illnesses are. It is important to realise that the therapist is basically re-educating the client into a healthier way of living, so it really depends on how far the individual wants to go in changing or improving their own life style.

A naturopath never claims to cure an illness, but instead she aims to help the body overcome the ailment itself. In cases of cancer, the naturopath helps the patient come to terms with the disease as much as she can, and tries to alleviate some of the condition, but never expects a total cure.

Naturopaths do say that their treatments are good for children, however, because the child has more natural vitality, and seems to respond to this type of treatment much more readily than an adult.

TYPES OF TREATMENT

These are the main treatments that a naturopath will usually recommend:

FASTING Contrary to popular belief, a fast is not a period of starvation. If done sensibly under supervision, the fast is an opportunity for overworked digestive organs to have a rest. You can fast on fruit juice, fruit, water or even on plain brown rice. Some people claim that the temporary lack of food boosts the immune system's resonse to disease. Others would claim that it works as a basic purification of the body.

HYDROTHERAPY Water treatments are very common in naturopathic practice. Treatments can include cold or hot applications of water for bathing, or use as sprays, compresses, packs, steam baths, ice poultices, or in irrigation of the colon. Enemas are also quite commonly used as they enable the bowel to be cleansed during the fast.

DIET A nutritious wholefood diet is usually recommended, with the minimum of processed artificial foodstuffs. Many naturopaths recommend a vegetarian diet, and one that is mainly based on raw foods. Where possible, people are also encouraged to eat organic food. Some naturopaths will recommend that you take vitamin supplements, but strict nature-cure therapists claim that they are unnecessary as you only need to eat healthily in order to get your minerals and vitamin requirements.

You might be recommended to follow the Hay Diet if you have digestive problems. Unarguably, nutrition is a fundamental part of health, and the therapist places great importance on getting it right. There is a whole range of nutrition therapies which now abound within complementary medicine and which originate from naturopathic principles.

AIR AND SUNLIGHT Getting out into the fresh air is good for the mind as well as the body. You might be advised to take air baths, which basically involve wandering about without any clothes on for a few minutes, so that your skin can breathe. Naturopaths also believe in the benefits of ionisation and might advise you to take a holiday in a spa resort, or a mountainous area with plenty of waterfalls.

Your naturopath should also be skilled in counselling methods, and be able to tell you about relaxation techniques and meditation where appropriate. As naturopaths perceive the importance of the link between mind and body, they will try to sort out any underlying emotional problems you might have.

> "The cure of the part should not be attempted without the treatment of the whole. No attempt should be made to cure the body without the soul and, if the head and body are to be healthy, you must begin by curing the mind."
>
> *Plato*

> "A wise man ought to realise that health is his most valuable possession."
>
> *Hippocrates*

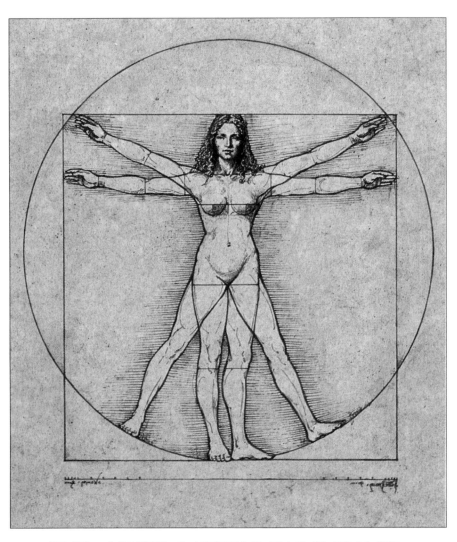

BRAVE NEW WORLD

Whether we like it or not, the so-called 'New Age' is here with a vengeance. But is it really so new? And has it got anything really worthwhile to offer?

The term 'New Age' is usually used to cover a huge variety of beliefs and activities, and — depending on the attitude of the person using it — can be used either as a term of approval or a downright insult. Generally, New Agers tend to believe in alternative (or complementary) medicine, self-help, spiritual awareness, equality of the sexes, respect for the planet and a sense of personal responsibility for the future.

Anyone can subscribe to New Age views. Famous British New Agers include the aristocratic Sir George Trevelyan (founder of the influential Wrekin Trust) and many stars of stage and screen, such as Charles

Dance, Sarah Miles and Kate Bush. Although many people tend towards New Age views naturally, many more people turn to them as a reaction to today's life style, which they see as overmaterialistic, empty and unfulfilling.

'New Ages' over the years

No matter how enlightened we may think we are today, throughout history other generations have had a similar sense of being pioneers in a 'brave new world'. The first Christians imagined themselves to be heralding the ultimate New Age, with their radically different message and practices. They also believed that they were living in what they called the

Latter Days, with the Day of Judgment just around the corner.

The coming of the end of the first millenium in 999 AD, seemed to provoke widespread panic and a certainty that the world was going to end. Strange religions and cults sprang up, allied to the belief that there were omens and signs predicting the end of the world everywhere. Since then the world has seen many new beginnings, and just as many false starts. Mankind seems to have an endless optimism and belief in the future, which is just as well, considering how badly many best intentions turn out!

The wisdom of the East

As a reaction to the materialism of the 1950s, there was a great upsurge in interest in spiritual matters and many people turned to the East for inspiration. In particular the 1960s saw the proliferation of gurus ('teachers'), who provided a new direction for those who had everything — the sixties group The Beatles, for example, who gave up the bright lights to sit at the feet of the Mahareshi and contemplate the wisdom of the East. Buddhist or Hindu thinking became extremely trendy in the West — and it still remains influential today among certain groups of New Agers.

Indeed, it was in the 1960s that the modern New Age could truly be said to have begun. The rise of Flower Power and the Make Love Not War campaign led to an increased awareness of the inner self and the popularity of meditation and spiritual seeking. The Beat Generation of writers such as Jack Kerouac and Allen Ginsberg emphasised the need to reject materialistic values, and the Human Potential Movement of the 1970s spread rapidly with its message of self-help and limitless personal potential. If nothing else, hope was born.

Go to any Festival of Mind, Body and Spirit in London — or any big city — and you will get a taste of what the New Age is all about. It may well prove to be an acquired taste, and one that you feel is not for you. There are usually hundreds of stalls selling crystals, dowsing rods, joss sticks, aromatherapy oils, meditation and self-hypnosis videos, and booths offering anything from a session of reflexology (specialist foot massage) to healing and instant enlightenment.

At best it may seem something of a circus to you — at worst, something of a con. But behind all the razzamatazz there is a central message, and one that is surely worthy of respect. The New Age is all about an attempt to harmonise mind, body and spirit ('holism'), and to treat the whole person, rather than just isolated symptoms or problems. It is also concerned with raising human consciousness, and putting you in touch with your Higher Self. Awakening this 'inner God' is believed to be magically transformative, so that anyone can become fundamentally changed for the better — given the right beliefs and techniques.

Enlightenment

Sometimes it seems as if hardly a month goes by without a new, improved system emerging (usually from California) to offer the world enlightenment. The latest craze is the Life Extension Plan (LEP), which aims to promote healthy, enlightened life well beyond the Biblical threescore years and ten. That may sound reasonable enough, but then along comes the Flame Foundation (originally from Arizona) with the promise, not just of long life, but of physical immortality!

However, despite the apparent craziness of much New Age thinking, there is usually something at the core of it which is worth digging for. For example, the emphasis on combating stress

New Age Success

The New Age may seem silly in many ways, but already it has had some major achievements.

By its steady insistence on the effectiveness of alternative therapies such as acupuncture and chiropractic, even the ultra-conservative medical profession has had to accept the New Age. As one GP put it: "People are voting with their feet and going to healers for help rather than coming to see me. I have to admit, I want to know why."

It would seem that we have the New Age to thank for the greater choice of health care that we have today, besides a greater awareness of environmental and women's issues. However, if the New Age is not to degenerate into just another welter of cranky religions and oddball food fads, then each of us has a responsibility to save it.

through meditative techniques, of learning to help oneself overcome illness by harnessing the power of the mind, and of protecting the environment for future generations, is surely worthy of consideration.

A Living Saint?

One guru who has achieved almost divine status among followers in the West is Sai Baba, an Indian holy man whom many revere as a 'living Hindu saint'.

An engagingly jolly personality, Sai Baba is most famous for his apparently paranormal production of objects from thin air, including hot food. He has also produced religious medals from nowhere for his Christian friends, and once materialised a *photgraph* of Hindu gods which he instructed his followers to dig for on a beach. He has also been seen in two places in the world at the same time – a phenomenon known as 'bilocation' – just like the Catholic saints of old. However, his most astonishing feat was raising a man from the dead – several days after he had died!

Investigations

Obviously such amazing feats have attracted criticism and scepticism. Intrigued by stories of Sai Baba's miracles, several western parapsychologists – a breed of investigators not known for their credulity – subjected him to rigorous examination for several years in the 1970s and 80s. One of these investigators, the Icelandic parapsychologist Erlandur Haraldsson, concluded that the miracles were genuine. Professor Haraldsson confessed to being utterly baffled by Sai Baba, but even under the most meticulous observation, the hot food appeared for visitors and the sick were healed, often dramatically.

During the early years of his fame in the West, Sai Baba was often regarded with suspicion by the New Age, who tended to prefer more contemplative and enigmatic gurus. However, he has become considerably more accepted recently, perhaps because some New Agers have tired of gurus who merely utter words of wisdom, going instead for one who – apparently – really delivers miracles.

Eating Naturally

Traditionally associated with health-food shops and sandal-wearing vegetarians, organic produce has shed its cranky image and is now readily available in supermarkets.

We often hear the word 'organic' — but what does it really mean? The term basically refers to matter which has been formed from living things. Organic farming, therefore, relies on natural compounds such as manure and rotted compost from plant matter to fertilise crops. These substances make a soil structure rich in humus and nutrients which are then taken up by plants. Soil fertility is built up by rotating crops and by planting legumes (members of the pea and bean family) which collect nitrogen from the air and transfer it to the soil.

In organic farming, pests and diseases are controlled without the use of chemicals. Natural predators are encouraged, and because these predators are not themselves poisoned with chemicals, nature's balance is thought to be maintained. Other methods used are mechanised weeding (rather than chemical weedkillers), the use of traps and barriers and the timing of crops to avoid pests. Other characteristics of organic farming are

the humane and responsible treatment of livestock and the practice of an extensive, mixed farming system (which means farming both crops and animals). This often comes as a surprise to consumers as there is a widespread and mistaken belief that organic food is purely vegetarian. But in fact, successful organic farming is essentially about creating a balance between crops and livestock.

The aim of organic farmers and gardeners is to produce food which:

● Has a superior flavour rather than a perfect appearance.
● Is grown using organic fertilisers and methods of pest and disease control.
● Contains no artificial hormones or genetically manipulated organisms.
● Is produced using methods which minimise damage to the environment and which encourage the proliferation of wildlife on farms.
● Treats animals as humanely as possible.
● Promotes positive health and well-

being in the consumer.
● Is never irradiated.
● Does not contain additives and is not overprocessed.

Why does organic food cost so much?

It cannot be denied that organic produce costs much more than conventionally grown food. This is partly because there is such a huge demand for it — and when supply cannot meet demand, prices are high. Secondly, because the demand is so great, about 60 to 70 per cent of fresh organic produce has to be imported from abroad where prices are higher to begin with. Thirdly, organic farmers receive no extra EC subsidies.

Under the EC Common Agricultural Policy, conventional farmers receive subsidies and a guaranteed price for their crops, regardless of how much or how little is needed or produced. Conventionally grown produce may appear to be cheaper, but as these subsidies are paid for from taxes, most of us indirectly contribute to them.

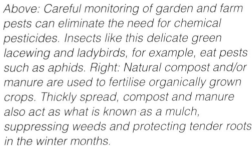

Above: Careful monitoring of garden and farm pests can eliminate the need for chemical pesticides. Insects like this delicate green lacewing and ladybirds, for example, eat pests such as aphids. Right: Natural compost and/or manure are used to fertilise organically grown crops. Thickly spread, compost and manure also act as what is known as a mulch, suppressing weeds and protecting tender roots in the winter months.

Is organic food really safe to eat?

You would think that if organic food is grown without resorting to artificial fertilisers and pesticides, it must be 'chemical-free'. In practice it is not that simple. We live in a polluted world and chemical residues drift across the planet on wind and water, sometimes persisting for decades. So even organic food can be contaminated by stray chemicals. However, the few chemical analyses which have been made of organic food show the samples tested to be free from contamination.

Some people may be put off by the fact that organic fruit and vegetables have a 'homegrown' look, in other words, you may be sharing your organic apple with a caterpillar! All fruit and vegetables, even organically grown ones, need to be washed thoroughly before use to remove any unwanted creatures and dirt.

Standards

In order to establish recognised standards of organic agricultural practice and food production, a number of organisations and programmes have

been set up. These include the Soil Association, Organic Farmers and Growers Ltd (OFG). None of them has been entirely successful in unifying standards but some progress is being made and there are now EEC regulations and UK standards.

Probably the most well-known organisation is the Soil Association, which was set up as long ago as 1946. Their standards define the principles and practice of arable, horticultural and animal production; crop rotation and management; the requirements for processing and distributing organic food; and the standards for manufacturing organic industrial products such as fertilisers, composts and plant protection products.

The Soil Association symbol is awarded to farmers and growers, as well as to food processors and industrial manufacturers, who follow the criteria laid down by the Association (see Useful Information, overleaf). In order to qualify for this seal of approval, a farmer's land must have been free from artificial fertilisers and chemical sprays for at least two years.

Why has organic food become popular?

There is nothing new or revolutionary about organic growing methods. In the past, farms were always mixed, with animals as well as food crops, so there was a plentiful supply of manure to recycle on to the fields. Then, in the 1960s, artificial fertilisers, chemical pesticides and weedkillers came along.

Suddenly, farmers began to increase their crops dramatically and market gardeners grew fruit and vegetables which were bigger and looked better than ever before. Pests and diseases became a thing of the past as regular spraying programmes were introduced. Those diseases or organisms which showed resistance were treated with newer, more powerful chemicals.

Eventually, consumers and environmentalists began to voice fears about chemical residues making food unsafe and destroying the balance of nature, but they were assured by the experts that all the chemicals were government safety-tested and any that failed to meet the stringent requirements were rejected. But consumers and pressure groups continued to worry, particularly as the testing methods for some of the early pesticides were a lot less stringent. Farming methods are being questioned and changes demanded.

At the same time farmers, gardeners and scientists have begun to acknowledge both the catastrophic effects of these chemical methods on nature's balance and the truth of the old saying 'you must put back into the soil as much as, or more than, you take out'. So now we appear to have come full circle — enlightened farmers and market gardeners are returning to organic methods and organically grown food is increasingly available in supermarkets and shops.

Although organic food has been available for many years, it was usually regarded as a 'fringe' product. Its recent widespread upsurge in popularity is for a mixture of reasons. Many of us buy it because we are increasingly concerned about our health and wish to reduce the risk of exposure to chemical residues. Some of us buy it because we care about the environment. We believe that organic growing methods make ecological sense and are better for the planet. And for some people, buying organic food is an important trend of the 'caring nineties'. They buy it in order to be 'seen to be Green'.

Whatever the reason, there is no doubt that sales of organic food have risen dramatically in the past few years. A market research survey carried out by

Mintel in 1990 found that 72 per cent of consumers were interested in buying organic fresh fruit; and Safeway found that 57 per cent of us were willing to pay 10 per cent more for organic food.

Where can we get organic food?

At one time, supplies of organically grown produce were limited to health-food shops, or you had to go to the grower to find what you wanted. Supermarkets used not to stock organic produce because supplies of home-grown fresh produce were intermittent and growers had problems with large-scale distribution. Supermarkets also demanded blemish-free and uniformly shaped produce, believing that this was

what consumers preferred. Because organic produce tends not to conform to these requirements, shelf space allocated to it was non-existent or minimal. Instead, we were confronted with rows of uniform but often tasteless fruit and vegetables.

However, the supermarkets have tried to overcome the problems associated with sporadic supply by importing from larger organic growers abroad. They have also found that consumers are obviously willing to ignore the odd blemish or bite out of a leaf. As a result, some of the major supermarkets now have a reasonably sized organic section. Although the supermarkets originally did much to lift

GROW YOUR OWN

If you want to escape supermarket shrink-wrapped produce and enjoy utterly fresh, flavourful fruit and vegetables, you could try growing your own using organic methods.

Even if you think you do not have time or only have room for a row of pots on a windowsill, gardening can be immensely rewarding. It is also a vital part of the green revolution.

There are plenty of books and magazines about organic gardening and the Henry Doubleday Research Association (see Useful Information, overleaf) provides its members with excellent advice and support.

If you don't have room to grow vegetables in the garden, consider getting an allotment through your local council.

the image of organic food, many local growers now feel that the produce they import is expensive and of inferior quality. As a result, some growers also feel that the supermarkets' involvement is doing damage to the public's perception of organic food.

If you find that the organic produce in your local supermarket looks a bit tired and old, you may do better to try an organic farm or market garden if you know of one locally. Many of these have small shops attached with a good range of produce on sale.

Does organic food taste better?

According to blind tasting trials carried out earlier this year by *The Independent* newspaper, organic food is a winner. The difference in flavour and texture between conventional and organically grown carrots was considered 'stunning', although the difference was less marked in potatoes. Organic Comice pears were 'sweet and aromatic' while the conventional ones were 'tough-skinned, tasteless and grainy'. In the baked goods category, cakes made with organic eggs, butter and flour had a much better flavour and lighter texture.

Surprisingly, organic meat fared less well in the trials, with chicken only marginally on top and steak being considered inferior. The panel concluded that although the organic fresh fruit and vegetables tested were infinitely superior to conventional produce, organic was not necessarily a guarantee of quality. Much depends on the skill of the growers in producing quality food.

Is organic food more nutritious?

Not much is known about the nutritional differences between organic and conventionally grown food and much more research is needed. However, it is possible to make a few generalisations.

Conventionally produced food usually has a 20 per cent higher water content. This is why some varieties of fruit and vegetables are so large, and why bacon oozes liquid when you try to grill it. The increased water content not only accounts for lack of flavour but also suggests that, weight for weight, fewer nutrients may be present. Organically produced food tends to have a more concentrated flavour, and also has a higher vitamin C and magnesium content.

PRODUCE THAT CAN BE ORGANIC

The term organic food includes not only fruit and vegetables, but also dry goods such as cereals and pulses, wine from grapes which have been grown by organic methods, and meat and dairy produce from animals which have been reared on a diet free from hormones and antibiotics.

- Flour
- Wholegrains, flakes and rice
- Breakfast cereals and oats
- Crispbreads
- Pasta
- Preserves, vinegars and condiments
- Fresh and dried fruit
- Fruit juices
- Vegetables
- Herbs
- Pulses
- Nuts
- Tea and coffee
- Crisps and snacks
- Milk
- Butter
- Yogurt
- Baby foods
- Cheese
- Meat
- Poultry
- Eggs
- Oils
- Wine
- Beer
- Cider

Organic Recipes

Ratatouille (4)
2 organic aubergines, chopped
2 organic courgettes, chopped
1 organic green pepper, chopped
1 organic onion, sliced
9oz (250g) organic tomatoes
3 cloves organic garlic, crushed
1 tbsp (15ml) fresh organic basil
2 tbsp (30ml) organic olive oil
salt and pepper

Put the aubergine and courgette into a colander, sprinkle with salt, and leave to stand for 30 minutes. Place a plate inside the colander and press firmly to squeeze out moisture. Skin the tomatoes, squeeze away the seeds and chop. Heat the oil in a saucepan and fry the onion and garlic for 10 minutes. Wipe the aubergines and courgettes. Add the rest of the vegetables to the pan, season, cover, and simmer for 40 minutes.

Risotto Romanie (4)
6oz (175g) organic brown rice
4oz (110g) organic carrots, diced
8oz (22og) organic leeks, chopped
4oz (110g) cooked organic ham
3oz (110g) organic mangetout
6 organic tomatoes, peeled
1 organic onion, diced
2 tbsp (30ml) organic olive oil
salt and pepper

Heat half the oil in a saucepan and add the onion, rice and chopped tomatoes. Cook gently, stirring occasionally, for 10 minutes. Add 1 pint (550ml) of boiling water and simmer gently for 30 minutes or until the rice is tender and the water absorbed. Heat the remaining oil in a pan and cook the carrots and leeks for five minutes before adding the remaining ingredients. Cook for a further three minutes, then add the rice and season.

Make No Bones About It

Prince Charles is a great believer in osteopathy – it is one of the most established and respected forms of complementary medicine available in this country. But what is osteopathy, and is it all that different from physiotherapy or chiropractic?

Osteopathy is a form of holistic medicine which revolves around the belief that the functioning of the skeletal structure of the body is fundamental to good health. The bones and joints of the body, and the way they interconnect, give the body its structure.

Osteopaths believe that if bones are out of place, or joints inflamed, the rest of the body will be adversely affected. Therefore, the osteopath will diagnose and treat the person's structural fitness and then, by using his hands to manipulate different parts of the body, will encourage it to regain its balance, (sometimes known as its homeostasis), so that good health can return to the person.

What are its origins?

Modern-day osteopathy began in 1874, when Dr Andrew Still, an American doctor, developed a system of manipulative medicine which was designed to realign any structural deviations and abnormalities. Still believed that the human body was self-healing, and that it had to have an uninterrupted nerve and blood supply from all the body's tissues if it was to function normally. So, for example, curvature of the spine or a muscle spasm would cause blockage of nerve and blood flow, which would obstruct the body's ability to heal itself. Osteopathy shares the belief of all holistic forms of medicine — that the body has its own healing energies. The idea of manipulating the body to

Musicians often find that hours of practice puts undue pressure on joints, and osteopathic treatment may help.

achieve better health is a much older idea than Still's. Chinese writings dating back to 2700 BC refer to manipulation as a healing art, and it is thought that the ancient Egyptians may have used similar techniques.

Hippocrates, widely known as the father of modern medicine, wrote in about 400 BC: "It is necessary to know the nature of the spine, what its natural purposes are, for such a knowledge will be requisite for many diseases."

Complementary therapies

Osteopathy undoubtedly shares much in common with chiropractic methodology. They were both founded at about the same time, and are both manipulative therapies. The major difference between the two is that chiropractors use more x-rays and other equipment and focus much more on the health of the spine as the key to the health of the patient.

Osteopathy is also different from physiotherapy, although again, they do share some methods in common. Qualified physiotherapists use heat, cold, exercise, massage, manipulation, electricity and light to rehabilitate patients after illness or injury. However, a physio, unless working privately, is under the direction of a doctor, who retains overall responsibility for the patient. Osteopaths work independently and not usually in collaboration with doctors, although many GPs do recommend their patients to them. Indeed there have been efforts to start a state register of osteopaths, to give them the same standing as doctors and dentists.

So what does an osteopath do? Basically she uses her hands to treat her patients, employing a variety of techniques to realign bones and joints and loosen tight muscles. There are no set techniques for an osteopathic treatment — many osteopaths develop their own way of working according to their experience and physique, and according to the needs of their patients.

For people with tense muscles, the osteopath will first of all try to loosen up the muscle fibres with massage-like techniques. If a joint is limited in its range of movement, then the osteopath will articulate or repetitively move the joint, with the aim of increasing its flexibility. The most well-known osteopathic technique is the high velocity thrust, which produces the alarming clicks and cracks as bones are quickly put back into place (most osteopaths will warn you first if there is going to be a 'pop' or cracking of joints). Some osteopaths are adept at using gentle release techniques, to help ease away stress in tissues.

What happens in a consultation?

As with most forms of complementary medicine, the first consultation takes an hour or so, and during that period you will be asked about your medical history and given a thorough physical examination. The osteopath is very interested in how your life style affects your posture and health, so her questioning will focus on such areas as your job, what exercise you take, and what type of physical complaints you have suffered from in the past. Osteopaths often treat people who have developed joint problems

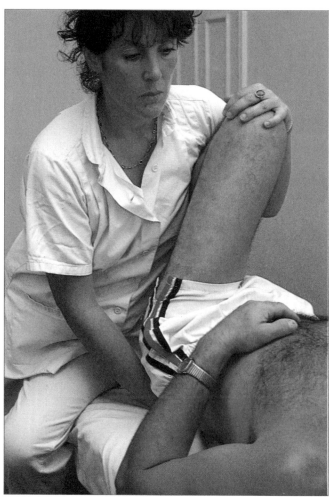

An osteopath at work on a bad back, examining the flexibility of the joint between the backbone and the hipbone.

CRANIAL OSTEOPATHY

Cranial osteopathy involves manipulating the bones in the skull to affect the health of the patient. It is rapidly becoming accepted as another tool in the osteopath's range of skills, and as a type of healing in its own right.

Cranial osteopathy, or cranio-sacral therapy as it is also known, is a specialised form of manipulation involving the bones of the skull. It was developed by a student of Dr Andrew Still, a man called Dr William Garner Sutherland, in the early part of this century. Sutherland discovered that the bones of the skull are not fixed, but can move slightly. Although these movements are tiny, people can be trained to detect them through their hands. Cranial osteopaths believe that by adjusting the position of the bones, which may have been displaced through injury or even when being born, positive changes to health can be affected.

This type of work is very different from normal osteopathy as it involves only gentle holding – no manipulation of any sort. The therapist is trained to hold the head and feel the pulsing of the cerebrospinal fluid in the brain and in the spine – therapists claim to detect all sorts of information about the state of the body, and even feel the movements of the gut while just holding the head! Cranial osteopaths still treat all the other parts of the body, but they tend to specialise in head injuries. One of the commonest problems they deal with is that of people who had difficult births and were delivered with forceps.

By readjusting the bones in the skull, which have been distorted through the birthing procedure, many symptoms can be affected. The therapy is very effective on babies or young children, who seem to respond particularly well to this reassuring form of healing.

Cranial osteopathy is, its proponents claim, suitable for many forms of illness, particularly complicated ones which have a range of symptom patterns such as ME, gastro-intestinal disturbances, and menstrual difficulties in women.

Osteopaths who have trained in cranial osteopathy with The Cranial Osteopathic Association have the letters MCrOA after their names. Quite a number of unqualified people are now practising cranio-sacral therapy too, and although many of them may be natural healers, and excellent therapists, you should check their credentials before you book an appointment.

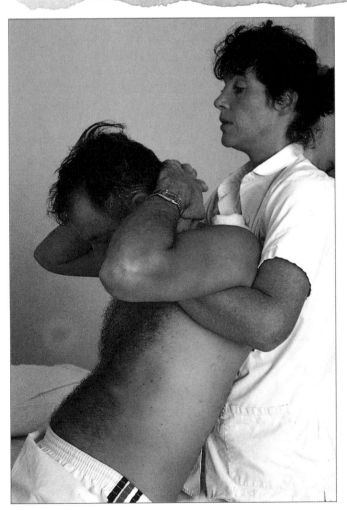

The 'lift off' technique helps to mobilise the upper spine of patients suffering from a bad back.

through sitting at a keyboard for long periods of time, or musicians, who hold postures while practising and incur joint problems as a result.

You will then be asked to remove your clothing down to your underwear, while the therapist examines you. Firstly, she will be trained to observe your posture to see if she can spot any imbalances in the way you are walking or holding yourself. Many people have the habit, for example, of putting all their weight on one leg, which leads to a shortening of the muscles in that leg. The osteopath may ask you to move in a certain way, or walk around the room, while she watches you.

The next stage is to assess with her hands the state of your muscles, a technique known as palpation. Key to any examination is a close look at the state of the spine, testing the movement of each vertebra and looking for tenderness, stiffness or displacement in any areas. When the osteopath is satisfied with her physical examination, she may recommend you have x-rays or blood or urine tests, to help her reach an accurate diagnosis.

What does the osteopath treat?

As osteopathy is a holistic form of healing, osteopaths claim that they can treat and cure many types of illness that don't necessarily relate immediately to a joint problem. However, the vast majority of work that the osteopath does is on bad backs, and it is a very effective form of treatment. Other musculo-skeletal injuries which are treated are strains, sprains and slipped discs, plus diseases such as arthritis, lumbago, sciatica, wry neck, tennis elbow, frozen shoulder, neuritis and many others.

As osteopathic theory states that improving the structure of the body can affect the functioning of the organs, then osteopathic treatment may help in other conditions. Some people find that after their initial joint problem has been cleared up, further treatment has a beneficial effect on another area of their health, such as migraine, asthma,

TREATMENT IN PREGNANCY

Osteopathy can often help when mothers-to-be are experiencing the stresses of pregnancy.

Many pregnant women suffer from low-back pain when carrying a child. and this tends to get worse towards the end of the pregnancy. The fact that they normally put on about 28lbs (12.7kg) in weight exacerbates any postural problems they have. In addition pregnant women also have potential problems because of the softening of the ligaments around the pelvis which naturally occurs in preparation for childbirth.

If you go to an osteopath while pregnant, she will use gentle techniques designed to cause the body as little stress as possible. She will also take into account your obstetric history before she does any treatment. Osteopaths claim that they can ease such pregnancy-related problems as indigestion, haemorrhoids, and aching feet and ankles.

constipation, period pains, heart disease and digestive disorders.

Osteopaths don't consider that they can treat everything, however. Although they perceive that the spine is fundamental to healthy functioning of the body, they do recognise the importance of such factors as genetic inheritance, diet, environment and psychology, and will refer people to other specialists when they consider their treatment is unsuitable.

Many people go to see the osteopath for just one or two sessions, to sort out a particular joint problem. Some, who suffer from bad backs, go on a regular basis, to keep their back functioning. Osteopaths recommend that you have regular check-ups with them if you are doing a hard, physical job or a regular sporting activity, so that they can make sure that no problems are lurking undetected. They also recommend that you consult them if you are trying to 'retrain' your body and sort out any bad posture habits by using a system such as the Alexander Technique. An early consultation enables them to prepare your body by loosening muscles and adjusting joint positions, so that you are more likely to achieve lasting change to your posture over a shorter period of time.

How to find an osteopath

Osteopaths can be found working independently, but many now get referrals from doctors. The cost of a consultation varies depending on where you live, but the first appointment will be more expensive - and it will take longer - than subsequent visits. You may be able to get cheaper treatment by contacting one of the training schools,

which may have an out-patient clinic run by students.

The osteopathy establishment is relatively clear about the status of its members, and as the technique has been recognised for many years, it has a reputation for respectability. Although every osteopath has his or her own particular way of working, all training is basically the same. Some therapists are now specialising in cranial osteopathy (see previous page), but this is the only deviation from mainstream osteopathy.

As with other forms of complementary medicine, therapists are often skilled in another therapy: some practitioners, for example, combine naturopathy with osteopathy. Such osteopaths will be interested in changing your diet and looking at other healing techniques which might help your particular condition.

"If a mechanic is so particular to inspect every part and principle belongng to a steam engine for the purpose of getting good results, can you as an engineer omit any bone in the body and claim to be a trustworthy engineer? Can you say that any part has no importance physiologically in the engine of life. Remember your responsibility in the sick room. You must reason or fail."

Dr Andrew Still

Andrew Taylor Still was born in Kirksville, Missouri in 1828. He first trained as an engineer but later went to medical school and became an army surgeon at the Front during the Civil War. After watching helplessly while his three children died during an epidemic of spinal meningitis, Still became disheartened with orthodox medicine and began his own experiments and research. His breakthrough occurred in 1874 when he successfully treated a child suffering from dysentery by reducing tension in the contracted back muscles. By the time Still died, osteopathy was recognised in every state of America.

YOUR HEALTH

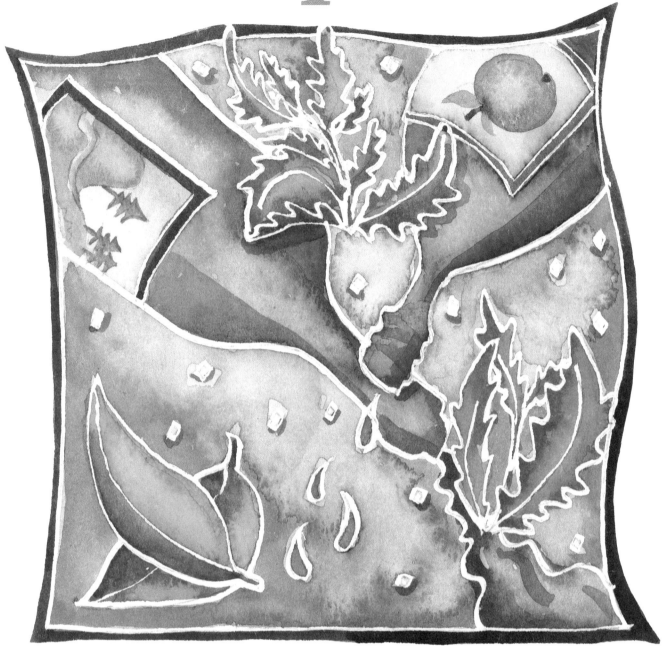

MINTY FRESHNESS

The oil of the peppermint plant is perhaps the most fragrant and well known of all the mint family. It is believed to have been cultivated by the ancient Egyptians and the ancient Greeks are said to have used it both as a spray and as a bath oil. It was the Romans who first introduced peppermint to Britain. They used it to decorate their tables and flavour their sauces. Later, during the 17th century, peppermint was widely cultivated in the area around London.

Peppermint comes from a small plant (mentha piperita) which is grown in temperate climates. The plant has hairy leaves that have a slightly red

If you are feeling a little under the weather or if your skin is feeling tired and irritated, then peppermint may help to liven you up. Its refreshing and cooling ingredients have many uses in a wide range of preparations.

tinge and it produces spiky, lilac-coloured blooms. It's easy to recognise the peppermint plant as it has a purplish stem that reaches a height of about 90cm (35 inches). It can sometimes be seen growing along the sides of streams, ponds and rivers.

Refreshing oil

One of the main uses of peppermint is as an aromatherapy oil. This essential oil is extracted from the leaves of the peppermint plant and used in the manufacture of a wide range of cosmetics and toiletries, including minty mouthwashes, perfumes, soaps and toilet waters.

The main constituent of peppermint is menthol, which is antibacterial and anaesthetic, and which will help to improve the blood flow when it's applied to your skin.

Peppermint oil is particularly effective when a few drops are added to a warm bath. If you've had a hard

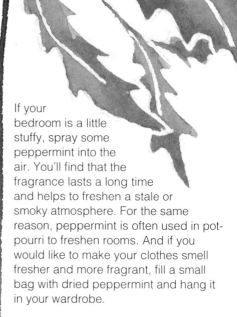

RECIPES FOR BEAUTY

HAIR RINSE

4 tbsp. dried peppermint
2 pints (1.15 litres) water
2 pints cider vinegar

Boil the dried peppermint in the two pints of water, then cover it and leave it to simmer for about 10 minutes. Remove the pan from the heat and leave the mixture to steep for an hour. Strain and add the cider vinegar. Bottle the mixture and leave it for 48 hours before you use it. Wash your hair and then add half a pint of water to the liquid and use it to rinse your hair. This rinse will help to remove soapy particles from your hair and will leave it smelling fresh and fragrant. If you use the rinse regularly, it will also help to prevent dandruff.

HERBAL BATH

4 tbsp. dried peppermint
1 pint (570ml) water
1 pint (570ml) cider vinegar
2 tbsp. dried basil

Add the cider vinegar and water to a saucepan and heat the mixture until the liquid is almost boiling. Add the dried peppermint and basil, cover the pan and simmer for about 10 minutes. Remove the pan from the heat and leave the mixture to infuse for eight hours. Finally, strain the liquid, bottle it and put a label on it.

Add half a pint (285ml) of the herbal mixture to your bath and relax in the refreshing aroma.

day at work, a peppermint bath will refresh tired skin and help you to relax. It can even help you get to sleep. While you're relaxing in the bath, you'll also be breathing in the oil's beneficial properties, so make sure you close the bathroom window and door to contain the soothing vapours. This will ensure that you get the maximum benefit from this treatment.

As it's so relaxing and invigorating, peppermint oil is also used in massage oils which are very refreshing when they're smoothed into your body. Peppermint is also a mild astringent so this treatment has the additional benefit of helping to invigorate your circulation and tone your skin, giving it a healthy-looking glow.

In addition, using peppermint is an excellent way to soothe tired and aching feet. If you've been on your feet all day and they're sore, treat yourself to a peppermint foot bath. Fill a bowl with warm water and add a few drops of peppermint oil to it. Then sit back and soak your feet in the aromatic mixture — you'll be amazed at how much better this treatment makes you feel.

Fragrant inhalant

Peppermint is very good at clearing congested nasal passages and it's therefore a common ingredient in inhalants. A few drops of peppermint sprinkled on a handkerchief will work wonders when inhaled, but adults should only use it in moderation and for a short period of time or the peppermint will begin to lose its effectiveness. Peppermint inhalant should not be used near babies or by adults with asthma or breathing difficulties.

If your bedroom is a little stuffy, spray some peppermint into the air. You'll find that the fragrance lasts a long time and helps to freshen a stale or smoky atmosphere. For the same reason, peppermint is often used in pot-pourri to freshen rooms. And if you would like to make your clothes smell fresher and more fragrant, fill a small bag with dried peppermint and hang it in your wardrobe.

Variety of uses

Peppermint is used in a wide range of medical preparations, including treatments for headaches, bruises, sprains and irritated or itchy skin. It's effective in the treatment of travel sickness, toothache, fatigue, flatulence, indigestion and asthma. It can act as a stimulant for the nervous system, pain reliever and insect repellent. You should remember, though, that if your skin is inflamed or sensitive you should be sure to use it only in a low concentration. Otherwise it may be too harsh, triggering off an adverse reaction.

In addition, peppermint is an excellent breath freshener and is included in many mouthwashes. If you've just eaten some onion or garlic or have been drinking alcohol and are afraid your breath smells, chew some peppermint to help kill the odours. Alternatively, rinse your mouth out with one of the many refreshing mouthwashes that are available.

The leaves of the peppermint plant may also be infused as a tea and drunk for its cool, fresh, minty flavour. The tea will help to freshen your breath, as well as acting as a mild sedative. Peppermint tea is particularly effective when it's drunk after a large meal as it will help to settle your tummy and prevent indigestion.

A CRY FOR HELP

Some experts believe that early trauma and the suppression of negative emotions can well up inside us and cause various illnesses and disorders. These are said to be relieved through primal scream therapy. But what is this therapy? And who can it help?

Nobody has a life totally without emotional pain. Everyone suffers a bereavement or some form of rejection or neglect at some time in their life, and few of us can truthfully say we know how to cope — either at the time or later. So the pain enters our subconscious until, with the passage of time, it festers and begins to make us ill.

In the 1970s American psychologist Dr Arthur Janov developed his 'primal scream' therapy after he had a strange experience with one of his patients. As he says: "I heard something that was going to change the course of my professional life and the lives of my patients. What I heard was an eerie scream welling up from the depths of a young man lying on the floor during a therapy session. I can liken it only to what one might hear from a person about to be murdered."

Janov discovered that this scream was "the product of some unconscious, universal, intangible wound...that most of us carry around and which never seems to heal..." He began to search for the sources of that internal agony, which took him to investigate the depths of the unconscious.

Early pain

Since Janov first developed his primal scream therapy, thousands of patients from over 30 countries have benefited from it by being released from their 'primal pains' of early neglect, abuse and lack of love. And the sad discovery was that most people have this kind of pain festering away inside.

During his research, Janov became aware — years before it was actually proven — that repressed emotion such as anger, frustrated love and despair eventually caused illness. It is now acknowledged, for example, that repressed grief destroys the auto-immune system and as a result allows cancer to develop.

It is not just the emotion itself, however, that can cause sickness of the mind and body, but the repression of that emotion. In the West the expression of extreme emotion is thought of as embarrassing, and something that should be kept away from civilised society. Compare the average British funeral to the scenes of uninhibited grief at an Arab interment, for example. In the UK if a mourner is overcome with emotion they are hurried away out of sight — not to save their face, but to prevent further embarrassment for the other mourners.

Janov says that 'pulling yourself together' and 'putting on a brave face'

A Pain In The Neck?

Dr Arthur Janov believes that almost all illnesses are symbolic forms of a cry for help.

Today most doctors admit that the mind can influence the body and its resistance to illness – but some primal scream therapists go further than this. They believe that, due to the suppressing of strong emotions, the body can manifest illness as if it's playing charades, turning metaphors about their buried feelings into real physical symptoms.

For example, you may secretly feel that something – or someone – in your life is a 'pain in the neck'. And that is precisely how it will make itself known to you! Other classic 'physical metaphors' which could be treated by primal scream therapy include:

● **'I can't put my foot down'/'I should have taken a stand'** becomes the inability to walk, often manifesting as a mysterious pain in the toes or feet.

One woman woke up in the middle of the night with such a severe pain in her big toe that she screamed. Her GP referred her to the hospital for tests for gout and arthritis – both were negative. But she was laid up for two weeks, until she found herself telling someone about a situation at work. "I just couldn't put my foot down," she said. As soon as she realised the connection, the pain faded.

● **'I can't face it'** can manifest as sight disturbances or eye trouble. This is your subconscious mind trying to tell you that you need to look at some aspect of your life that you are avoiding.

● **'Seeing red'** repressed anger can show itself symbolically in unexplained rashes. British healer Matthew Manning is among a growing number of New Age therapists who believe that many disorders are the result of secret anger, including allergies and arthritis.

● **'I'm itching to...'** buried frustrations can surface as itching, often as part of the angry rash syndrome.

● **'A gut reaction'** is a common term for a real condition. Most of us know how fear, nervousness and shock can make us sick, give us diarrhoea and a host of other digestive problems.

● **'A lump in the throat'** hidden or denied grief can allegedly manifest as a sore throat.

is often disastrous. The terror, rage and despair has no outlet, so it forms a tight knot inside, which may eventually become the 'tight knot' of a tumour.

Letting it all out
In primal therapy the patient is encouraged to relive her trauma, to go back to her birth, to relocate all those long-hidden emotions — and to express them. Sitting on large soft cushions in a dimly-lit room, the patients talk back through their birth and childhood, missing nothing out.

Most patients cry during this therapy, although sometimes the hurt they are recovering is so deep it will take them months to be able to loosen up enough to express it. Janov says that many children, especially boys, are forbidden to cry for fear of being thought a 'cry-baby'. For such people, being able to cry will mark a real turning point in their therapy.

As Janov says: "Tears are the expression of need." To admit you have a deep need means that you are beginning to ask for help, and this in itself is part of the healing process. You don't have to scream in modern primal therapy, but if, in the process of 'deep weeping', a scream wells up, then you are encouraged to let it out.

Many patients find that one scream is not enough to shift the entrenched emotion that has accumulated for many years — they sob and scream compulsively until it is all out in the open.

Critics call crying and screaming in this way self-indulgence, and of course it can be, but essentially this behaviour is seen as a necessary part of healing. Janov says that "suffering happens at the same time as healing", so the pain of

the scream is also the beginning of the end of the pain.

Any therapy can eventually become a habit and a crutch to help you through life, sometimes even becoming an addiction. But primal therapists are no keener to prolong the therapy unnecessarily than anyone else. They see therapy as a finite activity — something that has a beginning, middle and an end. The screaming (if it happens at all) is merely a catalyst for the healing process.

Dr Janov sums up the aim of the therapists: "Instead of repression we liberate. Instead of symbolization we take symbols to their correct home in feelings. Instead of constructing a defence we dismantle one. Instead of a system that is progressively closing down we are engaged in opening it up. It liberates the warmth we are all born with. We all have the capacity to be that child who is open, warm, curious, engaging, unafraid, daring and alive.

That is not just the capacity of children. It is a human quality we must try to recapture."

Useful Information
Book
The New Primal Scream by Dr Arthur Janov (Cardinal Books)

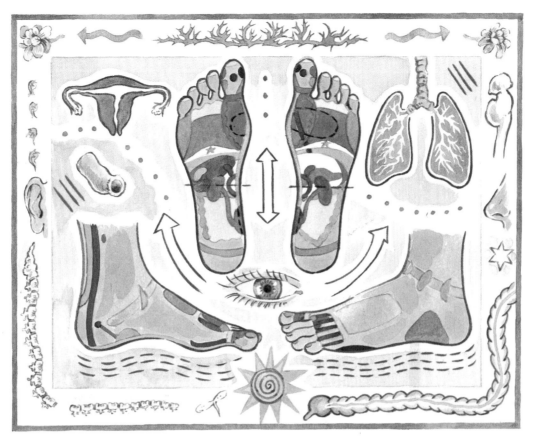

Feet First

Foot massage has been used as a form of pressure therapy in China for at least 5000 years, and has developed into a modern science called reflexology. But what exactly is reflexology and how can it help you?

Reflexology, also known as zone therapy, is a form of holistic medicine which attempts to harmonise all three elements of well-being: mind, body and spirit.

Linked with other ancient oriental therapies, such as acupuncture and acupressure, reflexology is based upon the belief that good health is governed by the homeostasis (balance) of the physical, spiritual and emotional energy which flows through invisible channels, or zones, in the body.

When these zones are blocked, we become ill or experience pain and discomfort. Reflexologists claim to be able to stimulate the body's self-healing responses to eliminate not only the painful symptoms (as in conventional medicine) but also the energy blockage — the cause of the illness itself.

Where does it come from?
Ancient texts, drawings and artefacts provide evidence that many ancient civilisations — including the Chinese, Egyptians and Indians, and even the early Russians — used a form of pressure therapy as a way of promoting good health. And evidence has recently come to light that some African and American Indian tribes are practising a form of reflexology today.

In the West, modern reflexology has developed from research into early 'zone therapy', which was conducted by the American physician and surgeon Dr William H Fitzgerald in 1913. Treatment by zone therapy included massage of areas on the feet, hands and tongue, although further research by another American, Eunice Ingham, led to the belief that the feet were the most effective areas to work on.

A British nurse called Doreen Bayly worked hard throughout the 1960s and 70s to create interest in reflexology in the UK and Europe, and started a training school called the Bayly School of Reflexology where her teachings are

still continued today (see Useful Addresses). The modern method of reflexology is rapidly growing in popularity, and there are thousands of qualified reflexologists currently practising in the UK alone.

What can reflexology do?
As there is a corresponding reflex on the foot for every part of the body, many reflexologists claim that, theoretically at least, they can treat any disorder. Generally, it is accepted that reflexology improves blood circulation and the efficient functioning of the nervous system, the lymphatic system, the kidneys, the colon and the skin.

The massage treatment involved in reflexology is extremely effective in countering the effects of stress and tension, and can be so relaxing that people have even been known to fall asleep during a session! As it is already accepted within the medical establishment that a large proportion of

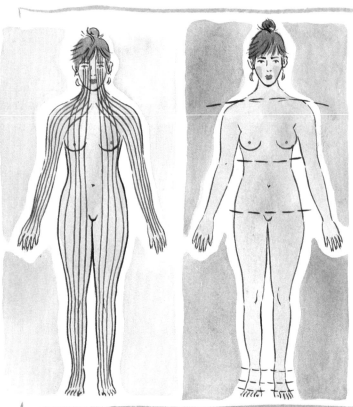

How does it work?

According to reflexologists or zone therapists, the body is divided into different zones.

Reflexology works on the principle that there are 10 longitudinal zones of equal width (five either side of the central line) (see far left), which run down the entire length of the body from the tips of the fingers to the tips of the toes, including the head and neck. There are also three transverse zones which cut across the body – one in line with the shoulders and collarbone, the second in line with the waist and the third in line with the pelvic floor (see left).

All of these zones are mirrored in both the feet and the hands, which contain reflex points that correspond to every organ, gland and part of the body. Feeling the feet or the hands (the feet are now used the most, as they are thought to be most responsive) can help a reflexologist to define the position of the blocked energy within the body and so diagnose the problem.

Massaging the appropriate reflex point can unblock the energy by stimulating the nervous system and blood circulation, promoting self-healing and relaxing the energy pathways. The body's natural balance then returns and the pain is reduced.

all diseases and disorders are stress-related, reflexology can only be beneficial to the vast majority of people.

Reflexology is believed to be particularly effective in treating problems such as backache, migraine, menstrual problems, allergies and insomnia. Although a reflexologist does not claim to be able to *cure* any major disorders, the relaxing and vitalising effects of reflexology are also known to be beneficial for people with diseases such as cancer, Parkinson's disease and multiple sclerosis.

Visiting a reflexologist

So just what can you expect when you visit a reflexologist? Before starting the massage, the reflexologist will take a detailed medical history, making notes about any major illnesses or conditions that you have had in the past. You will also be asked about any symptoms that you are experiencing at the time, even if they are seemingly unconnected.

Most practitioners like you to sit in a reclining chair, with your feet comfortably supported upon a stool. This means that you are extremely comfortable and relaxed, and it also enables the reflexologist to work on your feet without bending too much.

The reflexologist will examine your feet, paying particular attention to their texture, colour and temperature, as it is believed that the condition of your feet

and the condition of your body are strongly related. You will then be given a general foot massage to relax you.

Under pressure

Powders and creams are often used in the massage. Every area of the foot is worked systematically with the thumb. This can take a long time, as each pressure point is no more than the size of a pinhead.

Particularly sensitive areas may feel painful when the pressure is applied, indicating the problem areas. The pain goes away as soon as the pressure is taken away. The pressure is only 1–2.3kg (2–5lb), firm but bearable.

Some reflexologists go on to finish with a relaxing overall foot massage, often with aromatherapy oils. After the session, which usually lasts for about an hour, you may feel the characteristic light sensation in your feet, and will probably be very relaxed and tired. However, some people experience a sudden burst of energy.

Side effects?

Reactions to reflexology vary, but you may experience any of the following:
● A desire to urinate more frequently. Your urine may even have a different colour or odour. Many reflexologists advise their patients to drink lots of fresh water after a session to flush out the excess toxins from the body.

● Increased bowel activity and/or flatulence.
● Increased perspiration.
● The nose, throat and lungs may increase secretions of mucus, causing a blocked nose and coughing.
● Sleep patterns may be disturbed and dreams become more noticeable.

It is important to remember that these are short-term reactions as your body attempts to improve its balance. They are nothing to worry about.

> " If you're feeling out
> of kilter,
> Don't know why or what
> about,
> Let your feet reveal the
> answer,
> Find the sore spot,
> work it out."
>
> *Eunice Ingham*

> " I have two doctors -
> my left foot and my right."
>
> *Anonymous*

YOUR HEALTH

Deep Body Treatment

Rolfing is a little-known system of deep tissue body work. Rolfers claim to loosen up parts of the body that you didn't even know you had, creating better posture in the process.

Rolfing is a system of massage which is virtually unheard of in this country. Its founder was a woman called Ida Rolf and she developed a system of deep manipulative work that realigns, loosens and harmonises the body. Rolfing aims to reorganise the body's structure by loosening up the connective tissue called the deep fascia, which envelops all the major muscle groups of the body. The rationale is that the fascia are often thickened and shortened because of poor posture or injury, and to achieve better posture, this sort of work has to be done. Rolfers claim to be able to make deep and permanent changes to the body by their hands-on work. As evidence they take photographs before and after a treatment, and their clients

do seem to make remarkable changes in their posture.

Dr Ida Rolf (1896-1879) began her investigation into the human body from an initial background of biochemistry and physiology. She came upon the idea of Rolfing, or structural integration as it is also known, during her search for solutions to family health problems. She saw a connection between how the body's structure affects its function, and went on to develop a technique to alleviate structural defects.

She originally aimed to relieve painful conditions by her work but soon found that she could also improve general functioning and psychological wellbeing. As Rolf worked with people who were trying to change themselves and their posture, she saw that any real

change in the body could only be affected if the tissues were manipulated as well. She reasoned that any attempt to change behaviour alone would mean that the new muscular habit would be working against the strong resistance of the tissues, making permanent mental change virtually impossible.

What does a Rolfer do?

During a Rolfing session, which lasts between an hour and an hour and a half, the therapist will gently work on the body's connective tissues network, known as the myofascial system. The system supports the skeleton and connective tissues, positions the bones, determines the direction of muscle pulls and of movement, and gives the body its shape.

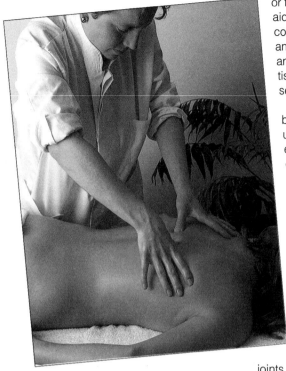

A Rolfer has to exert a great deal of pressure in order to massage the deep connective tissues.

The Rolfer will work on the body systematically, starting at the feet, so that he or she checks all the tissues in the body for shortening. The Rolfer believes that shortening and tightening of the fascia is often the cause of many deep-seated postural problems. As the body's muscular system works in pairs, if one muscle is damaged, then compensatory tightening will occur in its opposite number. Thus a pattern of tension can arise from one damaged part of the body.

The aim is to free the shortened fascia, allowing the muscles to return to a balanced relationship and the body to release the compensatory tensions that it has developed.

A Rolfing session

Rolfers usually give people 10 sessions of work, which they believe is sufficient to sort out most body problems. The first session consists of evaluation of the client — photographs might be taken for later reference, to confirm the changes that have been made.

The therapist will ask the client to remove outer clothing and to lie on a table. The therapist, using the hands sensitively, applies pressure at various points to release the deep fascial tension. The client may be asked to breathe into the area being worked on or to make specific movements, to aid the therapist's work. The combination of applied pressure and synchronised responses frees and repositions the conective tissues, and thus aligns the body's segments.

Rolfing isn't exactly massage, but it is quite similar. The Rolfer uses his or her hands — and even elbows and knees, pressing deeply at times, and it can be quite a painful experience, but it can also be quite relaxing. The first seven sessions remove strain from specific areas of the body such as the lower back, neck, knees and so on, while the remaining sessions organise and align the body as a whole. People who have been Rolfed report having raised energy levels as well as feeling easier and happier with their bodies. Movement is freer, as if the joints have been lubricated.

Reaping benefits

A Rolfer will treat anyone who is suffering from posture-related conditions, which therefore includes many people. Back problems and other disorders which haven't responded to conventional treatment are often the Rolfer's work. Rolfing is also used by dancers and sportspeople who are concerned with their ease of movement as it relates to their performance.

Rolfing came to public awareness in the 1960s when it was seen as a very hardline treatment, involving a lot of pain and not much sympathy. These days Rolfers are a lot more gentle, and more in tune with the emotional side of the clients. Rolf managed to identify a pattern of emotions relating to the body. Feelings of neglect and abandonment appear to be related to chest tension, the upper back releases strong feelings of anger, while jaws hold sadness, hips repressed sexuality and shoulders burden and responsibility.

There aren't many Rolfers around — perhaps only half a dozen in the UK — and there is no recognised institute to act as a publicity agent for them. If you are interested in finding a Rolfer, make sure they are qualified from the Rolf Institute, based in America. Prices for a treatment range from £35–60, depending on which part of the country you are in.

ALTERNATIVE CONNECTIONS

Rolfing may not be well known but it has similarities to other therapies.

Rolfing shares some of its philosophical background with other postural therapies.

The Alexander Technique (see page 9) agrees with the Rolfer's basic premise, that deep personal change has to come from releasing tightly held muscles all over the body, but it differs in that Rolfing looks at re-aligning the body in order to change the personality, while the Alexander Technique looks at changing long-established mental patterns in order to create physical change.

Bioenergetics is another type of deep massage and movement-orientated system. It shares the Rolfer's philosophy that emotional issues are just as much related to posture as physical issues are, however bioenergetics focuses mainly on emotional release to accompany the physical.

Hellerwork is a recent development from Rolfing. Joseph Heller was an experienced Rolfer who believed that dialogue was an important part of treating a patient, so he incorporated discussion and counselling in with his physical treatment. His therapy also advocates the importance of giving clients basic education about movement and postural problems (again, similar to Alexander work). There are only a few practising Heller therapists today, although the treatment is gaining popularity.

Overcoming pain

Rolfing can occasionally be painful but, according to Ida Rolf, you shouldn't let this put you off treatment because the pain can be overcome - "the way to get off the pains is to go into the pain, to make it as tough as you know and all of a sudden it isn't there."

YOUR HEALTH

A GENTLE FRAGRANCE

Do you have sensitive skin? Or are you simply looking for a subtle fragrance? Rose-water has been popular for centuries and is still a common ingredient in a wide range of cosmetic products.

Rose-water is a slightly perfumed, colourless substance that is easily obtained by distilling rose petals. It almost certainly came from Ancient Persia where the earliest emperors filled the streams which surrounded their gardens with the aromatic essence. Although the art of distilling rose-water was not introduced to the West until the 10th century, the French lost no time in beginning to manufacture it on a large scale shortly after it was introduced.

Rose-water is widely available from chemists and from the beauty counters in most department stores. However, many of the floral waters available today are synthetic, so if you want to make sure you're getting the real thing, give the bottle a good shake to see if the water foams. If the foam lasts for more than 30 seconds, it's likely that the rose-water is synthetic.

Making your own

If you would rather make your own rose-water, you'll be very pleased to know that it's an extremely simple process. All you need to do is add 30ml of rose essential oil to 4.5 litres of distilled water, and shake it well. Then pour the rose-water into a bottle and store it in a cool place, making sure it's kept away from direct sunlight.

Rose-water has been highly valued for over 2000 years and still forms the basis of many skin-care creams, lotions and tonics. For example, it was a fragrant ingredient in the first cleansing cream which was made by the Greek physician, Galen, in 150AD. This cream also contained olive oil, water and beeswax. The water evaporation from the cream made the skin feel cool, and it soon became known as cold cream.

Because of its moisturising properties, rose-water is usually one of the main ingredients in skin-softening

RECIPES FOR BEAUTY

ROSE CLEANSER

4 tbsp almond oil
20g beeswax
3 tbsp rose-water

Melt the almond oil and beeswax in a bowl over a saucepan of boiling water until they're thoroughly blended. Then remove them from the heat and beat in the rose-water one drop at a time until the mixture has completely cooled. Pour the mixture into a labelled bottle and store it somewhere cool. Use the cleanser twice a day as part of your regular skin-care routine.

TONER

17 tbsp rose-water
5 tbsp pure alcohol
1 tbsp glycerine
10 tbsp witch hazel

Mix the alcohol and the glycerine together, making sure you beat the mixture well. Then add the rose-water and witch hazel. Whisk it thoroughly until it has all blended together. This recipe will make about one pint of rose-water toner. This is a gentle product that's particularly suited to normal to dry skin.

LAVENDER

6 tbsp rose-water
1 tsp lavender oil
285ml (1/2 pint) pure alcohol

Pour the lavender oil and rose-water into the alcohol. Then shake the mixture well and pour it into a bottle. Store it in a cool, dark place so it doesn't lose its beneficial properties.

Leave the lavender water for at least a month before you use it, shaking the bottle every day. (The more time you give it, the better it will be.) The lavender water is light and subtly fragranced – it is ideal for wearing on warm summer days.

ESSENTIAL OIL

Many of the benefits of rose-water are due to the beneficial properties of the rose oil it contains. Rose essential oil is very fragrant and has a wide range of uses.

Rose essential oil has been considered precious for many centuries, and it is claimed that it was actually discovered in Persia in the early 1600s. The story goes that as part of the celebrations for a wedding feast, a moat was dug around the garden and filled with rose-water. As the married couple were rowing across the moat, they noticed that the sun had caused a layer of oil to form on the surface of the water. This oil was removed and was discovered to contain a highly concentrated perfume.

Rose essential oil is used in a wide range of scents and beauty preparations, and has a number of beneficial properties. It is good for the circulation, and can be used to treat stress, headaches and indigestion. It also acts as an effective relaxant, antidepressant, astringent and antiseptic.

creams. It is commonly contained in products that treat and help to heal chapped skin. One of the most popular of these creams is made from a combination of rose-water and glycerine, and is very effective when it's applied to sore and chapped hands.

Rose-water also has many other uses. It can be used as a freshening mouthwash and as a good rinse to clear your hair of dry skin flakes and the residue of shampoo. And if you have tired and aching hands, you'll find it's very refreshing to wash them in rose-water. In addition, rose-water is used in many products to treat and help skin abrasions, and is an ingredient in gentle, moisturising soaps. It is also often present in a range of perfumed waters, colognes, face masks, shampoos and a variety of luxurious bath treatments.

Freshen up

Another of rose-water's important uses is as a toner. Along with lavender water and orange water, it has been used for many years as an effective skin freshener, and it was one of the very first toners to be used.

Rose-water is so mild it can be used on its own or diluted with mineral water, and because it's so gentle, it's suitable for all skin types. However, rose-water is the most effective on skins which are dry and sensitive because,

unlike some of the stronger astringents, it does not contain alcohol and will therefore not overdry the skin. If you combine it with witch hazel, you will get an effective toner for normal to dry skin.

To get the most from your rose-water toner, pour a little on to a piece of cotton wool and gently smooth it over your face. You'll find it very effective in removing stubborn traces of grime and dead skin cells, and it will leave your face feeling refreshed and healthy.

SAGE STRUCK!

Are your teeth a little stained? Or do you have a few grey hairs? Sage is an aromatic herb that's easy to get hold of, and has a variety of cosmetic and medicinal uses.

Sage (Salvia officinalis) is a versatile herb that originally came from southern Europe. It is delicious to eat, refreshing to drink and extremely aromatic.

Sage has also been used since ancient times for medicinal purposes. It was particularly favoured by the Chinese, who in the 17th century would trade three chests of China tea for one chest of sage leaves. The Romans were so impressed by the herb they called it 'sacra', as they believed it was sacred and encouraged conception.

Sage is a perennial plant and it has distinctive greyish-green leaves which are oval in shape. It also has pretty bluish-violet blooms which appear at any time from early to mid-summer.

Seeds and plants are widely available, and you should find them on sale in most large plant shops and garden centres. You can buy fresh and dried herbs in most food shops and herbalists.

Cosmetic uses

In addition to its medicinal properties, sage is astringent, aromatic and very refreshing. And these are a few of the reasons why it's used in such a wide range of cosmetic and skin-care products. One of its most popular uses, though, is in hair rinses and shampoos for brown and greying hair.

When it's applied to greying hair, sage will darken the white hairs and help to disguise them, while enriching and conditioning at the same time. It also helps to stimulate the blood circulation in the scalp, encouraging hair growth and leaving your hair looking healthy and in good condition.

Sage is also commonly used in a selection of mouthwashes and gargles, and has been used to clean the teeth for many years. Before toothpaste was

Sage has long been known as a herb with both medicinal and culinary properties. It is widely available, and easy to grow yourself.

developed, people used to scrub their teeth with sage leaves. This helped to keep their teeth stain-free and it also strengthened their gums. Sage is still used in some toothpastes today. It's very effective and will keep your teeth clean and free from plaque, while leaving your mouth feeling fresh and healthy. Sage is also antiseptic so a good gargle with it will help to keep sore throats and infections at bay.

Skin care

Oil from the sage plant is extracted and included in a variety of bath treatments, perfumes, lotions and soaps. Sage is astringent so it will help to deep cleanse the skin and remove stubborn grime, sebum and dead skin cells.

Sage also helps to ward off coughs and colds, so if you're feeling a little under the weather, make a sage infusion, add

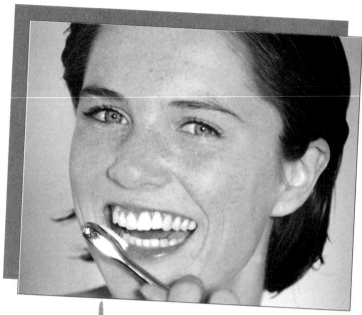

RECIPES FOR BEAUTY

TOOTHPASTE

2 tablespoons fresh sage leaves
2 tablespoons sea salt

Put the fresh sage and salt in a bowl and crush them with a pestle until they've formed a fine powder. Place this in a warm oven and leave it to bake. When the mixture is hard and well baked, remove it from the oven and pulverise it again. Then store it in an airtight container.

Use the sage toothpaste twice a day to get rid of harmful plaque and unsightly stains. It will leave your teeth white, and your breath sweet and fresh.

SHAMPOO (for brown hair)

3 dessertspoons dried sage
1.7 litres (3 pints) boiling water
6 tablespoons castile soap
2 eggs
cider vinegar

Boil the water and add the dried sage. Put the lid on the saucepan and leave the mixture to simmer for about 20 minutes. Strain the mixture and throw away the sage leaves. Shred the castile soap and add it to the infusion. Whisk it well until the soap has completely dissolved. Then remove the pan from the heat and leave it to cool. When it has cooled sufficiently, beat in the eggs a little at a time. Whisk the mixture until it's well blended and then pour it into a labelled bottle and leave for 24 hours to settle. Remember to shake the bottle well before you use the shampoo.

Shampoo your hair with the sage mixture and then rinse it thoroughly in a mixture of eight parts soft water and one part cider vinegar. Condition your hair as usual. This shampoo will help to give brown hair a healthy sheen, emphasise your natural highlights and darken any grey hairs.

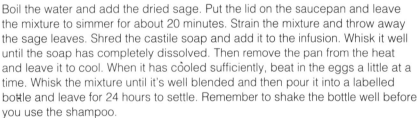

GARGLE

50g (2oz) fresh sage
570ml (1 pint) boiling water

Infuse the fresh sage in the boiling water and leave it for about 15 minutes. Strain the mixture to get rid of the sage leaves, and then bottle it. Use this mixture to gargle with four times a day, using half a cup at a time – it will freshen your mouth and sweeten your breath.

it to your bath and relax. You'll be surprised at how much better you feel afterwards.

As sage is so easy to get hold of, it's simple and cheap to make a variety of cosmetic treatments at home. You can make an infusion with it by pouring boiling water over it. Use a bowl of hot water infused with sage when you're having a facial sauna to help revive and cleanse your skin. Or add it to a vapouriser and treat your bedroom to a refreshing fragrance.

Medicinal treatments

Sage has been used for many years as a general tonic to remedy a number of different complaints. And long before Indian tea was heard of in Britain, our ancestors used sage leaves to brew a refreshing drink.

Sage helps to reduce swelling, alleviates nervous complaints, is antiseptic and has an antifungal action. It is also a diuretic, so sage tea before or during a period may help you to loose that bloated feeling.

A sage gargle, as well as sweetening your breath, can be very effective for treating laryngitis and mouth sores. It can also be combined with peppermint and rosemary to treat headaches. And it's just the job for treating anxiety, tension, depression and general tiredness. Sage may also be used to treat irregular menstruation and to relieve any irritating symptoms of the menopause. However, it should not be used during pregnancy, or in large doses for long periods of time.

LOOKING GOOD

The Pressure Of Life

Shiatsu is a Japanese therapy which is said to relax and revitalise the body, aiding diagnosis and treatment of many common disorders. But what exactly is shiatsu, and how does it work?

S hiatsu — literally 'finger pressure' in Japanese — is a manual therapy which involves applying pressure to various points on the body known as 'tsubos'. It is said that, if practised regularly, this therapy can be used to prevent disease and restore health and vitality, as well as diagnose and treat many ailments.

Sometimes known as acupressure, shiatsu has evolved by combining the Chinese therapy acupuncture, the Japanese relaxation massage 'anma' and gentle manipulation and stretching techniques from modern physiotherapy and chiropractic.

Although many of its techniques have been in practice for hundreds of years, shiatsu was only recognised as a therapy in its own right by the Japanese government in the middle of this century, when their Ministry of Health and Welfare stated that the therapy is thought to "correct internal malfunctioning, promote health and treat specific diseases".

How does it work?

The theory behind shiatsu is very similar to that of acupuncture, and is based upon ancient Chinese philosophy. According to this philosophy, there is an energy flowing throughout the universe known as Ch'i (Ki in Japanese). This energy flows through our bodies along 12 energy channels called meridians, which are each associated with a specific vital organ or part of the body.

When this energy flow becomes blocked due to injury, emotional stress or an imbalanced life style, we tend to develop physical ailments such as aches, pains and stomach upsets, as well as symptoms of depression and moodiness.

Practitioners of shiatsu claim that they can relieve these conditions by applying pressure to certain points on the body which lie along the meridians. The Ki is believed to accumulate or flow particularly close to the surface of the skin at these points, and this pressure is thought to stimulate the energy flow and free the blockage, unlocking tension and restoring full health.

'Pleasurable pain'

A shiatsu session with a qualified practitioner usually lasts for about one hour, and should take place on a firm surface in a warm and peaceful room. This is usually in a special shiatsu clinic, although some practitioners prefer to visit their patients in their own homes.

During the first session the practitioner will usually take a detailed case history and attempt to diagnose specific problems by checking 12 special pulses which correspond to the meridians. She may also gently feel the abdomen to assess the quality of the energy and the 'balance' of the internal organs.

Once a diagnosis has been made, treatment can begin. This is not necessarily in any fixed order, although some therapists do have a set procedure that they prefer to follow. The patient spends some of the time lying on her back, some time lying on her front and the rest of the time sitting up so that the practitioner can work on the shoulder area.

Pressure techniques are usually exerted through the fingers or thumbs, although some therapists may also use their elbows, knees and even feet! The sensation for the patient is often described as one of 'pleasurable pain' with the resumed energy flow giving a feeling of relief as the pain is reduced after the treatment. If the patient experiences extreme pain when pressure is exerted on certain points, this is taken to be a good sign as it indicates where the energy flow is blocked. At the end of the session, the practitioner may also offer advice on diet, exercise and life style.

The benefits of shiatsu

There are many benefits to be had from shiatsu, although it is believed to be most effective in treating and diagnosing everyday disorders and minor ailments rather than chronic illnesses. The deep pressure used in

LOCATING THE TSUBOS

Although in the West, shiatsu massage is generally practised by qualified practitioners, the Japanese have long regarded it as a form of home therapy to be used upon themselves and members of their family.

Listed below are just some of the 'tsubos' or pressure points of the body which are worked on in shiatsu – you should know when you have located a tsubo, as it will feel tender when you apply pressure.

The hands and arms
● Firm pressure on the centre of the palm boosts energy levels generally.
● Squeezing the flesh located between the thumb and forefinger enhances the general feeling of wellbeing, as well as relieving toothache, headaches, constipation and painful periods.
● Using pressure on the crease of the elbow improves circulation, respiration and digestion, and encourages the flow of lymph which works to eliminate body wastes.

The abdomen
● Also known as 'Hara', the abdomen is extremely important for helping practitioners diagnose and treat general energy imbalances. Using pressure on a point just below the navel relieves stomach disorders.

The back, neck and shoulders
● Working several pressure points located across the top of the shoulders and at the base of the skull relieves stress and tensions in the neck and shoulder area, and also soothes headaches and cold symptoms.
● Applying pressure to the points between the shoulder blades stimulates the circulation and helps to relieve symptoms of anxiety and insomnia.
● Using the elbow to press deeply down either side of the spine aids the respiratory, circulatory and digestive systems.
● Working on the middle of the back aids digestion.
● The lower back is associated with the kidneys, and controls water retention.
● Working on the points close to the 'sacral dips' (the

dimples located near the hips at either side of the spine) is said to be extremely soothing and relaxing for women and helps alleviate period pains.

The legs and feet
● Pressing deeply on the point at the side of the buttock muscle helps to treat sciatica and pain in the lower back.
● Pressure just behind the Achilles tendon (right) will help to ease low backache.
● Working on a point below the ball of the foot eases dizziness and painful periods.
● Intense pressure on the soles of the feet helps to stimulate the kidneys. This is sometimes done by the client lying face down while the practitioner walks upon the soles of her feet!

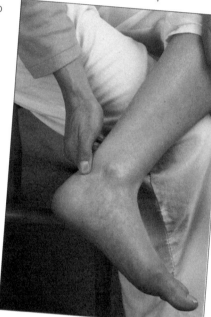

The face
There are several pressure points located on the face:
● The temples – promotes serenity.
● Below the eyebrows – relieves extreme tiredness.
● The centre of the cheeks – reduces any painful swelling.
● The jawbones – aids the efficiency of the digestive system.
● The bridge of the nose and edge of the nostrils – eases nasal congestion.

shiatsu is thought to relax and stimulate the body, with particular effects upon the circulatory, nervous, lymphatic and hormonal systems, as well as helping to release toxins and deep-seated muscle tension. Specific complaints which can be treated include:
● Sciatica.
● Headaches and migraine.
● Digestive disorders, including diarrhoea and constipation.
● Toothache.
● Menstrual problems.
● Rheumatic and arthritic complaints.
● Respiratory illnesses — asthma and bronchitis, for example.
● Backache.
● Catarrh and sinusitis.

● Insomnia.
● Low energy levels and fatigue.
    In order to get maximum benefit from the treatment you mustn't drink alcohol or eat heavily on the day of treatment — and don't eat anything for at least an hour before the appointment. Don't take a hot bath on the day of treatment. You should wear a loose tracksuit or leggings and T-shirt. Take along any details of current medical diagnosis or medication.
    Treatment is said to leave a feeling of calm and wellbeing, and is particularly good in treating any stress-related disorders.

Useful Information

Books
The Shiatsu Workbook by Nigel Dawes (Piatkus).
Acupressure For Common Ailments by Chris Jarmey (Gaia Press).

Addresses
Shiatsu Society
14 Oakdene Road
Redhill
Surrey RH1 6BT
Tel: 0737 767896
Provides information on local registered practitioners. Members of the Society receive a quarterly newsletter which also gives information on classes for people interested in learning basic shiatsu techniques, as well as more in-depth courses for those who wish to follow a professional career in shiatsu.

YOUR HEALTH

Sea Power

Most of us love to be beside the seaside, but did you know that the sea is said to have healing properties? Thalassotherapy uses sea water and sea products to promote health and healing.

The term thalassotherapy comes from the Greek word 'thalassa', meaning sea, and the therapy uses the properties of sea water to enhance the body's power to heal itself. Thalassotherapy has close links with hydrotherapy, which also uses the power of water to heal.

Hot and cold baths of sea water were quite common at coastal resorts in Victorian times, and nature cures using the sea have been used by people for thousands of years. Our use of the sea for rejuvenation has been at an unconscious level for a long time. Many people feel instantly better for going to the seaside — the ozone produced by crashing waves can be particularly invigorating.

In Europe, the power of the sea to heal is now being exploited by special thalassotherapy resorts which have been established to use sea water in a much more sophisticated form.

According to enthusiasts, thalassotherapy works because the mineral content of the sea is very similar to our blood plasma. (Blood plasma is responsible for feeding and strengthening all cells to enable the body to function healthily.) Therapists claim that when sea water is heated to blood temperature, the minerals present in the water are absorbed into the skin and penetrate the bloodstream, enhancing the mineral balance of the body and making the person feel rebalanced and healthy.

Many conventional doctors and dermatologists dispute this theory, however, but this doesn't seem to deter the many people who pay to have a thalassotherapy treatment.

What does it involve?

A trip to a European thalassotherapy centre is more of a health-farm experience than a medical one. The benefits of being by the sea and breathing in coastal air are said to be as beneficial as the treatments themselves. At thalassotherapy centres, beauty treatments using sea water and seaweed are also given on a daily basis. They range from the pleasant to the uncomfortable, and the therapist will usually recommend a course of treatment for you to follow throughout your stay there.

The more vigorous type of treatment is 'douche a jet', in which a high pressure hose is sprayed over your hips, thighs and bottom to stimulate circulation and to treat cellulite. Both hot and warm sea water are used for this type of treatment. A 'bain bouillonnant' is a jacuzzi-type treatment in which you sit in a bubbling bath which directs tiny pressure jets of water all over the body to relieve tension. Being massaged in a shallow bath of warm sea water is one of the standard treatments offered, and you are encouraged to take aqua-aerobics sessions in sea water to help tone and stimulate the body.

One of the more luxurious treatments involves being covered in a

DIY THALASSOTHERAPY

You don't have to pay a fortune in order to indulge yourself in a thalassotherapy treatment.

You can buy seaweed preparations and sea salt quite easily to create a healing sanctuary in your own bathroom. Most cosmetic manufacturers now produce many different scrubs, gels, soaps, muds and bath preparations containing sea products.

● Try a warm bath in salty water to relax tired muscles. Epsom salts or sea salt can be added to a bath to promote relaxation. Remember to shower off the water, however, preferably alternating between blasts of hot and cold water to stimulate the circulation.

● If you want to go for something more luxurious, try a body scrub such as Montagne Jeunesse Seaweed and Mineral Body Scrub. Wet your skin and scrub in firm but gentle circular movements, concentrating on dull or dry skin patches. Then try soaking in a bath using Creightons' Ocean Harvest Creme Foam Bath and apply lashings of Creightons' Ocean Harvest After Bath Moisturising Lotion to complete your treatment.

● Dead Sea products are also said to be excellent at promoting wellbeing and rejuvenation. If you can't personally take a trip there (Cleopatra is said to have bathed in the waters to maintain her glamorous looks) then buy Ahava Mineral Mud and apply to the body for 20 minutes or so. Rinse off and bathe in a warm bath with Dead Sea Discovery Mineral Crystals.

● You can also apply sea products to your hair to pep it up. Cosmetics to Go claim that their Kalite Sea Salt Scalp Scrub is effective in revitalising a sluggish scalp.

● Eating seaweed is another way to benefit from the sea, but buy packed products or use food supplements such as kelp – collecting your own from polluted beaches isn't to be recommended.

● When by the coast, try walking thigh-high in the sea to tone and help improve circulation in the hips and thighs.

One word of caution, though. With increased levels of pollution around most of the European coastline, it is as well to be aware of the dangers of bathing in pollution-filled waters. The resorts in Brittany even advocate drinking sea water, which probably isn't wise. If you are going to enjoy your own sea cure, make some enquiries locally about whether the water is polluted or not, and make sure you go to a beach where it is known that the water is clean.

thick, warm seaweed paste and then gently wrapped in plastic sheeting and blankets. This algae wrap is wonderfully relaxing and good for the skin and circulation. Some centres will also offer a sea-water floatarium, where you can float your troubles away.

Who benefits?

Thalasso cures are supposed to be beneficial for people with arthritis, rheumatism, lumbago, sciatica, cardiovascular disease, circulatory disorders, stress-related illness, fractures, and dermatological conditions such as eczema and psoriasis. In France, where the top thalasso centres are to be found on the Brittany coast, qualified doctors will work with clients in the centre to decide on suitable treatments.

Where to go

Thalassotherapy is relatively expensive, and, as the majority of thalasso centres are in Europe — particularly France — it is usually necessary to travel in order to experience the delights of sea-water treatments. If you feel like treating yourself, however, a good place to visit is Thalgo La Baule on the Brittany coast. For a more casual — but still expensive — trip, visit the Italian spa towns of Abano and Montegrotto, which specialise in similar treatments using the local thermal waters and fango mud instead of seaweed. To experience British-style thalassotherapy, you can go to a health farm or beauty salon which uses freeze-dried sea water and special packs of seaweed products for its treatments. For thalassotherapy on a budget, visit your local coastline and spend some time relaxing and swimming in the sea, or treat yourself at home.

The Dead Sea in Israel is a popular resort for thalassotherapy enthusiasts as they believe that Dead Sea mud is extremely beneficial both for the health and the skin.

" Surely it is a wonderful sight to take a stroll on a lovely summer's day and see people enjoying the healing powers of the sea and breathing in the ozone-rich air... our health will improve if we can bathe and swim in sea water and enjoy the benefits of the natural minerals contained therein, as well as enjoying its cleaning effects."

Sam Miller

Perfect Harmony

**The word 'yoga' comes from the ancient Indian language of Sanskrit and means 'union'.
But what exactly is yoga? And how can it improve our health?**

Yoga is an art or discipline which is thought to have been practised in the East for at least 5000 years. Traditionally, it is used as a means of promoting health and spiritual development by attempting to unite the body and mind in perfect harmony. Although the origins of yoga are not certain, it was first formalised and recorded in 200 BC by the Indian guru Patanjali. In the East there are many different forms of yoga — including

Raja yoga which aims to master and reject negative emotions, and Mantra yoga which uses chanting as a way of achieving unity through sound. Each type of yoga combines practices to form a complete philosophy.

The type of yoga most commonly known and practised in the West, however, is Hatha yoga, which aims to attain harmony through the use of physical postures and special breathing and relaxation techniques.

How to be perfect

Although yoga was originally designed as a spiritual path — a way of attaining 'enlightenment' — many people in the West are turning to yoga as an effective form of exercise. Enthusiasts claim that it can increase overall fitness, stamina, weight loss and flexibility, as well as self-discipline, self-esteem and self-control. As each part of the body learns to work in harmony with the rest, it is possible to achieve a unique sense of

SALUTE TO THE SUN!

This sequence of coordinated movements is easy to learn, and gives you an idea of the way in which yoga can help you to exercise and relax.

You can use these sequences after your limbering-up exercises, either to pep you up first thing in the morning or to refresh you after a long working day. You can compose your own sequence if you want to, but you must remember to counteract your movements — if you bend your back one way in a particular posture, you should follow with another posture that bends your back in the opposite direction, for example.

Salute To The Sun is one of the first sequences ever to have been devised. The series of poses was traditionally practised at dawn in India, and can be very stimulating if performed before breakfast. If you can't do it outside, try to do it in front of an open window.

You should aim to have a continuous flowing movement from one pose to the next, although at first you may need to concentrate on each individual pose in order to perfect it before moving on to the next one. Try to keep your breathing as regular as possible, inhaling and exhaling evenly.

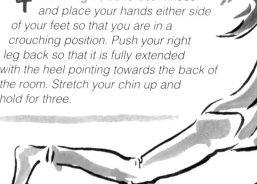

1 *Stand up straight with your feet together and your hands in a praying position in front of your chest. Try to avoid tensing your shoulders and creating a hollow with your back. Close your eyes and feel yourself relax before moving on.*

《 2 *Breathing in deeply, raise your arms above your head and bend backwards as far as you can, feeling the stretch along your spine. Try to keep your balance as you hold for a count of three.*

3 *Now breathe out as you sweep your arms down, bending at the waist. Try to touch the floor with your hands, bending your knees if necessary. Those of you who are very supple may even be able to rest your head on your shins! Relax and hold for three.*

4 *Breathing in, bend both knees and place your hands either side of your feet so that you are in a crouching position. Push your right leg back so that it is fully extended with the heel pointing towards the back of the room. Stretch your chin up and hold for three.* **》**

balance and relaxation, banishing the tiredness and aching limbs that are a sign of stress and tension resulting from modern-day living.

Many people also believe that regular yoga practice can be extremely effective in the prevention of many illnesses. It is claimed that just 10 minutes of yoga a day can increase the life and energy flow to every part of the body — preventing the muscular rigidity which so often leads to stiffness, pain and sickness.

As well as many general stress-related disorders, yoga is reputed to help in the prevention of:
● Asthma.
● Arthritis.
● Diseases and disorders of the digestive system including dyspepsia, ulceration and constipation.
● Bronchitis.
● Dysmenorrhoea.
● Hypertension.
● Migraine.
● Sinusitis.
● Backache.
● Diseases of the nervous system such as multiple sclerosis.
There are three main aspects of Hatha

yoga practice: breathing techniques, postures and relaxation.

Breathing (pranayama)
Most people use only a small fraction of their lung capacity in breathing, hardly expanding the ribcage at all. But yoga followers believe that learning to breathe properly is essential for good health. And if the breath is controlled and used effectively, its energy can have a positive influence on both the body and mind.

There are many special yogic breathing exercises which are aimed at specific results such as exhilaration, relaxation, concentration and the more efficient functioning of various organs. Many of these techniques are only taught to advanced students, as it is thought that you need to have immense bodily control to be able to deal with some of the rapid changes and effects such exercises can bring about.

However, the first stages of breathing control can be learnt by anyone. The type of breathing that you should practise as a beginner is called ujjayi, and should be very slow and deep, using the whole of the lungs. Try lying down on the floor with your hands resting on your lower ribcage, and feel it expand and contract as you inhale and exhale. Always try to breathe in and out of your nose, and avoid straining as you do so. Concentrate your thoughts as you do any breathing exercises, and always make sure that your posture is correct if you are sitting upright.

After the breathing exercises, and before starting the postures, you should do a few stretching or limbering-up exercises to warm up your muscles and loosen your joints in preparation for the demanding postures. This will cut down on the chance of pulling a muscle or injuring a joint, as well as reducing stiffness after the session has finished.

5 *Breathe out as you bring your left leg back to mirror your right. Keep your spine straight, supporting your body with your arms. Hold for three.*

9 *Breathe in and step forward with your right foot. Stretch your left leg behind you and keep your chin up. Hold for three.*

6 *Breathe in and then out again as your allow your knees, chest and chin to touch the floor, with your bottom in the air. Hold for another three.*

7 *Breathing in, place your body flat on the floor, push up with your arms and raise your head. Try to keep your shoulders relaxed as you count to three.*

8 *Breathe out now as you slowly bring your body up into an arch, pulling your stomach in. Keep your heels on the floor if possible, and hold for three.*

10 *Breathing out, bring your left leg forward so that you repeat step 3.*

11 *Repeat step 2.*

12 *Finish back where you started, repeating step 1.*

Try to do specific exercises for various areas of the body, such as ankle circles, arm swings and waist bends.

Postures (asanas)

Postures, many of which are named after animals, are designed to free tension, improve flexibility and increase strength and energy. It is also said that they are effective in overall muscle toning, weight control and relaxation. Specific postures massage different parts of the body, and can have various effects on certain organs.

Asanas should be learnt gradually, each one being perfected before you move on to the next. Follow the steps slowly and smoothly — maintain the pose for as long as is comfortable and then release it slowly, keeping control over your body. Concentrate on your breathing once you have mastered the posture itself, trying to exhale and inhale evenly.

As a general rule, you should breathe in when you go into a posture and breathe out as you release the posture. Whatever you do, don't tie yourself in knots — if any of the positions feels at all strained, you must be doing something wrong or pushing yourself too far. If you are finding a particular posture difficult, try to relax your body more fully — increased tension will only make your muscles seize up even more, and may damage them. Move out of any pose immediately if you feel any sharp pains or become very tired. Rest your back on the floor and relax.

Have a brief rest after each asana, and alternate more vigorous postures with more restful ones. Your limbs and joints may ache at first — this is only natural with any form of exercise which is new to you — any aching parts should be stretched briefly before you move on to the next position.

Relaxation

Ideally any yoga session should end with at least 10 to 15 minutes of relaxation, although you should also aim to relax for at least five minutes between each posture. This has the effect of refreshing you both physically and mentally, and it also allows you to release any accumulated tensions you may be suffering from.

Make sure that you can have at least 10 minutes without any disturbance and lie down, supporting your neck and head with cushions. If you suffer from backache, bend your knees so that your waist flattens against the floor, or rest your calves on a sofa or other soft surface. Wrap yourself up warmly, as your body temperature will drop when you are lying still and your muscles will tense up if you get cold.

Try to block any outside thoughts from your mind as you lie completely still. Concentrate on your breathing, keeping it as even and rhythmical as possible. Try to imagine the tension slipping away.

Yoga at home

You can practise yoga at home — there are many good books and video tapes available, but it is best to combine home practice with a class taken by a qualified instructor (see Useful Information, overleaf).

THE LOTUS POSITION

The ideal basic pose for breathing and meditative sessions is the well-known lotus position (padmasana), as it allows the spine to remain extended and the body relaxed for long periods at a time.

The lotus position is good for the circulation in the abdominal and pelvic area, toning the spine and internal organs.

Start by sitting on the ground with your legs straight in front of you. Bend your right leg and lift your right foot with your hands, placing it sole upwards on top of your left thigh, close to the groin. Then take hold of your left foot, bending the leg at the knee, and ease it under your right leg into the half lotus position.

Once you are comfortable in this position, you can go on to try the full lotus position, in which the left foot is eased up to rest on the right thigh. Stay in the position for as long as you are comfortable.

To start with, simply rest your hands on your knees. An experienced teacher can show you how to do stretching exercises (left). To come out of the position, ease your feet out and shake your legs gently to relieve tension. Repeat the exercise with the legs reversed.

This position takes considerable practice. If you find it too difficult at first, simply try sitting cross-legged or upright in a chair with your spine straight and your body relaxed.

The object of yoga is to balance yourself and use each part of your body systematically and symmetrically, so if you can't attend a class for any reason, you should perform your yoga exercises in front of a mirror so that you can watch your movements.

Try to start your yoga session first thing in the morning, before breakfast. If this isn't possible, make sure that you allow at least three hours after a main meal, or one hour after a light meal, before starting your exercises. Try to practise once a day, even if only for 10 or 15 minutes. Alternatively, a longer session once or twice a week will suffice.

You will need a quiet, warm but airy room, with no distractions to disturb your concentration. A non-slip surface such as a hardwood floor is ideal, with a mat or rug for protection for your bones. Try to avoid deep-pile carpets, as they can cause you to lose your balance easily. A pleasant atmosphere is also very important — some people like to play soft music or light a stick of incense, while others like to practise out of doors for maximum effect.

Always wear loose, comfortable clothing (preferably made of natural fibre) which will not restrict your movements. A leotard and footless

tights are very good — they allow you or your teacher to see if your body is correctly aligned when you are performing the postures. And make sure that you remove your shoes — bare feet will stop you slipping or losing your balance.

Yoga for beginners

It is important to stress that anyone can do yoga — it doesn't matter if you feel you have a limited capacity for movement. Lots of practice will gradually loosen you up and make you much more supple.

In the meantime, take things slowly and try not to overstrain. Don't worry if you can't complete a posture at first, especially one of the more complicated ones. It is much more important to focus on how your body *feels* in any position, and sense the benefits that the yoga is bringing. Try to locate any areas of stiffness or flexibility as you do the exercises. Always spend time on movements that you can't do easily as well as the ones you like most — this is essential for you to achieve a good sense of balance in the movements and exercises that you do.

> " In yoga,
> the asanas or postures
> lubricate the body.
> They keep the
> muscles and joints running
> smoothly,
> tone all the internal organs,
> and increase
> circulation without
> creating any
> fatigue.
> The body is cooled by
> complete relaxation,
> whilst pranayama
> or yogic breathing
> increases prana,
> the electric current.
> Fuel is provided by food,
> water and
> the air you breathe.
> Lastly, you have
> meditation
> which stills the mind,
> the driver
> of the body."
>
> *Vishnu Devananda*

YOUR HEALTH